Praise for *Mastering Mentoring and Coaching with Emotional Intelligence*

"The *purpose of the book* is clear—to assist the mentor/coach in "*acquiring the necessary mindset*" which will enable the mentor/coach "*to be a good coach or mentor*". In order for a mentor/coach to lead his protégé to her enhanced state of expertise and success, the mentor/coach must first be aware of his own mental mapping that drives his states and behavior in the context of coaching. And, secondly, the mentor/coach must be able to access the structure of the mental maps that drive the limiting behaviors of his protégé.

"The mentor/coach will find the book an easy read with superb directions and exercises as to how to apply the technology to mentoring/coaching."

—**Bob G. Bodenhamer, DMin**, author and international trainer

"This book tackles the distinctions between trainer, coach and mentor with the clarity which demonstrates the deep understanding of the authors for each of the individual roles. A must have book for mentors. The book has clear and easy to follow models which have been overlaid on several corporate mentor/protégé examples, thus the reader can select the most suitable model for his/her situation. An impressive demonstration of the clarity which pervades the book is in the example of the safety-net metaphor."

—**Curly Martin**, international coach, trainer and author, Achievement Specialists LLP

"For mentors, coaches, clients, and HR people alike, this how-to book teaches you the ancient art of mentoring. Contains very practical, clearly presented and easily applied tools. An essential read if you want to acquire the mindset that will enable you to be a good coach and/or mentor in the widest possible circumstances and contexts."

—**Julian Russell**, a leading UK executive coach and the founder and Managing Director of PPD Consulting Ltd, business leadership development specialists

"A well-researched compendium of processes and questions, through which coaches and mentors can take their clients and protégés."

—**Shelle Rose Charvet**, author of *Words That Change Minds*

"This is the best book I've read on the subject, because it is holistic, clear to understand, easy to follow, and with enough depth to satisfy seasoned mentors and coaches.

"The authors have a way of drawing techniques and best practices from different business disciplines – as well as others - and put it all together in a useful, logical, and effective manner. In many cases, they better explain concepts that have been around for a while, than they were ever explained by the original authors."

—**Richard Juneau**, consultant, trainer and coach

Mastering Mentoring and Coaching with Emotional Intelligence

Patrick E. Merlevede
Denis C. Bridoux

Crown House Publishing Limited
www.crownhouse.co.uk

First Published in 2003, under the title *HRM themaboek Mentoring and Coaching* by ced.Samson, an imprint of Kluwer Uitgevers, authored by Patrick Merlevede. The first English Edition of 2004 is a reworked and expanded version by Patrick E. Merlevede and Denis C. Bridoux and Stephen Wilkinson-Carr.

Published by

Crown House Publishing Ltd
Crown Buildings, Bancyfelin, Carmarthen, Wales, SA33 5ND, UK
www.crownhouse.co.uk

and

Crown House Publishing Company LLC
4 Berkeley Street, 1st Floor, Norwalk, CT 06850, USA
www.CHPUS.com

First published 2004; reprinted 2004, 2006

British Library Cataloguing-in-Publication Data
A catalogue entry for this book is available
from the British Library.

10-digit ISBN 1904424082
13-digit ISBN 978-190442408-6

LCCN 2003103578

Printed and bound in the UK by Cambridge Printing

About the Authors

Patrick E. Merlevede

After working some years for a knowledge management consultancy firm, helping companies to figure out what was the secret of their success, Patrick decided to focus on the human side of knowledge management. Since 1997 he has been helping organizations worldwide by combining principles from emotional intelligence with the best practices of human resources. Some of the most visible results are the book *7 Steps to Emotional Intelligence* and the jobEQ.com website. He is one of jobEQ's founders and the driving force behind jobEQ's research and development. He is available for consulting, keynote speeches and training related to issues covered in *7 Steps to Emotional Intelligence* and in the Increase your jobEQ book series.

More about Patrick Merlevede:

www.merlevede.biz

Contact Patrick at Patrick@merlevede.biz or visit one of his websites.

Denis C. Bridoux

An international NLP and Neurosemantics Master Trainer/Developer and a Meta-Coach with the International Neuro-Semantics Society, Denis also operates as a mentor and consultant in the UK. He is the director of Swift Changes, formerly known as Post-Graduate Professional Education. His breadth of culture has enabled him to build bridges between very diverse disciplines and to enrich NLP even more as a result and he closely collaborates with L. Michael Hall, the internationally renowned creator of neurosemantics. Unique in Europe, his Master Practitioner training was labelled "undeniably the most interesting currently available in the UK". Marrying humour, intellectual rigour and flexibility to enable his participants to learn easily and effortlessly, his enthusiasm for the subjects he presents is contagious. He is currently working on a book on the "Itinerary of Change" presented in this volume.

To contact Denis, call +44 7939 623054, or mail him at: denis@outcome.demon.co.uk. Alternatively, visit his website, www.swiftchanges.com, or write to: Swift Changes, P.O. Box 506, Halifax HX1 5UF, UK.

Stephen Wilkinson-Carr

With a background in military intelligence and a keen interest in Executive Success, Organisational Development and Corporate Governance, Stephen Wilkinson-Carr is Chief Executive of Solutions Consulting Ltd, a UK based management development consultancy.

A Neuro Linguistic Programming Master Practitioner, MBA, Business Mentor and Executive Coach, Stephen is committed to the development of people at all levels in business. He uses an in-depth understanding of the way people are motivated to facilitate personal development in specially tailored career transition, organisational change and personal marketing programmes throughout Europe.

He can be reached on +44 797 664 4485 and at:

solutions.consulting@blueyonder.co.uk

Contents

Acknowledgments

This book is the result of a collaboration that started in 2000, when Denis offered to help me (Patrick) with the English translation of *7 Steps to Emotional Intelligence* (Merlevede, Bridoux and Vandamme, 2001). Since then, we have been in a kind of living-apart, writing-together relationship, with Denis living in the UK and me living in Belgium. In general we would like to dedicate this book to all persons who have been mentor or coach to one of us in the past and to those who will be mentoring and coaching us in the future.

There is something to learn from each experience in life.

Even if sometimes it's hard to appreciate going through an experience, may we wish you many interesting learnings!

Patrick Merlevede

I'd like to express my gratitude to all persons I've met in the past twelve years, since I left the cocoon of the university and had to start thinking about earning a living. Somehow, each person, whether they played the role of teacher, mentor, coach, customer or student, or even competitor, have added to my experience. Maybe I haven't thanked them at the time, but I'd like to take this occasion to set that straight.

Some people deserve a special mention. First of all, I'd like to thank my wife, Evelynn, for the ten years of marriage we have shared so far and for our wonderful son. I hope reading this book will be useful for him when he grows up. Secondly, I have to thank Peter Van Damme and Steven Warmoes, for being employers who knew how to mentor me and who gave me many training opportunities, including some training with Robert Dilts, the originator of some models that appear in this book. Apart from Peter, I also have to mention the two other members of jobEQ's initial core team: Serge Deprez and Brian Van der Horst. Over time they have deeply influenced my thinking, in their roles of colleague, mentor, coach, and sponsor.

Denis Bridoux

I wish to address my gratitude to all the people living or dead who, directly and indirectly, mentored and coached me, even if they didn't know it, especially my mother, who instilled in me the belief of perfectibility and the desire for high standards, Kay Woollard who supported my development from the 80s onwards, Adam Christie for his critical eye, all my NLP and NS colleagues, Richard Bandler for installing resourceful self-beliefs, L. Michael Hall for our constructive discussions and meetings of mind since 1997, and, finally, for the authors JRR Tolkien *(requiescat in pace)* without whose inspiration I wouldn't be writing this and David Zindell for the breadth of his spirit.

Preface

You have in your hands a book on *Mentoring*. It's a book about how to effectively communicate expert knowledge, experience, and skills to another. This is great from the point of view of the protégé. Why? Because as a relational process, mentoring can accelerate learning, model and replicate expertise, and demonstrate the right attitude for the protégé to absorb—the attitude that in turn makes the skills magical.

I'm delighted to see this new work from Patrick and Denis following their previous work on emotional intelligence, *7 Steps to Emotional Intelligence*. This book, in fact, is a natural next step, a kind of *7 Steps for Effective Mentoring*. The mentoring relationship described here is one that arises from the emotional intelligence of self-awareness, self-management, and a caring ability and willingness to invest oneself in others. Here they make explicit a wide-range of critical facets of the mentoring process.

Even more important are *the powerful mentoring tools* that the authors provide. If all you want is a book that talks about mentoring, this isn't the book. The authors *do* much of what they describe—they mentor the reader to become a skilled mentor. They provide processes, patterns, and tools for transferring high quality knowledge and skills. In the business context, this enriches the activities of management and HR, to groom bright new talent for higher level responsibilities, to fast track early adaptors and change-embracers, and to create relationships of trust and loyalty.

Since mentoring is all about passing on one's expert knowledge and experience, this book is especially valuable to leaders, senior management, executives, and anyone who has developed specialized skills. The focus here is practical—transferring specialized knowledge, developing critical skills, and translating knowledge to action.

To facilitate that, I'm pleased to note the new development that Denis Bridoux has made of the Neuro-Semantic *Mind-to-Muscle pattern*. This is a premier pattern for translating great ideas in our heads to felt, experienced reality in our muscles and neurology. "Embodying great meanings" is at the core of Neuro-Semantics. Here you will find the *Mind-to-Muscle* process expanded and nicely refined in the "Itinerary of Change" pattern. By this pattern you can coach yourself or another to *feel* in your body what you know and decide in your mind.

While the text here frequently uses the term "coaching", this book is about *using coaching as a methodology* for communicating and enabling the protégé. To that end, those involved in coaching will find this a valuable book integrating and using numerous neurolinguistic models for mentoring: Perceptual Positions, Well-Formed Outcomes, SCORE, COMET, Precise Questioning, Value Hierarchy, and more. May you enjoy your explorations and become a highly skilled mentor and/or effectively coach others for mentoring.

L. Michael Hall, PhD, Psychologist, Author

What This Book is All About

INTRODUCTION

Ever since we started training and coaching people to increase their emotional intelligence, we have been getting requests to help to increase the emotional intelligence of organizations as a whole. In this book we aim at helping you to increase your own jobEQ in such a way that you can help others to increase theirs and thus to achieve better results together. As you'll notice in the section to come, we will invite you to learn more from the experiences you have already had, in a similar way that mentors use their experience to help others to become better at their jobs.

From caterpillar to butterfly

When you were a child, you may sometimes have wished you had an older, wiser friend whom you could trust, whom you could go to for advice or to share your triumphs with, who could perhaps just give you a shoulder to cry on or act as a bouncing board for ideas you had—in short, someone who would listen, a patient confidant of the good and the not-so-good days.

Or, perhaps, you were one of the lucky few who did have such a friend in whom you could confide when you had problems or just difficulties. You would visit them, open your heart and, as you talked, as if by magic, your problems would seem to sort themselves out. Difficulties would be turned into challenges and, yes, you could now face them with renewed assurance and resolution, triumphing against the odds and, possibly, even other people's expectations.

What would it be like if you could offer somebody else such support so that they might get enough chances to succeed? This could be a new colleague at work, a pupil or student, or

Oprah Winfrey has had the benefit of a mentor in the person of Maya Angelou.[2]

"Since the moment I opened *I Know Why the Caged Bird Sings*, I've felt deeply connected to Maya Angelou. With each page, her life seemed to mirror mine … Meeting Maya on those pages was like meeting myself in full. For the first time, as a young black girl, my experience was validated. And it still is, only now I sit at Maya's feet, beside her fireplace, hardly believing that, years after reading *Caged Bird*, she is my mentor and close friend. When we met in Baltimore more than 20 years ago, our bond was immediate. We talked as if we had known each other our entire lives; and throughout my twenties and in the years beyond, Maya brought clarity to my life lessons. She speaks of what she knows …

Now we have what I call a mother/sister/friend relationship. She's the woman who can share my triumphs, chide me with hard truth and soothe me with words of comfort when I call her in my deepest pain. When I am with Maya, unimportant matters melt away—her presence feels like a warm bath after an exhausting day. In our hours together, we can set aside all pretensions and just be: two women barefoot in a living room, sharing the most intimate parts of our lives."

maybe a relative, a member of your sports team or art group, or anybody else for that matter.

How would you like to make this kind of a difference in the life of another, so that they can access resources within them that even they may not know they have, so that they can address the challenges of living and working in the twenty-first century, so that they can grasp with both hands the opportunities they see coming their way, so that they even might find opportunities they weren't aware of, so that they can shine and share with the world all that they have to offer?

What would it be like for you to know that you have been instrumental in the development of a special human being?

How would *that* be for you?

In case you didn't know, *that's* what we call mentoring, and we will show you how you can do it to your satisfaction and that of your protégé.

Many famous people who have significantly contributed to the world have had the benefit of a mentor, without whom they would not have been who they were, done what they did or had what they had. Indeed the world would be a much poorer place if the concept of mentoring had not occurred.

Very few people actually are one hundred percent self-made. If you look closely you'll probably find a mentor behind virtually every significant person you know in life (even if that mentor might not have had that "title"). A website, called *The Mentor Hall of Fame*[1] has made a list of famous mentor–protégé pairs and even a quick browse through this makes edifying reading.

As you are engaging on the road to mentoring, you, too, are part of the long chain of learning that stretches back to well

---

[1] See http://www.peer.ca/mentorpairs.html

[2] See http://oprah.oxygen.com/omagazine/200012/omag_200012_maya_b.jhtml

before known history began. And how does it feel to realize this?

For all you know, you, too, may appear on this list one day.

Before you engage on this path, imagine the future now: try it out for size. Allow yourself to dream. Ask:

- What will it be like once I become a great mentor and advise people in the best possible way?
- What will it be like for other people to benefit from my mentoring skills?
- What will it be like for my organization?

Action

If you want to become a mentor, you may want to take the time to ask yourself the following questions:

- If somebody was mentoring me, or had been mentoring me at a given time in my life, what would I have wanted them to have been like? In what terms do I think of them? What metaphors come to my mind that would best represent what I would think of them as?
- What would I have liked them *not* to be like? What metaphors arise here?
- How would I have liked them to behave toward me? *Not* to behave toward me?
- What values would I have liked them to display that would have enabled them to help me become the best possible me?

Draw a mindmap of what the subject represents in your mind.

Who should read this book

When we set out to write this book, we started by discussing who would be reading it. We hope that you can identify with one or more of the following categories.

- If you are starting in coaching or mentoring, this book can be used as introduction to the subject.

- If you have some experience in mentoring or coaching, this book can help to expand your skills.

- If you are on the receiving end of coaching or mentoring, this book may help you to sort out what you can expect, what approach would best fit your needs and how to identify a coach or mentor who will help you on your path.

- If you are active in the human-resources department, this book may help you to use coaching and mentoring as development programs aimed at making employees more successful in what they do today or in what will be expected from them in the future.

- If you picked up the book because you like the cover enough to make you want to browse, or because your intuition told you that this might be what you need, we hope you like the juicy morsels of food for thought we offer you throughout.

- Finally, if you got this book because one of your friends recommended it to you, then it is probably meant for you!

Whatever reason you chose to start reading, welcome to the coaching and mentoring path toward more jobEQ!

What is the book's subject?

In the process that led to the creation of this book, the questions we may have been asking ourselves most often are: "What is mentoring? What is coaching? Where is the line between these two subjects and other ways to help others with their personal development, such as training and counseling?" To answer these questions, we went back to where the terms originally come from and how they evolved, consulted most of the domain's literature as well as our friends and colleagues and had lengthy discussions.

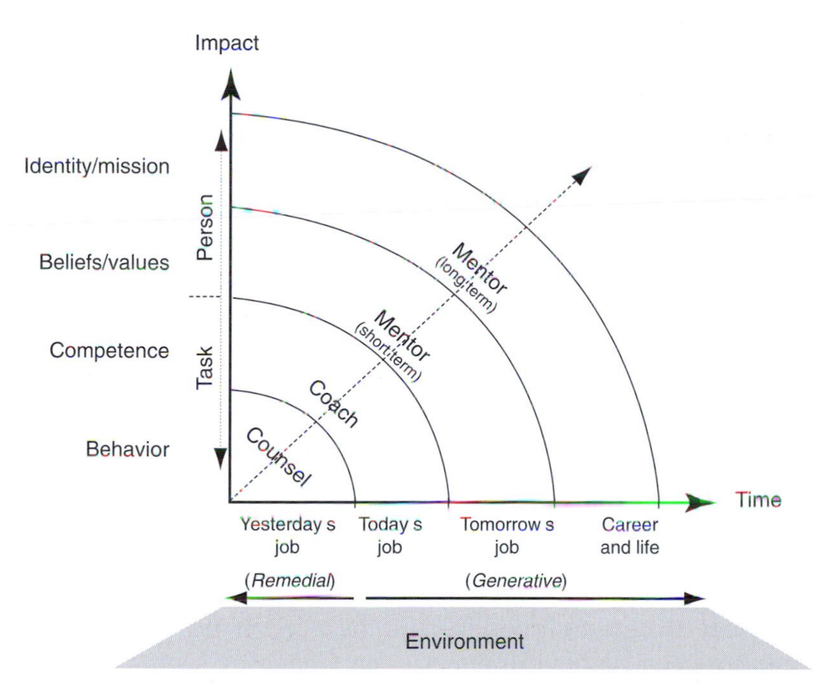

Figure (i-1)

Figure (i-1) allowed us to structure our thinking and to work out what we wanted to cover in this book and what we would leave out.

First of all, we found out that most counseling has to do with solving yesterday's problems, often by looking at what happened in one's past life. Much of it seems inspired by the many therapeutic traditions coming from an era where therapy focused on what is broken in a person—and why it is broken.

Second, much of the literature we reviewed before starting on this book doesn't perceive any difference between *coaching* and

As we will discuss in the first part, mentoring is an ancient art, which predates coaching by over 2,000 years. This is another reason why, apart from promoting the mentoring attitude, we'll often choose the word "mentor" instead of referring to a mentor-coach.

mentoring. Some refer to a coach-mentor, mentor-coach, using hyphens or strokes to express the interchangeability of the titles.

Third, we found that coaching as it is done in companies often has a short time frame, figuring out what is needed to function better in today's job, while other forms of coaching, such as life coaching, have a longer attention span, but operate from outside the framework of work.

Fourth, counseling and coaching are often carried out by paid professionals. In these cases, if the protégé is footing the bill, the vested interest of the coach may get in the way of the personal development of the protégé. Most of mentoring is done on a voluntary basis, with no direct financial benefit to the mentor.

Fifth, in the work context, if funded by the company, the focus will be the company's future, instead of that of the individual. Company-funded mentoring programs tend to focus on tomorrow's job, while people who get themselves a mentor outside their work environment are focusing more on their career as a whole instead of just considering tomorrow's job.

Finally, we found that you learn to be a coach, but you become a mentor because of your experience. Coaching seems to be the subject of training—people are taught coaching skills—while few mentoring programs exist.

Three developmental roles in business

While the trainer can be seen as having knowledge, the coach brings know-how and the mentor has wisdom. A way to optimize the use of these resources is shown opposite.

In this book we decided to go for the positive approach, focusing on what you want to achieve, starting from today. From that perspective, the question as to where coaching stops and mentoring starts is just a matter of definition, creating an artificial boundary. The distinction we choose to make is that

Trainer	Focus on knowledge and skill transfer	Train when there is a clear hole in the person's knowledge about the subject. Set up a training course when there are more people having to learn the same skills.
Coach	Focus on skill usage and competence development for the current job	Coach when the person has the knowledge, but doesn't get the results. Short term: enable the person to get direct results, be action-oriented, resolve competence problems, provide day-to-day help so that the job is done to standard (or better).
Mentor	Focus on person, personal development	Mentor to prepare a person to do a job (before the person actually needs to perform the job) or retain a high-potential employee. Long term, career-oriented, not specifically focused.

coaches tend to be more focused on the *what* and the *how* and the mentor on the *why* and the *who*.

The book's themes

As a mentor, you need to help your protégé through four phases.

1. Figuring out what you want

This phase is about "handling intentions" in order to generate clarity. It involves answering questions such as "What's the goal of the mentoring or coaching relationship? Why do you want coaching? What do you expect to gain? Is it about obtaining a next career step? Is it about handling the current job better? What are the contradictory outcomes and intentions you have? How do you resolve those contradictions?" These questions need an answer before you move to the next phase, or else they will come back to haunt you, as the mentor, and your protégé. For instance, if you proceed on a path that contradicts other goals in life, this contradiction will turn against you later on, and may for instance explain why you don't act on your intentions or don't succeed.

2. Deciding what to do

The interventions you do as mentor or coach help your protégé to get from a goal to an action. This phase results in a clear, well-formed plan of action. Without a clear plan of where to go you may end up somewhere else or remain stuck at a certain point.

3. Making sure it happens

The mentor's job during this phase is to monitor progress in order to ensure that the outcome is reached. We have set the ball rolling—does it keep rolling in the right direction? Does it maintain its momentum? Are things done on time, on schedule, in the way they were intended to happen? If the previous phases of the process were successful, this phase is self-explanatory, because by now your protégé will know how to get what they want. Still, a plan cannot predict for one hundred percent what will happen, since we are always operating from imperfect and incomplete data. If something unexpected happens, often going back to Phase 1 or Phase 2 is appropriate.

4. The day after

At a certain point you conclude that the goal is reached or it isn't worth spending more energy in going down that track. Ideally, at this point, all that's left is documenting what we did and what we learned. Now it's time to live with the consequences. Now that you've got what you want, what are the implications? In most cases, because of the inherent complexity of life, when we reach an outcome, that state will have emergent properties, some side effects that were not anticipated What was the effect on others? What have we learned from doing it? This may lead to a next step, where you have to figure out what you want again. In other words, this results in a next loop through the four phases, as we can see in Figure (i-2). These four phases are also present in your own journey to becoming a better mentor or coach.

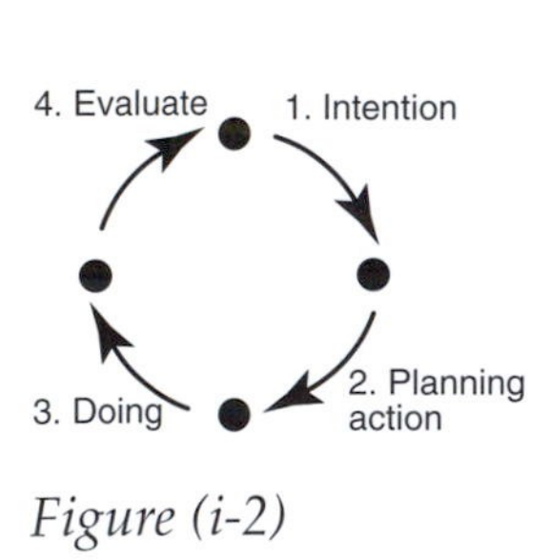

Figure (i-2)

How this book is organized

Richard Bandler, whom Denis experienced as a great trainer and mentor, once said that, before anything else, excelling in a given discipline is about having an *attitude*, a way of being, that helps us to achieve what we want. The *methodology* required to excel in this discipline fits within this framework, and the *technology*, the various tools and approaches one learns to apply with pertinence, fits within the methodology. Indeed, before we start anything we must want to do it and to do it well. Otherwise, why bother?

Christian and other ethical codes teach, "Do unto others as you would be done by." Therefore, before going out and applying some of the approaches we explain in this book, we recommend trying them out for yourself!

Therefore, we have structured this book to enable you, before anything else, to *acquire the necessary mindset* that will itself enable you *to be a good coach or mentor* in the widest possible circumstances and contexts. To do this, we will be asking you a wide range of questions, which only you can answer, instead of giving you ready-made solutions. As you read each of these, take the time to pause and formulate an answer in your mind. This is covered especially in Parts 1 and 3 of this book, where you will develop or refresh a mentoring frame of mind. The other parts of the book are more about the practicalities of coaching and mentoring and how *to do it well*. Interspersed throughout, you will find a range of processes we invite you to apply to yourself—or on your protégé, since these will work equally well with them—which will move you forward and ensure your satisfactory progress. In a way, you could say that this book will be a mentor to you, which will enable you to mentor others well. A meta-mentor indeed!

Starting from the Beginning

PART 1

Do you know how to guide a person and nurture their personal development so that they achieve what they want?

Do you know how to coax somebody into making the most of what they have, not only for their benefit but also for that of the people they interact with?

Do you know how to generate and sustain over time the best possible interaction with somebody that will freely allow the emergence and flowering of their creativity, excellence and success?

If you don't, or do, but want to do it even better, read on.

Mentoring—some background

Most English texts on mentoring tell us that the discipline originates from a character in Homer's *Odyssey* called Mentor—actually the goddess Athene in disguise—who accompanied the young man Telemachus on a search for his father Odysseus. Yet very little textual material in the Homeric texts actually justifies this transformation of somebody's name into a role and title. This brings us to the question, "Where does this myth come from?"

To find the answer, we have to go to France, to 1689. That year a French prelate, François Fénelon, Archbishop of Cambrai and foremost intellectual light in the country at the time, was nominated tutor of Louis the XIV's grandson and heir to the throne, Louis, Duke of Burgundy, then seven years old. It was felt that the young duke, considered a brilliant but unruly, unbalanced child governed by his instincts, would substantially benefit from the tutelage of the brilliant theologian and most forward-thinking Frenchman of his day. By the time Fénelon ended his work as educator of the duke in 1699, the young man had been transformed into a model potential ruler.

Unfortunately, we cannot know how much effect Fénelon's "mentoring" has had. The Duke of Burgundy died in 1712, during an epidemic of measles, which had taken his own father and his wife a mere few weeks before him. After Louis XIV's death in 1715, the throne of France passed to his five-year-old great-grandson and son of the Duke of Burgundy. Since Fénelon's ideas were adopted wholesale during the eighteenth century by the Enlightenment movement, the French Revolution might not have taken place had the Duke of Burgundy survived the epidemic, and the world would be a different place.

How did Fénelon carry out this transformation in the young nobleman? In addition to formal training in the classics, Fénelon stimulated his charge's imagination by composing texts that one would today label as "edutainment". Among this was a series of fables, witty *Dialogues of the Dead*[3], where, among many others, Socrates and Confucius compare their respective cultures. Key to our subject matter, there is a mythological adventure novel called *Les Aventures de Télémaque—The Adventures of Telemachus*—in which Telemachus, accompanied, as we have seen, by the older and wiser Mentor, conducts the search for Odysseus. Like the young duke, Telemachus is rash and impetuous, but full of goodness, which requires channeling in order to manifest only positive consequences for himself and others. The real hero of the story is actually Mentor/Athene—actually an autobiographical character—who will steer Telemachus through his journey, so that he can best learn about the arts and crafts of enlightened rulership along the way until, at the end of the story, he is ready to return to Ithaca and replace his father on the throne should the latter wish to wander off again.

First published in 1699, *Télémaque* had a phenomenal success first in France and then across Europe. With eight hundred editions of the text appearing in the eighteenth century alone, it was apparently the most widely read book of the age, so much so that, by 1749 in France and 1750 in England, the name Mentor had become a label that one applied to a skilled adviser.

The Lessons of Athene

There is much that we can learn by returning to Fénelon's original tale that will be pertinent to your requirements.

---

[3] Fénelon, F. (1700) *Dialogues des morts composés pour l'éducation d'un prince.*

Athene is the goddess of wisdom (and also of war). She knows everything that Telemachus might need to know. Does she appear to him as herself and impart her wisdom to him wholesale? Of course not, since the boy wouldn't learn anything through this and he would be forever dependent on her for instructions. Instead she veils her splendor and assumes the role and position of somebody else, a wise elder who has seen life, "been there and done that" (and literally got the mantle), as she feels that this familiar person will be better able to foster a spirit of self-reliance in the boy than an all-knowing busybody. Instead of imparting her wisdom wholesale to him, she gives him only the components that are strictly necessary to enable him to find out more for himself.

As a goddess, she would be most able to protect him well against any danger, but what would the boy learn from this? Instead, as Mentor, she lets him make mistakes so that he can see the consequences of his actions (or inaction) and thereby learn how to do things better next time. Should the worse come to the worst, she can always rescue him, and does once or twice, but only in extremis and without ever "getting out of role". She actually creates for him an environment where it is permitted to err, as the education Telemachus will acquire as a result of his mistakes will benefit him in the longer term. Indeed, much of their conversation actually enables the boy to review what's happened, what went well, what went wrong, what he has learned, how to do things differently next time, how to apply it back home, and so forth. All good questions you, in turn, could ask your protégé, and even yourself when reviewing your own interaction with them.

In addition to all that Athene offers Telemachus, there is much she offers us regarding how we can all become good mentors. The archetypal Mentor, she is the one that we should seek to emulate and model ourselves upon in order to mentor well without blinding our protégés with science or making them dependent on our wisdom.

For a full process to develop the mental attitude of a coach based on the Athene/Mentor archetype, see "The counsels of Athene" in the Appendix on page 211.

Exercise: Motivation to be a mentor

Write down your answers to these questions on a sheet of paper:

1. Why do you want to be a mentor? What is important for you about mentoring?
2. If you have a specific person in mind, why do you want to be a mentor to that person?
3. How do you expect your mentoring will help this person to develop, what will it be like when you look at the results in two years from now?
4. What kind of experiences do you consider worth sharing with this person? Where will you play a protective role? Where will you allow room to make mistakes?

As a way to help you discover your answers to these questions, we recommend to go through the experience yourself using "The counsels of Athene" process described at the back of the book.

The mentoring attitude

Although this book is about both mentoring and coaching, the attitude we adhere to ourselves is more of a mentoring attitude.

In the Appendix you'll find more information of what we learned from our interviews.

We inquired among people who had been mentored or who considered being mentored how they perceived the ideal mentor. Some of these explore different but by no means incompatible avenues. This is how they responded, describing their ideal mentor as:

- someone who has been there before
- somebody who knows, who is familiar with the world, or with my discipline
- someone who takes me by the hand and guides me through a new territory
- someone who asks me the questions I don't ask myself but ought to

- someone who gives me the feeling they are interested in my development
- someone who is not in competition with me
- someone I can trust
- someone I can confide in
- someone I click with on identity and value terms
- someone who appears to know me nearly more than I know myself
- someone who is there for me

The values on the right reflect the attitude we believe in, and these are also very helpful for building a great coaching relationship.

The key values we distilled from these interviews are:

- knowledge
- curiosity
- willingness
- relating
- unconditional regard
- trust

Of course, merely having the right attitude isn't enough, but it gives you a good starting point. Next to having the right attitudes and living up to the values in that box, the right *skills* are needed too, and, while these skills will be explained, we hope that self-examination will tell you how many of these required skills you already posses.

The history of coaching

Whereas as early as the late seventeenth century Fénelon helped to develop the concept of mentoring as grooming a person for high office, coaching itself is a much younger discipline. The term is derived from the name of a particular vehicle called "coach", a chariot of Hungarian origin, first developed in a town called "Kocs".[4] This particular chariot was built and designed during the reign (1458–90) of King Matthias Corvinus to transport the king and important members of the government. The coach became so successful that its design was soon exported to other countries.

What links, might you well wonder, could there be between a carriage and the profession of coaching? The only one that seems to make sense to us is that, in the seventeenth century, a

[4] Source: *Oxford English Dictionary*.

The word "coach" could have been quite a derogatory nickname for a meddlesome person.

However, there may be a better explanation. The term "cox", which denotes the person who steers or imparts rhythm to a rowing team is very ancient and may be related to the verb "to coax" which, among other things, means "to persuade, to urge (by gentle means)" (Oxford English Dictionary). As with the above, "to coax" also had a derogatory meaning until the 19th century, linked to manipulation.

Although the sounds for "coax" and "coach" differ, this is the same difference we observe in English between Northern English "fisk" and Southern English "fish", Northern English "ask" and Southern English "ash".

contemporary of Fénelon, the French fabulist Jean de la Fontaine, wrote a poem entitled "Le Coche et la Mouche" or "The Coach and the Fly", in which a fly is described as pestering a train of horses paining to pull a coach up a hill, and ascribing the success of the pull solely to its spurring efforts and "advice". It may be that the coach of the title was then transferred from the conveyance to the person who does the spurring and the advising.

Indeed, although it may have been applied for many years already, the word is officially recorded for the first time in the UK about the middle of the nineteenth century, initially as an irreverent nickname for a private tutor who prepares students for their exams. It soon lost its irreverence, however, to become a recognized title in British colleges. By 1880 the term also indicates the trainer of sport teams, probably starting with the illustrious sport of rowing. The first association for coaches was the American Football Coaching Association, founded in 1922, and the term in the US remained mainly used in sports. Almost all the books that appeared each year in the US on coaching between 1980 and 1990 still were sports-related.

Coaching was introduced in business as a metaphor. It fitted in the new mentality that was now expected from employees, who were becoming "human" resources. Indeed, till the 1960s most companies treated their employees as "appendices" to the machines. This changed under the influence of humanistic psychology, with proponents such as Carl Rogers and Abraham Maslow, as well as the organizational development specialists. Slowly, organizations started to realize that their staff were more than "intelligent machines" and that each person was unique and thus deserved a unique treatment.

Ken Blanchard's 1984 bestseller, *Putting the One Minute Manager to Work*, recommended coaching as a leadership style in order to obtain better results from people who have already achieved a medium level of competence. His advice was based on the work of Paul Hersey, who created the model known as *situational leadership*.

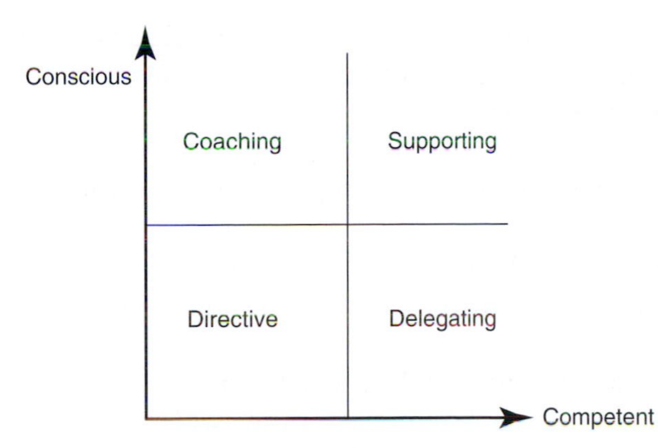

Figure 1.1: One way of presenting the situational-leadership model

The learning cycle often implies that the person will move from the lower left (unconscious incompetent) to upper left (consciously incompetent) to upper right (consciously competent) to lower right (unconsciously competent). In the lower left quadrant the competence is still low and the person is unconscious about it – it is recommended to use the directive leadership style.

In a nutshell, Blanchard and Hersey recommend you adapt your leadership style to match the level of competence of your employees. At first, when a person clearly lacks competence and may not even realize that there is still a lot to learn, they are "unconsciously incompetent" (indicated by the lower left quadrant of Figure 1.1). In this phase the manager has to be directive, giving the employee the exact procedure for the work that needs to be done.

After a while the employee will develop some competence (upper left quadrant of Figure 1.1), at which point the manager needs to switch to a more coaching leadership style, where they still closely monitor the work being done and still take the final decisions, but where they leave room for the employee, soliciting their opinion and motivating them to make a rational decision on *how* the desired results need to be achieved. The focus of this phase lies in creating an insight and awareness for the "why" of the assignment.

Once the person proves to be competent, the required leadership style changes again, becoming more *supportive*, and the person acquires more autonomy, especially when it comes to deciding *how* to do something and even to *what* to do.

Finally, when the person has proved able to handle this new freedom, you'll delegate the responsibility to the person and merely monitor their results.

Gradually, the use of the word "coaching" expanded from its narrow meaning in the Blanchard and Hersey framework to become a vague word covering all kinds of approaches. The 1990s saw a real boom of coaching and mentoring books. Today, every manager needs to be a coach, regardless of the competence level of their employees, and we diversified into "life coaches", "career coaches", "executive coaches", and so on. The amount of literature follows the trend: the number of coaching books in the English speaking world has risen to more than 130 books a year and 40 percent are business-related and cover business coaching, executive coaching, team coaching, career coaching, life coaching, and so on.[5]

What can the sport coach teach us?

Just as Mentor's story inspired us to learn about mentoring, sports coaches can teach us a lot about coaching. Notice how the team's performance can depend upon the coach who is leading it. Whether you look at American Football or at the soccer competition in the UK, you'll find that every year several football coaches get fired because their team doesn't obtain the desired results.

[5] We went to the Amazon.com website and counted the number of coaching books published between March 2002 and April 2003. You can repeat this exercise if you want to update the figure.

Exercise

Maybe you do some sports yourself or you remember a particular sports coach from your past. Or you may admire a coach from one of your favorite sports teams, be it football, basketball, cycling, whatever. Imagine for a moment that you are this coach. What would be their advice for you? Where does their approach differ most from how you tackle issues? What is there to be learned from this comparison?

Advice or area of difference

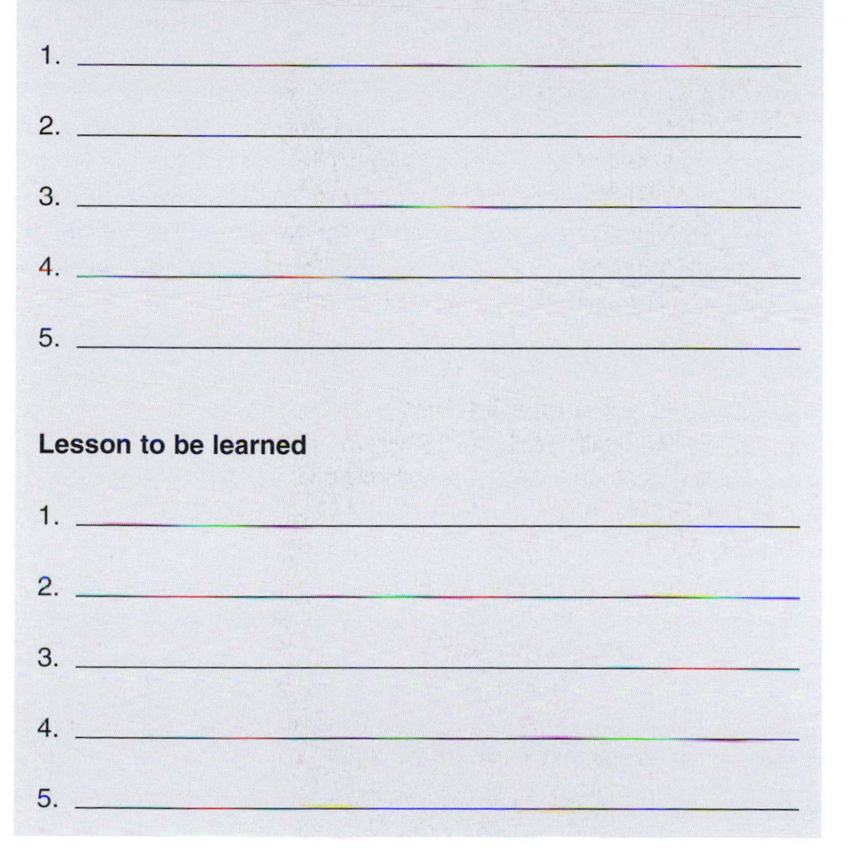

1. ______________________________
2. ______________________________
3. ______________________________
4. ______________________________
5. ______________________________

Lesson to be learned

1. ______________________________
2. ______________________________
3. ______________________________
4. ______________________________
5. ______________________________

Organizing the Mentoring and Coaching Processes

PART 2

This part puts the mentoring and coaching processes into more perspective. The first question to ask is: what can one expect to get out of a coaching or mentoring relationship? A second section walks through the lifecycle of a mentoring relationship. We continue with a section covering the idea of actively intervening in the protégé's career. The final section formalizes the mentorship idea even further, and deals with mentoring as a human-resource (HR) instrument for improving your organization's potential.

The contract/agreement

The Roman philosopher Seneca (4 BCE–65 CE) taught people that there is no favorable wind for those who do not know where to go. The notion of "contract" refers to getting a clear outcome for the coaching or mentoring and, although essential in a coaching context, it is desirable, rather, in a mentoring one. Which kind of outcome one can expect will depend much on the nature of the relationship. For instance, one can be using the term "coaching" to refer to some of the activities a manager does to help their subordinates reach their goals.

Assess the coach

Check for proven coaching competencies and for a reputation of "being a good coach" (values and attitude).

Decide whether you want the coach to have experience with the subject matter.

Does the coach have the necessary information specific to the organization (e.g. company culture, competence model)?

While it might make sense to consider the coaching contract in such a context also, it is certainly needed when the term "coaching" is used to refer to an independent person who is asked by the HR department to help an employee reach a specific outcome in a given number of coaching sessions (often five to ten meetings or telephone sessions over a rather short period of time).

A coach is often selected for their expertise within the problem area at hand, as well as for their coaching skills in general. For instance, many executive coaches have had a managerial role prior to becoming a coach. Even though it will enhance a coach's credibility if they can say that they have been there and done it, in our opinion coaches do not need to have done the job themselves previously in order to coach effectively.

Having good coaching skills, however, as will be explained in Parts 4 and 5, is crucial. Also, having an understanding of the organizational culture and goals, as well as adapting the coaching to the company's values and idiosyncrasies, is certainly needed.

Examples of coaching outcomes

This might be something as vague as "Helping while starting in a new function" or something as specific as learning specific skills or competencies:

- stress management, time management, burnout or anger management
- better communication skills (listening skills, presentation skills, communicating to a specific target audience (e.g. labor union, press)
- negotiation and/or conflict-management skills
- management skills (e.g. coaching, delegation, giving feedback)

Once it is clear on which issue the coach is expected to work, and whether it actually seems to be advisable to use coaching, you may wish to draft a short formal contract, in which you might to cover some of the following elements.

Coaching contract checklist

Have coach and protégé been briefed about the expected outcome? Will there be an intake meeting, with whom (HR, manager, protégé ...)?

Are price, duration and location of the coaching clear (what budget will be used to pay for the coaching, what are the payment modalities)?

How will the results of the coaching be evaluated (and by whom)? What kind of feedback is expected? What should be the content of the feedback? Does the coach have to present a formal report (if so, to whom)?

Contingency planning: what should the coach do if the coaching seems to fail (e.g. the protégé doesn't seem "coachable", the issue cannot be solved with coaching)?

The coach's assessment

Is the problem you're asked to help with a real coaching problem, or would training or management intervention be a better solution?

As a coach you might want to check whether the issue is really a coaching issue. Take the following examples:

- You are asked to coach a new business-development manager to improve their negotiation skills but that person has no negotiation experience and has never had any negotiation training.

- You are called in to help a technician to act in a more "customer-friendly" manner, while they actually have to cope with customers who are angry because the technician cannot fix the machine since the broken parts are not in stock and will only be supplied within a fortnight.

- You are asked to coach a salesperson in giving a less vague description of the company's product when making a quote. After a while, you might discover that the real reason why the salesperson has given a vague description is that it helps to push the company's products, even if these products do not match the customer's needs. Because sales commission is the motive, the sales staff lack an incentive to be more precise. Additionally, the manager might be reluctant to do anything about it, because doing so would threaten his or her fat bonus. The real flaw is the bonus plan, which doesn't take into account returned products or customer dissatisfaction.

It's clear that in these examples coaching may not be the most efficient use of resources and measures should be taken at other levels.

Problem type	Question to ask	Appropriate solution
Knowledge problem	Does the protégé know what should be done?	Training to increase knowledge might be less expensive.
Managerial problem	Can the protégé do something about the issue?	Consider adapting the organization or empowering the protégé.
Remuneration problem	Does the protégé benefit from acting as we would like them to act?	Consider revising the bonus plan so that it encourages the "right behavior" and corrects unwanted behavior.

Integrating coaching in the HR strategy

We have looked at it from the perspective of coaching a person within an organizational context. Instead of limiting yourself to such an ad hoc approach, we recommend that you integrate coaching with other HR instruments, such as competence management, training and development and the overall remuneration policy.

A competency model would be a useful foundation for other HR instruments. A person should be recruited only when they are considered suitable in terms of attitudes, values, and skills. Once the person is recruited, their training, mentoring, and coaching needs can be determined in order to fill the gap between the individual and the current and future needs of the organization; the individual's remuneration package can be set appropriately, possibly leaving some room for a premium, should they have some unneeded competences which increase their market value.

To maximize the added value of coaching, it should be embedded in the overall HR strategy instead of being used on a "one-shot" basis.

When a person receives training in a given subject because of a perceived competence shortfall coaching can be applied in order to further ensure that the new skills are put into practice and tasks can be set that will enable them to sharpen their skills and exercise their new "muscles".

Seven steps to ensure an effective mentoring relationship

Dividing the flow of a mentorship relationship into steps seems to be a research topic all by itself.[6] We do not claim to have the "ideal" number of steps and we know that in reality these steps may intermingle. After all, as Peter Senge, the author of the widely acclaimed *Fifth Discipline* and renowned systemic thinker, said at the First World Conference for Systemic Management (2001):[7] "A process design made for machines is perfectly predictable, but as engineers we had to learn that when you make a design for humans, you can't predict how reality will turn out afterwards."

One thing is sure: the relationship will have a start, a middle, and an end. It will also evolve over time, at first bringing partners closer, then gradually separating again. First there may be a growing admiration, then the independence of the protégé will grow again.

The importance of "chunking" the relationship—subdividing it into several steps—is that it allows you to point out some issues that may occur over a period of time as the coaching relationship develops. It may also enable you to identify why a relationship doesn't work as well as expected. You may, for example, skip a step in the mentoring process, and discover later on that not addressing these issues may explain why the relationship is going less smoothly than it could. Or maybe you and your protégé will discover that the relationship just doesn't work out, and that puts an early end to it.

---

[6] In her book (1996) *Le mentor: Transmettre un savoir-être*, Renée Houde compares how several authors chunk the mentoring process. Unfortunately, she chooses to explain how in her model three phases include all the rest. We are more concerned with the various process topics you'll encounter and therefore discerned a larger number of steps.

[7] First World Conference for Systemic Management, Vienna, 1–6 May 2001, organized by the Institute for Systemic Coaching and Training.

Characteristics of the protégé

Potential
The person has proved able to perform and wants more.

Willingness to learn
The person sees more potential in themselves and feels responsible for developing it, and is open to feedback and mentoring advice.

Step 1: Choosing a protégé

If it's up to you to choose, mentor a person because you admire them, maybe because you recognize something of yourself, because you know there is a lot of potential present or because you just know this person might learn a lot from you. All these reasons will work just fine as long as there is a willingness to learn from you on the part of the protégé. But they also include a danger: the purpose is not to mold someone in your image, or try to make them realize the dreams you *didn't* realize. The goal is to help the protégé realize *their* dreams. Maybe that's why mentoring will work better if the request to be mentored comes from the protégé.

In the case of the famous couturier Yves Saint Laurent, it was his mother who got in touch with Michel de Brunhoff, the editor of *Vogue* at the time, for him. In turn, Michel de Brunhoff opened the door to Christian Dior once he was convinced that young Yves and Dior would mutually benefit from this professional relationship. Often, mentors are chosen because they were the protégé's professor or supervisor before, because they are a friend of the family, or because they are amongst the stars of their profession.

If your protégé is a member of your own organization, there should remain some distance between the two of you. We recommend that you be at least two steps ahead of this person in terms of the career ladder and that the person work in a department other than yours, so that there should be no risk of your undermining their line manager.

Whom *not* to choose?

a. People you cannot respect or do not admire for their potential. In other words, people who are the opposite of the picture we have just painted.

b. Your children or life partner. Good mentoring requires objectivity, being able to see a person's weak spots, point them out and get them to work on it. It also requires having enough knowledge of the problem at hand (maybe knowledge of the industry or the company). When it comes to our loved ones, we could well be compromising our objectivity. It may be hard to avoid taking sides, because we are too much involved in their wellbeing and may also be too protective. The last thing they need is someone playing their "advocate", arguing for their rights, since in most cases this may mean throwing oil on the flames. Also, there is only a slim chance that you will be considered by, say, your child as "the" person in the discipline to turn to. More commonly, you're probably the *last* person suitable for the job!

Of course, we can have mentoring moments with our beloved ones, applying the mentoring principles from this book whenever this is appropriate. Some mentoring relationships have occurred within a parenting context (Mary Catherine Bateson was just as much mentored as she was parented by Margaret Mead and Gregory Bateson), a husband–wife relationship (there is evidence that Marie Curie, née Slodowska, mentored both her husband Pierre and her daughter Irène), and a loving relationship (Ruth Benedict was Margaret Mead's mentor as well as her lover). However, in order for these to work, the objectivity we referred to above was demonstrated and appears to be a prerequisite.

c. People you supervise. As a supervisor, you have an agenda other than as mentor: your agenda is linked to obtaining the desired results for your unit. At times supervisors will find this agenda "incompatible" with helping their collaborators grow to their potential, especially if that means that this person leaves your unit. It could also create other conflicts of interest between the wellbeing of the group and what's best for the individual. For instance, suppose other employees get the impression that your protégé is receiving favorable treatment.

Of course, a lot of mentoring principles also apply to any supervisory relationship: you should offer support to your staff, be their coach and give performance advice. So-called "nonmanagerial supervision" has a lot in common with both coaching and mentoring—you could even say that it *is* a type of mentoring.

Seen from the other side: characteristics of a great mentor

Partnership-driven
The mentor is not out on an ego trip, doesn't want to control or exercise their power.

Openness
There is a climate of trust, in which both parties can tell the truth without consequences.

Passion and generosity
The mentor loves to give others the opportunity to learn, and is passionate about sharing wisdom.

d. Your boss or your peers. The reasons why you should be careful about these kinds of mentorship relations are similar to what we looked at above. Also, there is little chance that you will be able to mentor these persons to the same degree as would be the case in a "normal" mentorship relationship, given that there will probably only be a fraction of the person's job you will know more about and the very least you'll need is the humility to realize this.

It may be possible, however, if the mentoring relationship occurs about non-work-related issues. The difficulty there may be more about what colleagues and other company members would say. Clear boundaries would need to be set up and any move involving the other person should be framed by a declaration of interest in order to pre-empt any potential malicious gossip. Therefore, if in doubt, abstain.

Reverse mentoring

At Picanol, the worldwide market leader in the production of weaving looms, each person in the management team has to choose a "reverse mentor", who has three characteristics:

- is of opposite sex
- for engineers, someone who isn't an engineer
- someone coming from a different country

The purpose of choosing a mentor who is different from you is that the presuppositions underlying your decisions will be challenged.

Step 2: Connecting

The key to success in the early stages of the relationship is a shared investment in the relationship between mentor and protégé. If everyone had "ideal" relationship skills, rapport building would always run smoothly. In reality, some people are more closed off and don't open up so easily. Others may find it harder to figure out how to make the most out of a relationship. There are also matters of personal, social, and cultural preferences, which may differ.

Rapport parameters

Checklist
What do you have in common or on what can you achieve an understanding?

- place
- interests
- attitude and values
- common history, stories (metaphors)
- vision for the future

For instance, while most people will agree that formal business mentoring probably takes place in the office, if it's a less formal mentoring relationship, there is no problem for, say, an American to invite someone to their home, something that is done less often in the UK, where a pub might be seen as a better place to communicate informally; and in France or Belgium, a good meal in a restaurant might be preferred.

So take some time at the beginning of the mentoring relationship to get to know each other as people, each with their unique strengths and weaknesses, their experiences and their aspirations. In Part 4, we'll present you with rapport-building skills, listening skills etc., that you can apply.

Step 3: Outlining the relationship

> To who does not know where he wants to go, there is no favorable wind.
>
> *Seneca*

Once a certain level of mutual trust is achieved, it's time to figure out what the mentoring will be about. Even if you consider the mentoring relationship an informal one, it's always good to have a goal in mind, because this clears up possible confusion and helps to match expectations with what's realistically achievable. At least it will focus your attention and generate a sense of commitment. Agree on issues for development:

> We are not in a position in which we have nothing to work with. We already have capacities, talents, direction, missions, callings.
>
> *Abraham Maslow*

- What needs to be done to maximize the protégé's potential over the time horizon considered?
- What new roles would the person want in the future?
- What challenges does this pose, given the person's attitude?
- What new competencies do they need in order to meet these challenges and come up trumps?
- How does all this relate to the whole person?

Three types of question to ask your protégé

What do you want to accomplish (as a next career step, from this mentoring …)?

How will having me as your mentor help you?

What can I offer you that you can't do/learn yourself?

Step 4: Getting to the bottom of it

> To be completely honest with oneself is the very best effort a human being can make.
>
> *Sigmund Freud*

Once we know what we want, there are two matters to settle. One relates to looking for potential roadblocks: how come we aren't there yet; is there something that has prevented the protégé from achieving these goals before? Part 4 will cover the SCORE and COMET models for dealing with this. Part 5 contains a section on limiting beliefs. Of course, a mentoring relationship has nothing to do with lying on Freud's psychoanalysis coach. Nevertheless, developing intra- and interpersonal skills needs addressing one way or another. So getting to the bottom of the issues must also be linked to the second type of issue: what practical, concrete actions can the protégé take in order to get closer to their goal?

When the protégé wants to change the subject, that by itself becomes an issue to get to the bottom of.

This is often the stage where your protégé may want to change or redefine the goals you are working on. Perhaps the rate of the change process in relation to the issue is too fast for your protégé and more time is needed to explore at a higher level before going into detail.

Another reason might be a shift in priorities, which makes the previous issue less important at this point in time. Whatever the reason, in such a case challenge the protégé to choose a matter that is really essential to them.

Step 5: Concrete actions

We have too many high-sounding words, and too few actions that correspond with them.

Abigail Adams, letter to John Adams, 1774

Ultimately, mentoring can work only when protégés take their own destiny in their own hands. As Henry Ford put it, "You can't build a reputation on what you are going to do." If a mentor helps too much, they do their protégé a disservice, because the protégé may end up relying on their mentor, or even become a kind of extension of the mentor, instead of growing to fulfill their own potential. Even when Christian Dior named Yves Saint Laurent as his heir, it was up to Saint Laurent to prove himself afterwards, and, given that he ran into trouble with the owners of the Dior *haute couture* house, it's clear he hadn't been prepared well enough for this, and he lost his dream job. Afterwards, it took him two years to get out of the deep hole he had fallen into and set up his own company.

Take chances; make mistakes. That's how you grow. Pain nourishes your courage. You have to fail in order to practice being brave.

Mary Tyler Moore (b. 1937), American actor

Once we get to the bottom, the question is: what steps (action points, concrete actions, job experiences, projects, challenges) will help the protégé to grow in the areas where this is needed for achieving the goals as they are set? For some of these, the mentor will play an active role, for instance as teacher, or by being the role model or maybe even by "sponsoring" the protégé, helping them to get a job. For other actions, the mentor is more of a guide, pointing out where to look for learning.

Based on the SMART acronym[8] and on research about what makes an outcome well formed,[9] we worked out the following template for planning actions:

SMARTEST actions

The three basic questions concerning actions are: What is the goal? How will you know you have reached it? What will you do to get there?

Once you find answers to these three questions, the SMARTEST criteria (which will be outlined in Part 4) will help you to check whether your outcome is well formed, and thus has a reasonable chance for success.

Step 6: Following up

If the protégé really believes in the SMARTEST actions they formulated, chances for success are actually quite large. Still, as Murphy's Law states, "If something *can* go wrong, it will." Maybe Charles F. Kettering,[10] inventor and co-holder of more than 140 patents, summed it up the best when he said, "Keep on going and the chances are you will stumble on something, perhaps when you are least expecting it. I have never heard of anyone stumbling on something sitting down."

The proof of the pudding is in the eating.

Only by not doing anything are you not making any mistakes, but then maybe not doing anything is a mistake all by itself.

Denis Bridoux

[8] The SMART acronym stands for "**S**pecific, **M**easurable, **A**cceptable, **R**ealizable and **T**imed" (also see Part 4).

[9] Our book *7 Steps to Emotional Intelligence* includes a full chapter entitled "Planning for Success". The "SMARTEST" acronym we propose here is the latest one of a series of coaching, mentoring, and planning projects Patrick Merlevede undertook for customers in Belgium, including Banksys and the City of Antwerp.

[10] Charles Kettering (1876–1958) was head of GM's research function between 1918 and 1947. He believed strongly in the combination of hard work, ingenuity and technology to make the world a better place.

One of the hardest things in this world is to admit you are wrong. And nothing is more helpful in resolving a situation than this frank admission.

Benjamin Disraeli (1804–81)

Apart from checking whether a project is still on track, an additional reason for including intermediate checkpoints in our prescription for SMARTEST action is that such checkpoints also present us with learning opportunities, which can be summarized in the following questions: "What went wrong? Why? What can we learn from this for the future?"

This holds even if you prefer to keep a mentoring relationship informal. In this case, a minimal interpretation of follow-up would mean that we at least want to obtain an extensive, honest answer to the "How are you doing?" question we usually ask people as a welcome. And the answer doesn't have to be negative in order to learn. After all, even if we tend to learn more from our mistakes, from time to time, it is nice to be able to step back and appreciate what we have achieved, to become conscious of the new competencies we have gained, or how we have changed, grown into a fuller person inside.

As the relationship evolves over time, this phase may gradually evolve from a discussion between "master and disciple" to one between good friends, or even peers, where situations are discussed to retrieve the learnings for both participants out of them. Thus, Margaret Mead herself was delighted to reconnect with her daughter Mary Catherine Bateson from a new perspective upon the latter's graduation, and she sent her a congratulation letter beginning with "*Chère collègue*".

I owe my success to having listened respectfully to the very best advice, and then going away and doing the exact opposite.

G. K. Chesterton (1874–1936)

Step 7: Get out of the way

Indeed, after a certain period in time, often somewhere between two and five years, the complementarity of the relationship between mentor and protégé will end and the relationship will become more egalitarian. Call it "Mission accomplished!" Of course, calling it an end isn't easy and researchers such as Kathy Kram found that it may take up to six months to get through this phase (Kram, 1983). If it takes too long to conclude the relationship, this may cause a feeling of disappointment for your protégé, who may have expected more than you have to give. The challenge for you is to find the right moment to set your protégé loose, so that your relationship can transform into a friendship that goes beyond the mentorship per se.

Career acceleration

The concept of "career acceleration", the fast track to success, makes sense if we think that somebody has learned what there was to learn in their current job, and, given the potential we perceive, we wish to move the person in a new job fast, because we think they will learn more by doing things they didn't have to do before and we have a professional opening that will offer them the right experience to cover their development needs.

Another reason for career acceleration is that those with high potential might leave the organization if they don't see what opportunities or new challenges there are for them. It's the potential we see in them that makes us want to pay those with high potential more than their colleagues doing similar jobs and that also motivates us to spend additional time and energy to develop them so that they are ready for their next assignment.

Do not be too timid and squeamish about your actions.

All life is an experiment. The more experiments you make the better. What if they are a little coarse, and you may get your coat soiled or torn? What if you do fail, and get fairly rolled in the dirt once or twice.

Up again, you shall never be so afraid of a tumble.

Ralph Waldo Emerson

Checklist: recognizing a high-potential employee

The major issue for an organization's HR managers and executives probably relates to the need to groom the next generation: who will emerge to lead your business in the next five to ten years? What are you doing about it now, so that potential leaders will be ready when it's time to step up?

For Jack Welch, CEO for General Electric from 1981 to 2001, the stars are "people who are filled with passion, committed to making things happen, open to ideas from anywhere, and blessed with lots of runway in front of them. They have the energy not only to energize themselves, but everyone who comes in contact with them." (Welch, 2001). We recommend designing your own checklist of elements you consider important. To get you started in writing down yours, the following

The 4 Es of General Electric (GE) leadership

Very high **energy** level

Ability to **energize others** around common goals

Edge to make tough yes/no decisions

Consistently **execute** and deliver on promises

example includes the elements of the jobEQ formula for success:

Results = Culture × Attitude × Competencies

Demonstration of **results**: Do we have objective evidence to call this person a top performer? Have they fulfilled major assignments?

Support of **company culture**: Can this person adapt to cultural differences? Is their behavior aligned with the company's values? Do they, in their behavior, demonstrate integrity? In what ways have they shown loyalty to the company? Do they relate to and identify with the management?

Attitude: Does this person have the attitude we expect of a future leader (e.g. eagerness for responsibility, seeking and accepting feedback, maturity of thought, thirst for knowledge, willingness to make a difference and to take risks, mindfulness of consequences, an eye to the long term, as opposed to wanting to make a fast buck)?

Competencies: Does this person have well-developed interpersonal skills? Can they mobilize people? Do they have accurate insight and a will to learn? Do they learn from mistakes?

Knowledge management: Does this person have a skill set that is valuable to the company in the future? Do they have a broad business knowledge? Is there a risk that they might leave the organization?

In order to find the limits of the possible, you have to go beyond, into the impossible.

Arthur C. Clarke

Of course, if all these elements were all 100 percent present, it would mean that no further development work is required! The "holes" a person has with regard to this map mark out where you need to focus your attention when mentoring, for instance by giving the person assignments to develop these areas on the job.

More than 80 percent of the people in General Electrics mentoring programs in 1999 were promoted by 2001.

Given a protégé's potential, we do not expect that they will spend the customary average three years or so on the next career step. They may actually already move on to their next assignment in less than two years. Some really specific assignments can even be as short as three months! The goal of carrying out one of these assignments is to give your protégé the opportunity to demonstrate that they have acquired a key learning or, as an ex-army chief once said, "to show their mettle in the midst of fire". Medieval lawyers called this "ordeal" or "trial by fire". Or, as Pablo Picasso said, "I am always doing that which I cannot do, in order that I may learn how to do it."

To get to the moon, you first have to dream you'll get there one day.

Denis Bridoux

Checklist: Choosing an assignment

The choice of an assignment implies finding answers to the following questions:

- What are the key challenges of the assignment?
- Does the person have the competencies required or do we expect that these competencies will arise during the assignment?
- How will the assignment help the protégé to stretch beyond their comfort zone and develop the competencies needed?
- How does the experience of this assignment fit in with their overall career goals (knowledge of different product areas, functional domains, etc.)?
- How will the assignment be followed up?

An important thing to realize from the onset is that, even if your protégé accepts the assignment and knows what there is to learn, it's not because they are given this assignment that they will necessary learn what they're expected to learn. They may learn something completely different.

Even if the results of the assignment are commendable, they may not actually have learned as much from the experience as expected, or even at all. It may well be that your protégé succeeded in reorganizing the situation, so that they managed using their strengths, instead of having to develop their weaknesses and, as long as it worked, what's wrong with that? Therefore, expect the unexpected and you won't be disappointed.

It is useful here, therefore, to distinguish two types of objective when setting up an assignment. One—public—is to do a job well. The other—related to the mentoring process itself—is about making your protégé try out something new and learn from it.

This is very important: playing to your strengths may indeed develop them further, but turning a weakness into a strength, or working on something one is not inclined to be very good at to begin with, will make far more profound qualitative *and* quantitative changes to your skills balance and what you can do with it. An unresolved weakness may sabotage an existing strength, whereas a weakness resolved will synergize with other resources and enable your protégé to contemplate going for things and succeeding in ways they might not even have dreamed about before.

Pitfalls of acceleration and their solutions

Image of favoritism

Explain your choice in terms of attitude and competence strengths as well as on long-term advantages for the company.

In order to avoid the idea from coworkers that your protégé gets unfair advantages, each person should ideally pass a normal recruitment cycle before getting the job. These elements should explain your choice in terms of attitude and competency strengths, as well as of long-term advantages for the company. When you compare the person with other candidates, having objective elements to explain why the protégé was chosen over others will defuse impressions of favoritism and, instead, present an image of fairness. Wouldn't a company doing this be worth working for? In addition, it may act as an incentive for the other coworkers: who will be next?

Time to prove

An often-heard complaint is that managers remain on assignments for only about three years. In the first year, they clean up the mess left behind by their predecessor, and everything that isn't as wished can be blamed on that person. During the second year, the person stabilizes his reorganization and during the third year they reap the benefits, leaving just in time before the bodies start to fall out of the cupboard. Their successor starts this cycle all over again, by cleaning up the bodies. This cynical and unresourceful frame of thinking contains several assumptions that need addressing point by point, once and for all:

The predecessor was no good and this one won't be either, or, if he is, it won't be for very long. Such a "blame frame" serves no one. It is only a counsel of despair that acts as a disincentive to work well. It encourages "burnout" and presupposes an imbalance of efforts and energies that is unnecessary if resources are sustained and well managed. Before speaking of failure, one should give others permission to succeed. When actual "failure" is there, it is rarely due to one person, but to a system that either got in the way or colluded actively or passively with its occurrence.

Revolution/reorganization is the only way. A frame of mind like this is very "either/or", good one day, bad the next. It measures success and failure as absolute and nonexistent (1 versus 0) and doesn't acknowledge that there is no such thing as absolute success or absolute failure, but always something in between. You don't build a house by putting a floor up and then pull it down to start again. Evolutionary change doesn't throw out the baby with the bathwater: it preserves the good aspects, creates a frame where the less good can be improved upon and sets up a structure that allows you to build on.

Good work can be done only remedially, and then not for long. Well-structured good work should work generatively in a way that is evolutionary. Any lastingly successful change work, either at individual or group level, finds ways of incorporating previous structures, sometimes even turning weaknesses into strengths.

The organization suffered by employing your predecessors. Although this may have been the case—on the other hand it may not—it doesn't have to be so forever.

Setting up a formal mentorship program in your organization

Resource

Margo Murray's *Beyond the Myths and Magic of Mentoring* (2001) covers in depth how to set up a mentoring process within your organization.

Setting up a formal mentorship program offers several benefits, which make it appealing for companies. Indeed, if the program is successful, one can expect a significant payback, with great effects for both the company image and its future, for instance through knowledge management.

Actually, since 1990 the need for mentoring and coaching only increased. Trends such as downsizing and business process engineering cut away many management layers in big companies and increased the workload for the remaining staff. Creation of jobs for "knowledge workers" increased job complexity, which in turn increased the workload of the manager, who in many cases already had to supervise more direct reports than before.

Another trend is the ever-increasing "globalization": the European Union effectively removed border controls during the 1990s and introduced the euro, which became a real currency in 2002. But, even in Europe, cultures and the cost structure of companies remain quite different from country to country. For many workers, the end result is an increased stress level, where even engineers, IT professionals, and back-office workers realize that their jobs might be moving to Eastern Europe or India if they cannot add more value than their foreign counterparts.

Part of the need for coaching and mentoring programs is to increase the coping skills of employees to deliver better performance in the face of these changing times. And there are also several additional positive effects, such as:

Coach to increase today's performance; mentor to develop, in order to capitalize on the potential.

jobEQ's mantra

High payback: Mentoring leads to increased productivity while being cost-effective. Smarter people give better solutions to the company's problems. Mentoring helps to develop the potential that is already present in your employees in a way that is far less expensive than formal classroom training. Given that, even in 2001, surveys indicated that some people consider they are using only 50 percent of their potential, the opportunity cost of not starting a formal mentoring program is huge.

Improved recruiting efforts: Even though most people realize that few companies nowadays can guarantee a long-term career, this only means that people now have to take their own measures when it comes to getting guarantees for their long-term development. So you can expect that more people will be looking for clues that a company is taking care of this long-term dimension. Having a mentoring program is far more credible than explaining a career path to someone, and makes this path more explicit.

Knowledge management, better retention, resource optimization, and succession planning: Since 1990 more and more organizations have become aware of the importance of doing knowledge management, and one of the often-cited techniques is "building talent pools". Well-known advocates of this approach are HR consulting firms, such as Personal Decisions International (PDI) and Development Dimensions International (DDI), who have specialized in assessment and leadership development for over thirty years. Demographics aren't helping, either: today's 25- to 35-year-olds are less numerous than the previous generation, so keeping them may be increasingly challenging, as there may be a demand for them elsewhere. When people move, they not only take with them more than the post they had, but also a treasure chest of information, networking resources, and practical tips, which, being stored in their heads, cannot be retrieved directly. A mentoring scheme can be a way of preserving and sharing this "soft" knowledge with others.

Of course, there are several differences between informal ways of mentoring, as we have been discussing above, whereby the larger part of the initiative to start a relationship comes from the mentor or protégé and is fully volunteered by both parties, and a formal program, where the HR department strongly promotes mentoring, or even where the organization links financial rewards to the program.

If the effort is more structured, the HR department (or those in charge of the mentoring program) will be involved in matching mentors and protégés. Such matching enables the HR department to ensure that the mentor assigned is strong in the areas where the protégé is seen as weak. It is clear that such formalization completely changes the motivational effects of the program. In best cases a protégé nominates three or four persons they would like as a mentor, but the matchmaking could also be inspired by a third party (the HR department, some nominations by the protégé's boss, an outside consultancy team ...).

In any case, both parties must be given the right to refuse to initiate the mentoring relationship without being reproached for so doing.

Making the case for mentoring

Point to consider

Even if you add the cost of paying a high performer a good salary package (according to market value), and providing them with enough training opportunities (and a mentoring program), this will be peanuts compared with the value they represent to your organization and the benefit this will bring.

As any book on high potentials will tell you, talented people are key to organizational success. The real job for leaders is to recruit top talent into their organizations, and to make sure they integrate well into the organization by acquainting them with its formal and informal structures (e.g. internal rules, values, structures, networks). Once this has succeeded, the leader's task consists of ensuring that these top performers remain highly competent. For corporate mentoring programs this represents the biggest added value. Unfortunately, studies show that both top executives and top performers themselves often neglect these aspects, often using "lack of time" as an excuse. As a result, many executives and high-level managers get limited support to do so in the organization.

Mentoring and coaching programs clearly can play an important role in tackling these issues. In addition to the advantages of ensuring the retention of high achievers, mentors or coaches can help top executives to increase their own self-awareness and flexibility and to motivate them to keep on learning. Most top managers may also benefit if their own mentor or coach helps them to keep track of their emotional intelligence, with special attention to the way top executives treat their collaborators. It may reduce their own stress levels and feelings of isolation. Validating other people around you creates a climate of goodwill. Commonly, people who feel validated will seek to reciprocate in kind and find ways of validating you also.

Calculating the return on investment (ROI) of retention

A rule of thumb is that the cost of replacement of a high performer will easily outclass one year of full compensation for that person, but be aware that some costs are hidden or will show up on other budgets. If you want to make the calculation yourself, here are some elements to factor in the equation:

Recruitment cost: Cost of attracting and hiring a high performer: a common figure is that it takes at least three months of salary to replace someone, and there is also the risk that the new person hired does not perform as well as the previous person, and even a 50 percent risk that the person won't hold the job for more than eighteen months.

Cost of absence of a high performer: The added value of a high performer is much higher than their salary and they create a bigger leverage than other employees. And there is also the stress caused to other employees (eventually through extra workload, and also by reduced morale) and lost opportunities because the high performer is missing for a period of time.

Cost of getting the newcomer up to speed: Time lost while the replacement is being trained (the first three months on a job are an "induction period") where the value added is lower than for a fully performing employee and training requires that others give up valuable time.

In addition, the departed high performer may have had some specific knowledge and skills that are hard to replace.

Resource

A great book on retention of talented committed employees is *Love 'Em or Lose 'Em* (1999) by Beverly Kaye and Sharon Jordan-Evans. Mentoring is just one of their 26 strategies for retention.

Making the case for remedial coaching, where you make sure the protégé has the required skills to do their current job at a high performance level, is even easier. All you need to do is to consider the cost of a job done below high performance level and compare that with the cost of coaching the same person to reach this level. For instance, if a good salesperson makes on average two sales a day and a weak performer makes only one sale, you are losing 50 percent of your possible sales volume. The cost of coaching that person for an hour a week will probably be much less than what you would have lost in sales. No wonder sales is one of the areas where coaching is most used and even considered as the most important task of the first line of management.

The push and the pull of mentoring and coaching

Mentoring and coaching programs can be initiated either by the HR department or by another formal sponsor in the organization (the push approach), or the initiative can come from would-be protégés themselves (the pull approach). These approaches are complementary.

Coaching and mentoring need = function (push, pull)

In a push approach, coaching or mentoring originates in a perceived gap between the actual situation and the desired situation we want a protégé to be in. Ideally, this perceived gap is based on a formal, well-studied competence model for the current position the person is holding (coaching) or a future position we have in mind for the protégé (mentoring). In both cases the initial trigger can be a formal 360-degree[11] feedback program or a full-blown assessment center, making the gap explicit. For coaching, the gap can also be perceived by examining why the person doesn't obtain the performance goals we set forth (either explicitly, or what we had hoped that the employee would achieve). The perceived gap is then filled by a combination of formal training programs and coaching or mentoring, and enforced by using carrots such performance bonuses and sticks such as threats of missed promotions or the risk of being fired.

This push approach is typically managed by HR and this causes many conflicts, for instance when the model used for the job doesn't correspond with the reality of the job.

Let us say a sales manager complained about the assessment center set up by HR, which led them to conclude that their best salespeople weren't fit to do the job! The cause of this problem was that HR used a standard questionnaire that measured competencies that were irrelevant to the job. No wonder the credibility of HR is quite low in some organizations.

Another typical problem is that training programs typically given by external trainers are not relevant to the needs of the employees. For example, a trainer presented a hard-sell approach to medical representatives of a pharmaceutical company. Experienced participants complained that this approach wasn't relevant for dealing with doctors, even if the trainer had previously worked as manager in the pharmaceutical industry. The high performers explained that such a pushy "sales" approach alienated medical doctors, causing them to say that they didn't have the time to meet the reps, which defeated the object.

In a "pull" approach we hope that the protégé will realize by themselves that they need to evolve, either because they risk missing goals or because they could do more than they currently achieve. This should be backed up with an encouragement of personal aspirations and ensuring that protégés take

A word of caution: the law of the averages

Standard competency frameworks, which are tested on many salespersons or managers in different companies, aim to present the competencies that are the greatest common denominator between all participating companies. However, if your company is unique, such standard framework will probably filter out the unique competencies needed by your employees to make this uniqueness work!

The key competencies for your company are exactly those that are above average and are to be found only in top performers, but they are lacking in weaker employees!

[11] For a full explanation, refer to page 41.

responsibility for their own learning. They will be looking at coaching, mentoring, training and even 360-degree programs as resources the company is offering them to reach their personal goals. Programs such as the current virtual universities, where e-learning is combined with coaching and mentoring opportunities, typically appeal to this group.

The company's real high potentials will typically be behaving in line with this pull approach. The more you hire people with a learning attitude, and the more you encourage personal responsibility for growth, the bigger the pull part of the equation will be.

The pull approach has its weaknesses as well. People with little ambition, who just want to do their job from nine to five, may be less ready to take up the pull, especially if their company expects them to use the virtual-university facilities outside of their formal job hours. Employees who lack accurate self-assessment skills may think that they don't need any further coaching or mentoring to do their jobs.

Wrapping it up: a checklist for a formal mentoring program

Mentor
What attitude, values and skills are expected? How will mentors be selected? Can we offer some compensation?

Protégé
Who gets a mentor (what are our criteria, how do we select, etc.)?

Combination
How can we match up mentors and protégés? How are outcomes set?

Is there a formal agreement? If so, what do mentor and protégé need to agree upon?

HR management
What are the program's goals? How and when will we evaluate it?

How does the program fit into the overall HR strategy?

What are our resources? (For instance, what support and training can we offer to the program? Can some of the mentoring be counted as working hours?)

Can we make the case for our program (cost–benefit analysis)?

Career management
De we require a formal development plan from the protégé? Is there a follow-up? Can we offer any additional benefits for protégés who are reaching their personal development targets?

Taking Stock and Moving Ahead

PART 3

As coach or mentor we will recommend our protégé to make a gap analysis, figuring out which attitude elements, values and skills are appropriate for the task at hand, and where they still have some work to do. In this part of the book we recommend you to do likewise with regards to what it takes to be a good mentor or coach.

Following this part of the book, we present you with a toolkit covering a range of short- and long-term developmental issues. We start this part with a questionnaire aimed at helping you to prioritize and choose which sections of the rest of the book will bring you the highest added value in terms of improving your coaching and mentoring approach. The rest of this part focuses on helping you move ahead. It will cover presuppositions, expectations and intentions. This material is useful for your own learning process as mentor or coach and can be applied as tools as well.

Behavioral observation: what you are already good at?

Most of the time, it seems easier to agree on "where we need to go" than on "where we are today". The problem with taking stock lies in getting all parties to agree with the appraisal of the current situation.

Self-assessment

Most of the competencies you'll need for mentoring are applicable in other contexts too. Therefore, we have used the

Instead of filling out this questionnaire on paper, we invite you to fill it out on the jobEQ website. Go to http://www.jobEQ.com/mentor

COMET methodology[12] to formulate the questions in the self-assessment so that they may also apply if you haven't yet done much mentoring. For getting the most accurate results on the self-assessment, fill out the questionnaire opposite with the following question in mind: "If someone else was asked to describe me, what would be their feedback on the following statements?"

If you fill out the questionnaire on the jobEQ website, the system will automatically calculate your score. Otherwise, here is the key to calculating your score.

Calculating your score

The questionnaire measures six critical areas that contribute to your specific skills in short- and long-term mentoring. To know your score for a skill area, you need to add up the scores for the individual questions that point to that skill area.

Step 1: Calculate your score for each question.

Next to each question, write your score: 0 points for an answer in the first column (with heading "never"), 1 point for an answer in the second column (with header "once or twice") and so on till you reach four points for a answer in the fifth column.

	Never	Once or twice	Occasionally	Repeatedly at various times	Extremely frequently
points	0	1	2	3	4

Step 2: Calculate your score for each area.

Add up the scores for the following questions:

[12] Created by Patrick Merlevede for jobEQ.com, 1999–2003 (also see Part 4 of this book).

In the past two months how often has this behavior been displayed?

The person:	Never	Once or twice	Occasionally	Repeatedly at various times	Extremely frequently
1 Is passionate about helping others to develop themselves	O	O	O	O	O
2 Admit their own mistakes and confront unethical actions in others	O	O	O	O	O
3 Articulates personal vision, mission, and values	O	O	O	O	O
4 Separates facts from interpretations, assumptions and opinions	O	O	O	O	O
5 Reads between the lines when others state their point of view	O	O	O	O	O
6 Takes a tough, principled point of view even if this is unpopular	O	O	O	O	O
7 Gives guidance in a way that is appropriate with the attitude and the current skills and knowledge of the person	O	O	O	O	O
8 Makes sure the action plan is specific, positive, and measurable	O	O	O	O	O
9 Analyzes the reasons for personal successes and failures, helps others to do likewise	O	O	O	O	O
10 Builds rapport and encourages open communication	O	O	O	O	O
11 Refers to the organizational mission and values when discussing alternatives and taking decisions	O	O	O	O	O
12 Handles difficult people and tense situations with diplomacy and tact	O	O	O	O	O
13 Knows how to make the most of current job responsibilities for further development and helps others to do so	O	O	O	O	O
14 Asks questions to clarify and ensure understanding	O	O	O	O	O
15 Strives to find win–win solutions	O	O	O	O	O
16 Takes other's emotions into account while communicating and adapts own emotions accordingly	O	O	O	O	O
17 Can be trusted with sensitive information and maintains confidentiality	O	O	O	O	O
18 Gives feedback, indicating specific observable behaviors	O	O	O	O	O
19 Helps others to identify and to deal with limiting beliefs	O	O	O	O	O
20 Networks inside and outside the organization in order to gain better information based on multiple perspectives	O	O	O	O	O
21 Helps others to formulate concrete and achievable actions	O	O	O	O	O
22 Has engaged in career discussions helping others to plan their careers based on values, attitude, and competencies	O	O	O	O	O
23 Adapts in order to persuade their audience with the right message	O	O	O	O	O
24 Supports responsible risk taking in response to business opportunities and person's growth	O	O	O	O	O
25 Aligns their behavior and personal goals with personal values and mission	O	O	O	O	O
26 Acknowledges differences within groups and between worldviews and acts appropriately to include them based on their merit	O	O	O	O	O
27 Spots and nurtures opportunities for collaboration	O	O	O	O	O
28 Builds trust through their reliability and authenticity	O	O	O	O	O
29 Asks for feedback to discover their own blind spots and helps other to do likewise	O	O	O	O	O
30 Uses stories and cases to illustrate the point they are trying to make	O	O	O	O	O
31 Leads a varied life, with time for all their interests	O	O	O	O	O

			Maximum score
FB	= 4 + 8 + 15 + 18 + 21 + 29 = __	(feedback, action plans, and conflict handling)	24
QA	= 5 + 9 + 14 + 20 = __	(question asking and analysis)	16
CO	= 10 + 12 + 16 + 23 + 26 +30 = __	(communication)	24
VM	= 3 + 11 + 19 + 31 = __	(values and mission, balance)	16
IN	= 2 + 6 + 17 + 25 + 28 = __	(integrity and trust)	20
CD	= 1 + 7 + 13 + 22 + 24 + 27 = __	(career development)	24

Interpretation of your score

The questionnaire was testing you for two types of skill.

Maximum score = 64

Short-term mentoring skills: **FB + QA + CO = ___**
This heading includes skills such as connecting with people, relating, feedback skills, formulating well-formed outcomes, asking questions, analyzing an issue, finding patterns, challenging persons to grow, adjusting communication, communicating metaphorically, etc. These skills are mainly discussed in Part 4.

Your FB score: _____

Maximum: 24

Feedback and conflict-handling skills
Giving good feedback and accepting feedback requires being able to separate facts from interpretation and deal with blind spots, and acting upon the feedback. Similar skills are needed for handling conflicts and turning them into win–wins.

Your QA score: _____

Maximum: 16

Analytical skills
The first task for analysis is gathering enough information, where question-asking skills come in handy. Once we have the information, we need to structure it, finding the pattern that connects.

Your CO score: _____

Maximum: 24

Communication skills
We never succeed in communicating all details of a subject, and there is always the risk of our being misunderstood. If you evaluate the quality of your communication based on the effect it has, this motivates you to adapt your message for your communication partner.

Long-term mentoring skills: **VM + IT + CD = ___**

Maximum score = 60

This heading includes skills such as formulating vision and mission, clarifying values and dealing with limiting beliefs, dealing with integrity and being congruent, balancing different areas of your life etc. These skills are mainly discussed in Part 5.

Motivation, values, mission, and balance

The worst that can happen is that you look back at your life and conclude that you haven't been doing the things you would like to have done, because you didn't have the time or lacked the courage to act in accordance with your values or pursuit of your mission in life. This competence cluster includes the necessary skills to avoid falling into these traps.

Your VM score: _____

Maximum: 16

Integrity and trust building

Are you willing to walk your talk, to go that extra mile to keep your promises? Your reputation and ability to inspire confidence are crucial for a constructive mentoring relationship.

Your IN score: _____

Maximum: 20

Career-development skills

Career development is one of the prime purposes of mentoring. It involves being able to find out what motivates your protégé, how they prefer to organize their work, and what they value or want for their future.

Your CD score: _____

Maximum: 24

Note: 360° and 720° feedback

Self-assessment has the inconvenience that some people may overestimate themselves (thinking their competence level is higher than it really is) while others underestimate their competence. Also, other parties may not perceive the competence that is there. So-called 360° feedback addresses these issues by having one's boss, subordinates, and colleagues make the assessment, hence the term 360°. Extended forms even take into account the feedback of the customer. "720° feedback" is a commonly used term in the HR world to indicate a retesting of people as a follow-up (e.g. after a training programme).

You'll benefit the most from the questionnaire when you use your scores to set the direction of your learning. After doing this self-assessment you will know on which mentoring skills covered in the two remaining parts of the book you'll have to focus.

You can generalize your own experience with this book to coaching in general: first one uses an assessment tool to figure out the gap between the current level of competence and the desired level. The assessment indicates for which topics coaching or training may be applied.

Expectations and how to manage them

When you embark on a new venture, you usually have some expectations of what you're going to get. This may be a positive or a negative expectation. How many people do you know who expect to fail at something and, as a consequence, don't even get started? In actual fact, whatever you do, consciously or not, you will create an expectation of what you're aiming to accomplish, or of what is going to happen. An expectation is a construct of the mind, conscious or unconscious, an extrapolation upon previous data, which you then project into the future. It is a type of belief one has about something that has not happened yet, about the future. Depending on individual parameters, your extrapolations can broadly be in two categories: similar to what went on before (more of the same), or different from what went on before (less of the same), or somewhere along this spectrum.

Some expectations are pretty solid. For example, you may expect to receive some mail today, because you have received mail before. Depending on the type of mail you expect you may dread it, eagerly await it, or just expect to get some mail. Depending on what happens, you may be surprised, relieved, or disappointed that the mail did or did not arrive.

Other expectations may be far-fetched and built on very flimsy ground indeed. How grounded in reality may be an expectation—acquired at a crystal-gazing session at a local fair—that you will inherit a fortune from a long-lost relative?

Thus, among other things, your expectation has evolved out of previous experiences, previous expectations you had, and the values that you have ascribed to these as a result. For example, if you value "fun", you will build "fun" into your expectation of watching a particular film or reading a particular book, mentoring a particular protégé or attending a particular training course. This, you will compare with what you get when you actually live the experience.

Even if you don't actually go through the experience because something or somebody will have prevented you, you will make a comparison between what you expected to get and what you didn't get and, in all probability, will probably not like not getting it if this was a pleasant expectation you had. On the other hand, if the expectation was not very nice, you'll probably feel quite relieved.

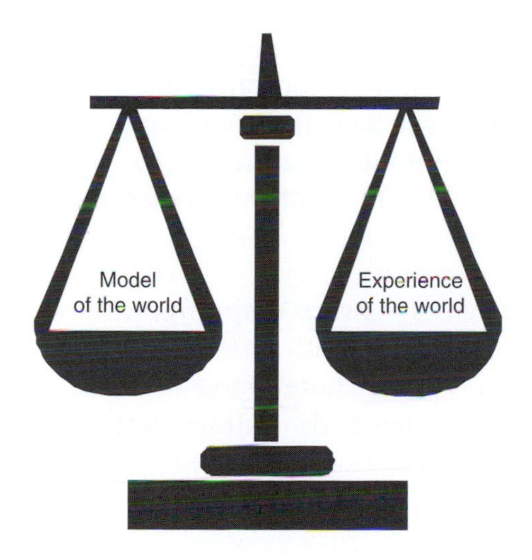

Figure 3.1

If your experience matches your expectation, you will get what you expected and feel what you expected to feel, no more no less. However, the experience will probably not stand out in your mind, because nothing actually stands out! Our mind encodes and searches for patterns of difference.[13] If there is

[13] Gregory Bateson (1972), *Steps to an Ecology of Mind,* itself drawn from Alfred Korzybski (1933), *Science and Sanity.*

little or no difference, there won't be anything to notice. It will be "just as you expected". You got what you expected.

However, should the experience give you more, or perhaps less, than you expected, it will stand out and you will feel this difference in you as an emotion that you will label as good or bad depending whether your experience gives you more than you expected or less.[14] The deeper the difference, the more intense the emotion. Thus, if our experience was not as good as we had expected and anticipated, we may feel disappointed, unhappy, or downright miserable. On the other hand, if our experience is better than we expected and anticipated, we may feel contented, elated, delighted, delirious, or even ecstatic.

We cannot help but compare our experience of reality with our construct of what this reality is about, our expectations, of situations, objects, people, the future. An emotion like nostalgia, for example is the result of a comparison, not between the past and the future as people commonly think. It is instead a comparison between an expectation we have of the future, built past experience, with the future as we experience it on a day-to-day basis as it manifests in the present (see following exercise).[15]

We thus compare our sensory mapping, what we experience of the world "out there", with our conceptual mapping, our model of the world "in here", and so what we expect, our hopes, aspirations, demands, extrapolations, etc., with ongoing everyday experiences. Any emotion we experience is therefore, paradoxically, always appropriate, since it reflects the

---

[14] Also drawing on the work of the general-semantics expert Alfred Korzybski, Michael Hall suggests that our emotions are the result of a differential comparison between the expectations that arise out of our model of the world and the experience of what has actually occurred (Hall, L. Michael, "NLP and General Semantics: The Merging of the Models", course commissioned by Post-Graduate Professional Education, London, 1998, 1999, 2000).

[15] Simone Signoret, the great French actress, played on this concept when she wrote her book *Nostalgia Isn't What it Used to Be*.

state of our model of the world at a given point in time and space.

Protégés quite commonly set up unrealistic expectations for themselves— i.e. expectations that do not correspond with the eventual experience— and come a cropper because it doesn't happen. So, if they go through a situation and experience a negative emotional evaluation of it, it may be a sign that they need to change their mapping tools and update their maps, so that they are truer to their experience of reality. This ability to modify our maps so that they become more true to the experience is a sign of our emotional intelligence and, as a mentor, you are in a unique situation to enable them to develop this all-important resource. However, it is itself contingent on your own ability to do so.

Some people who hear this argument may respond with an "all or nothing" approach and argue that such reasoning is only an invitation to have low expectations, to refrain from dreaming and have high aspirations, and may perceive this advice as a counsel of despair. If we had actually said that, it would indeed be the case, but this is not what we are inviting you to do. After all, dreaming is what got us to the moon, what got us out of our prehistoric caves, and often what keeps us going when what we currently have is not what we like—and you do want your protégé to dream, don't you? Indeed, if they did not entertain high expectations of one kind or another, you would probably see it as you duty to give them the means to do so, or to discontinue the mentoring process itself.

Instead, this is more an invitation to qualify our expectations, to texture them with achievability, to temper them with realism, so that the expectations we end up with are the highest we can have that will nonetheless allow for pleasant surprises. What your protégé wants is neither all "pie in the sky" nor no pie at all, but a pie on the plate that tastes even nicer than they expected when they tuck in with gusto, and they may offer you a slice of it also!

Creating more appropriate expectations

Compare two situations: one in which you were unpleasantly surprised and one in which you were pleasantly surprised. Just perceive them in sensory terms and leave your evaluations behind for a time. As you reaccess each memory you may find that they are encoded differently, with different parameters in each perceptual modality.[16] The representation of one may be brighter, or more colorful, or more 3-D, or more dynamic than the other. The picture you have of each may be situated differently before you: one may be nearer or further away, it may be bigger or smaller, it may be bordered or borderless etc. The sounds for each may vary also, in volume, pitch, resonance and so forth. The feelings are definitely different.

Now for each of these experiences there was probably an expectation beforehand.

Going through the parameters we mentioned above, compare each expectation in sensory terms with the experience you ended up having, first the pleasant one, which we will call A. Compare Expectation of A with Experience A. How do they differ?

Now do the same with the unpleasant one, which we will call B. Compare expectation of B with Experience B. How do they differ? Go through the parameters we mentioned above.

Now compare the two expectations by themselves, Expectation of A with Expectation of B. How do they differ? Go through the parameters.

Map across, one by one, the parameters of Expectation of A to Expectation of B.

---

[16] Perceptual Modalities are our senses. We encode our experiences in sensory-specific terms: Seeing (V), Hearing (A), Feeling (K for kinaesthetic), Smells (O for Olfactory), tastes (G for Gustatory). See our book *7 Steps to Emotional Intelligence*, (2001), Chapter 4.

Now with Expectation of B in its new parameters, how do you perceive Experience B?

Now give yourself the permission to learn from this and to create for yourself as resourceful expectations as possible that will nonetheless allow for pleasant surprises when you live them. What parameters would these expectations need to have to do that for you?

Test it out with another situation that hasn't happened yet. Check its parameters and adjust them accordingly.

There are, however, times when not having, not setting, or removing expectations is useful and appropriate so that anything that happens is a treat. Such an attitude is encouraged by many Eastern philosophies: it generates a state that is both of benign detachment and, at the same time, of deep association and belonging to the world. The lifestyle we live in our industrialized cultures, however, where all sorts of schedules and timescales are imposed upon us by our environment, is not most conducive to cultivating such states and we do not suggest you should adopt such an approach full time! After all, your protégé needs to set goals for themselves and to meet other people's goals as well, and so do you. Nevertheless, you may invite your protégé to give themselves some "treats" at some point in the day, the week, the month, the year, where they can set aside their expectations and just *be*. Such oases of "beingness" need not even take long, but they will emerge from them refreshed and revitalized every time.

Evidence has also shown that too-precise expectations are those that usually end up in disappointment. "The devil is in the detail," goes a saying. Give an expectation too many details and you will create so many opportunities for difference that at least one will arise that may mar your enjoyment of your experience.

When a new manager is hired, and your protégé may be one of these, they will begin full of beans, firing on all cylinders, hoping to accomplish major achievements within a limited time span. By pushing too hard, they may encounter resistance and, in the end, the expected results may end up even further off than expected. Demanding too much of themselves can have similar consequences. Myalgic encephalomyelitis (ME), also known as "chronic fatigue syndrome" or, more derogatorily, "yuppie flu", as a medical condition, has been strongly associated with people who do this. To sustain their energies longer, if appropriate, invite your protégé to extend their motivation further in order to reach their goal over a longer period of time.

Burnout syndrome research shows that employees often have a positive attitude toward work, but that their tolerance of frustration is rather low. Frustration is itself a result of expecting something to happen quickly and it doesn't. Another one of those!

As you are probably aware, the bigger the company, the more rigid and resistant it is to change. Although they may want to, your protégé cannot expect to reach a major culture shift within a few months on their own. Others in the organization need to change also so that they may support each other. Habits and procedures may require a major overhaul. Pushing the organization to change as a result of unbridled enthusiasm can backfire, as apathy and inertia prevail. Many new employees grow disaffected and despondent when this happens. In a worst-case scenario, they may even be dismissed because too many people feel undermined, affronted, or attacked by them.

The answer for your protégé lies in finding the right balance between push and pull, between diplomacy and taking the lead, between respect and confrontation. In such a situation we recommend you look for the positive intention behind the resistance that people may manifest, looking at the situation from their own perspective, and finding ways of integrating all such perspectives in the final resolution.

Suggestions for bringing reality and expectations closer to each other

1. Test your expectations against reality. Unrealistic expectations tend to come a cropper.

2. Make them more broad-brush than finely etched. There will be less difference to notice.

3. Allow for a longer timescale, rather that expecting too much in too short a time.

4. Find ways of matching your expectations with somebody else's: they will also work at their end toward making it work.

A good process to bring reality and expectations together is called *conditional opening*. It allows a person to "come down to earth" in relation to some expectations they may have, and to ensure that they can achieve what they set out to accomplish.

Conditional opening
(©2003 Denis Bridoux from Connirae Andreas)

1. Invite your protégé to identify a project or dream that they see in absolute, all-or-nothing terms, or which is perhaps expressed in terms that appear vague, abstract or woolly to you.

2. Ask your protégé what this project would bring them and identify the outcomes, known as meta-outcomes, that may be hidden behind this outcome. If their mind goes in several directions, lead them toward the one that appears to depend on them only or that lies within their sphere of influence.

3. Present yourself honestly as someone who can't give them the moon, and ask them, if there was an intermediary outcome which would satisfy them, what it would be.

4. Ensure it depends only on them; or, if it depends on other people or external circumstances, ensure that they feel directly responsible or instrumental regarding these people or external circumstances.

5. Ask your protégé whether achieving this would sufficiently satisfy them with regards to their initial objective. If not, ask them what would make it satisfactory.

6. When the outcome is satisfactory, check its ecology by ascertaining it will have only positive consequences, both for your protégé and anybody else involved.

7. Ask your protégé to imagine having achieved this outcome already and to comment on it. Test ecology again in this time in the future.

Confidence to act as if

Stockdale Paradox

Faith in reaching vision

and

Confronting the most brutal facts of reality

Striving for perfection may be the greatest enemy of giving something a try. Nobody is perfect, and there are always things one could do better. Hopefully, it doesn't stop you from getting started. In the book *Good to Great* Jim Collins writes about Admiral Jim Stockdale, who was captured during the Vietnam War and remained imprisoned for eight years. Stockdale tells us that the optimists didn't survive the prison camps in Vietnam. They would be saying, "We'll be out by Christmas", and then Christmas would come and go. This would oblige them to say, "We'll be out by Easter", and again Easter would come and go. By the time the new Christmas season came along, they would be so depressed at being in captivity without any possibility of freedom that they died through lack of morale.

Among the best leaders, Jim Collins encountered a similar healthy notion of having a long-term vision in mind, but at the same time taking into account the current harsh reality, and he came to call this the Stockdale Paradox. The best example Collins gave us is the story of Darwin E. Smith, the in-house lawyer who became CEO of Kimberly-Clark in 1971, despite a board member's serious doubts about his qualifications. Over twenty years, Smith turned it into a great company and at the end tells that for most of that period he had been working hard to get qualified for the function and to live up to the expectations of the board.

I never stopped trying to become qualified for the job.

Darwin E. Smith, CEO of Kimberly-Clark

Much of Parts 4 and 5 of this book appeals directly to the conscious mind. You will be presented with rational techniques designed for working on short- and long-term mentoring and coaching issues. One of the key learnings of emotional intelligence is that you can be more successful if your unconscious thinking processes aim to achieve the same outcomes as your conscious thinking. To help you use both parts of your brain, we added the following section on presuppositions.

The presuppositions you want to have

Presuppositions are a type of belief that we hold implicitly. You may say, "But I don't believe in some of these." And that's fine with us, because you don't have to! Presuppositions are a funny thing, and so is the human mind, because sometimes just pretending that you believe in them will be sufficient. Many disciplines, including mathematics, have assumptions and postulates that are unprovable and yet people have to accept them as a given. This is the case here also.

So what would you like to pretend that would make a positive difference for you and for your protégé? It may be about yourself, about them, about the professional environment where you operate, about principles that would be worth adhering to, such as, perhaps, ethics or professionalism.

Some protégés have told us, "When I worked with my mentor, I felt safe to err, because even my erring would be put to good use. I felt as if there was a safety net ever ready to catch me should I fall. The safety net went when I was ready and confident, and that was OK too. It would not have been OK had it remained any longer."

As a mentor you will need to create such a safety net for your protégé. This is a key task The opportunity to experiment in safety is invaluable and assignments that enable them to put theory to practice without too much risk will boost their self-confidence and embolden them to tackle more challenging issues.

Too often are we expected to get things right first time these days, despite the fact that a lot of higher education still doesn't offer the opportunity for practical or field work. Yet, owing to the pressures of industry, ever more bent on quick returns, graduates are often expected to apply this theoretical knowledge as soon as they are in post and, of course, to know instinctively how to do so, like a duck that takes to water. If this works out, fine. If not, their reputation may be tarred forever.

So, apart from the sheer practicalities involved in selecting pertinent assignments (see Part 2), how do you create such a "safety net"? What does it consist of? What constituent materials form its warp and weft? Simple: it is made of presuppositions, operating assumptions that we take for granted, which are a given in the context.

For example, take creating a context of, say, respect: what would mentors need to take for granted in order to respect their protégés? You will probably need to presuppose that, among other things, they:

- are individual human beings
- are repositories of some knowledge and skills
- are entitled to their own thoughts, feelings, and opinions
- are engaged in a process of evolution
- are more than they seem
- are the seed of somebody magnificent
- have their own boundaries
- have their own motivations
- have a sense of their own integrity
- can receive respect
- can be trusted

However, it takes two to tango. A mentoring relationship involves another person, namely yourself: what do you need to take for granted about yourself in order to respect your protégé? Perhaps you can, for instance:

- respect yourself
- respect another person
- appraise someone dispassionately
- trust your own judgment
- value difference

And what do you need to take for granted about the relationship itself? Perhaps that it:

- can be more than one way
- can be balanced
- can be complementary
- can be generative
- can be synergistic, i.e. the whole is greater than the sum of its parts
- can be mutually rewarding

And what do you need to believe about the wider system that you are both a part of? Perhaps that it:

- acknowledges effort
- is supportive of your effort
- stands to gain
- is resilient
- values what new blood can offer
- seeks to achieve synergy within itself

To continue the safety-net metaphor, if the presuppositions you need to have about your protégé form the warp, those about yourself are the weft. The interaction of the two forms the skein, the system, the net, which in turn requires a supporting structure, poles, struts, hooks etc. in order to operate effectively, the wider system, the team, the company, and, ultimately, wheels within wheels, the community, the culture, the country, the world.

Write down a list of what you would *like* to presuppose, to take for granted, about yourself, about your protégé, about your relationship, about the wider systems and the systems beyond those that would make it work for all parties involved.

Make this a rich list, with perhaps at least a dozen presuppositions in each category.

Then say them to yourself and act in accordance with them for an hour or so.

Notice the difference in your behavior, your thought processes, your feeling patterns, how you express yourself, how you relate to other people near you, how you think of people further away. How would it make things different? Do you like this? How does it feel to realize this?

Now that you know, keep it going and, every so often, take stock of what it gives you.

You can, if you want, be more specific about what you are aiming to accomplish. For example, do this with the most pertinent frames you would like to set, or about the ideal "safety net" for your protégé.

A very good process to incorporate abstract concepts, principles, and ideas in your body, so that you live them instead of just thinking them, and walk your talk easily as a result, is called "mind-to-muscle". It was developed by the neurosemanticist and meta-analyst L. Michael Hall and will be of equal use to mentor and protégé alike.

This process will enable you to turn highly informative, insightful, and valued principles into neurological patterns. This naturally occurs in life when you acquire a new skill and develop a sense of unconscious competence about an activity, such as riding a bicycle, swimming, driving, or when a baby learns to walk or to speak.

Initially, learning how to cycle or swim may take a substantial period of time and effort in order to get the required strategy and patterns of the movements right and the necessary coordination deeply imprinted into your motor system. Yet, by practicing and training, you acquire some competence, and gradually your learnings become incorporated, as it were, into the very fabric of your muscles themselves, which develop to respond appropriately, so that you stop being conscious of what you do and "just do it", at a level of unconscious competence. Your motor system now runs the show without involving your intellect and frees you to do other things—such as talking on your cellphone while rollerblading!—so that you now reap the benefits of having acquired that skill. At this stage, you have translated principle into muscle.

The same process holds true for any expertise, excellence, and mastery in all other fields, be they sports, mathematics, teaching, surgery, selling, public relations, mentoring, or coaching. We begin with a principle, an abstract concept, an understanding, an awareness. We explore its meaning for us and gradually translate it into something that makes sense to us, so that we can make it ours and live by it. By the end of the process, we have made it part of our system in such a way that not only do we think it, but we also feel it, we enact it, we speak it, we gesture it without even thinking. It has been translated and incorporated into "muscle memory".

People have found this especially effective to apply when carrying out a modeling project, whereby you model a person's particular skill or inner resource. It has been applied many times in as varied a range of modeling projects as resilience, leadership, wealth building, selling excellence, and learning. This can easily be done on your own. Since it involves talking aloud to yourself and gesturing, we suggest you adjourn to a place where you can be on your own.

Mind-to-muscle process

1) Identify a principle (concept, understanding) regarding mentoring/coaching that you would like to live by without even having to think about it, one that would benefit you and others.

What concept or principle about mentoring or coaching do you want to integrate into yourself?

Describe your conceptual understanding of this principle. What do you know or understand about this that would serve you? Start by extemporizing, perhaps looking upward.

State it in a clear, succinct, and compelling way. Now state it by finishing the statement, "I understand ..."

2) Describe the principle as a belief.

Would you like to believe that? If you really, really believed that, would that make a big difference in your life? How would it benefit you to believe it?

State the concept by expressing it as a belief, looking ahead of you. Finish the sentence, "I believe ..."

Now state it as if you really did believe it, with the expressiveness of voice and the gestures of that belief.

If you were expressing what you believe about this to a deaf person, what gestures would you make?

Enact your belief with your gestures.

Notice what you're feeling as you say that again.

3) Reformat the belief as a decision.

Would you like to live by that belief? (Yes.) You would? (Yes.) Really? (*Yes!*)

How does it feel to realize this?

Will you act on this and make it your program for acting? If so, state it as a decision.

Choose to do this. Restate the belief by saying, "I will …", "I choose to …"

"From this day forward I will … because I believe …"

4) Rephrase the belief and decision as an emotional state or experience.

State the decision again noticing what you feel, the emotions that your having made this choice arouse in you.

What do you feel as you imagine living your life with this empowering belief and decision?

Be *with* those emotions; let them develop and expand.

Put your feelings into words: "I feel … I experience … because I will … because I believe …"

5) Turn the emotions into actions to manifest your decision.

Finish the sentence, "The one thing that I will do today as an expression of these feelings, to make this decision real, to get this started is …"

And which one thing will you do tomorrow? And the day after that?

6) Step into the action and let your mind figure the implications and consequences of this new way of operating.

As you vividly imagine carrying out this one thing you will do today, seeing, hearing and feeling what you are experiencing while doing this, what do you believe about that?

7) Loop the process to integrate it in your system.

What have decided about that?
What do you feel about that?
And what will you do as a consequence?
How does it feel to realize this?
And what do you understand about that?
Because you feel what?
Because you've decided what?

Because you believe what?
And what other thing will you do?
And so on—you will know when to stop.

Developing compelling intentions: the itinerary of change

Have you ever wondered about the following?

- What's the difference between people who accomplish something and those who don't? Those who do have a strong desire to do so.
- What is the difference between people who have a strong desire and don't do anything about it and those who do? Those who do have compelling intentions.
- What's the difference between people who have compelling intentions and don't manifest them in the world, and those who have compelling intentions and do? Those who do want to.

- What's the difference between people who want to do things and don't, and those who want to do things and do? Those who do have a sense that they can.

- What's the difference between people who can do things and don't, and those who can do things and do? Those who do feel they have the permission to do it.

- What the difference between people who have the permission to do things and don't, and those who have the permission to do things and do? Those who do decide or choose to put some will into it.

- What's the difference between people who choose to do things and don't, and those who choose and do? Those who do act on their choice; they put their choice into motion.

- What's the difference between those who put their choice into motion and don't carry it through, and those who put their choice into motion and do? Those who do have mechanisms in place to sustain their effort over time.

- What's the difference between people who sustain their effort and don't complete things, and those who sustain their efforts and take their project to a conclusion? Those who take their project to a conclusion know when to stop.

This is the structure of the chain:

Desire ➔ Intend ➔ want ➔ can ➔ allow ➔ decide/choose/will ➔ put in motion ➔ sustain the effort ➔ complete

Although the order of the verbs may vary from person to person, whatever we seek to accomplish in life, whether large and small, for ourselves or others, we are somewhere on this chain in relation to it. You could say that it is our strategy for accomplishing things.

Notice, incidentally, that in this chain the key components are not necessarily the individual verbs, but the arrows that cause you to flip from one to the next. What you need to identify is,

"What specifically causes the flipping?" so that you can't stay there any more but have to move on and can't get back. These arrows therefore, represent "must/have to".

Take desire. Every change begins by a dream, an aspiration. Without a dream, we wouldn't have gone to the moon. "I have a dream!" said Martin Luther King, and this dream led to the end of segregation in the US. Desire puts us on the road to change. It's the first step on this road. Without a desire, there is only apathy.

Take intentions. You may know the saying, "The road to hell is paved with good intentions." Does this mean we should not start the journey with good intentions about where to arrive? Not at all, because we wouldn't know where we want to go! It simply means that we often have many intentions that we don't carry through, that never move from your mind to the world or that peter out before reaching a satisfactory outcome. Often, this occurs because we lack the initial impetus to make us want to get off our backsides and manifest them. Other people can provide further impetus and, as mentor, you will be able to do so. But even better than doing so would be to show your protégé a way to fuel and turbocharge their own intentions, so that they can do it by themselves. You may want to take them through the process below to do so.[17]

Start by asking yourself, "Where am I in relation to my project?"

If you are still at the level of intentions, ask yourself, "What will doing this do for me, for other people, for the company/community/country/world? What else? What else?" Write each of these answers at the bottom of a page in wide format, using a different-colored pen for each. Get between five and nine intentions. Fewer, and you may not get enough energy out of it; more and you'll end up confused.

[17] This process is derived from two neurosemantic processes developed by L. Michael Hall, the "meta-pleasuring" process and the "mind-to-muscle" process.

Repeat, asking this same question, "What will doing this do for me?" about one statement at a time, and climb up the levels of intentions until you feel you can't get any higher. If the outcome is in relation to other people, the company, the world, reflect it in the question and ask instead, "What will doing this do for others [etc.]?"

Then move on to the next intention and repeat the process. You may find that some will merge at some stage, but this is by no means universal.

Now revisit your initial intention. How much more motivated do you feel now in relation to it? How much more do you really want to achieve this.

If you're at the "want but can't" level, ask yourself, "What would make it possible for me? What else? What else?" Too often we narrow our choices and limit our options. Find one that will definitely move you on. Quite commonly, we limit our choices by creating an all-or-nothing situation, and choosing an outcome that is too big or would require too much effort. If this is the case, find a way of breaking down the outcome into more manageable components, which will make it easier to chew on. Remember that the journey of a lifetime begins with a single step. When you reflect on your outcome differently you may find that what may have once seemed impossible gradually becomes possible.

If at one stage you start saying "but" and refer to some constraints, you've moved on to the next link in the chain, the "can but won't allow".

There are times, of course, when hierarchical authority prevents us from doing things, but at other times, although even the external constraints are supportive, we still feel we won't do it. Some people say, "If I allowed myself, I would do such and such a thing ..." It's as if *inner permission* is lacking. Ask yourself, "What do I need to do to get inner permission?" Considering the external constraints, "What would allow me to do it nonetheless?" "How could I feel I've got permission to do it?" Ask this question, perhaps looping it, repeating it in relation to the previous replies as you did above with the intentions, until you feel that it's now only up (or down) to you and that you can.

Then manifest your desire to implement it. Verbalize your decision. In *Star Trek: The Next Generation*, when Captain Jean-Luc Picard wants something to be done, he tells Commander Ryker, "Make it so, Number One!" When a course is set, he says: "Engage!" Find a similar symbolic way of manifesting your decision, your choice, your will, your commitment. If necessary, accompany this by standing up and taking a step forward as you do so.

If "maintaining the direction" is the issue, ask yourself: "What do I need to keep focused on getting there? What would allow me to stay on track?" This will act as your compass.

If "sustaining the effort" is the issue, ask yourself again: "What would enable me to sustain my effort? What else? What else?" Again find one that compels you. Apply the looping/repeating again if necessary to fuel this energy. Find in you resources that motivate you, that galvanise you. If necessary, revisit your chain of intentions to see how manifesting it has enriched you and to validate the journey so far. Why stop there if you have gone this far. Come on, you're nearly there.

Finally, some people don't know when to stop. Even we, the authors of this book, can be tempted to cram ever more, tweak and polish forever. We're not perfect—who or what is? But then if we hadn't somehow said, "That's enough; that's fine as it is; that will do; we can always do a Volume II or a second edition ...", you wouldn't be reading us now. People who stop have a mechanism inside their mind that enables them to evaluate and to relate their project to the outside world, with its constraints and priorities, which is where it will end anyway. This inner system doesn't carry out this evaluation in absolute terms, but in impersonal and relative terms, not necessarily "the best for me", which would invite the perfectionist in each of us to keep going for ever, not in terms of "the best ever", but "the best for here", "the best for now". So ask yourself, "How does my project fit the outside world? What will enable me to say, 'Enough is enough, at least for now'? What criteria do I need to apply to let it go, set it free, let it loose on the world with a light heart?"

Incidentally, a mentoring project itself is like this and will go through the chain above, which gives you a structure as to the itinerary of change, and at which specific stage you are at any moment in time. Whether as mentor or protégé, you yourself will go through such a process, and how does it feel to realize this?

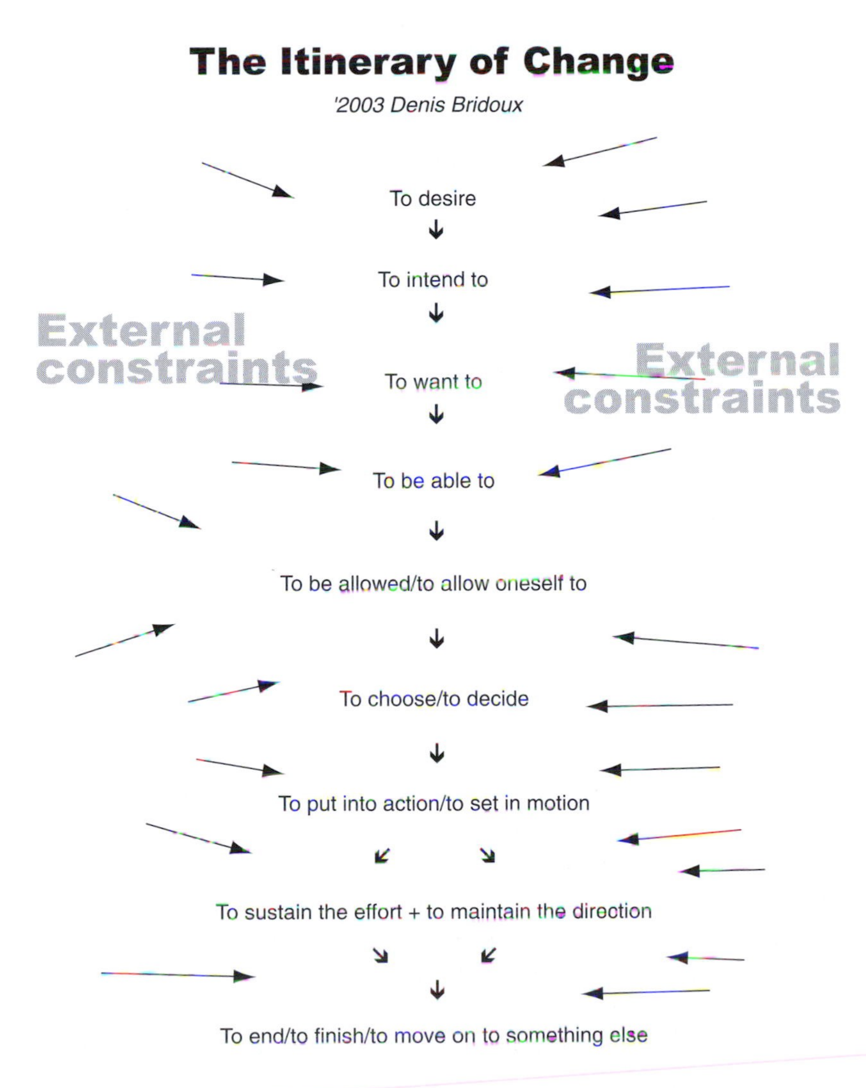

Short-Term Mentoring Skills

PART **4**

Critical skills for mentoring include being able to communicate well, asking questions to figure out where your protégé wants to go, where they come from, and where they currently are on their path. It also requires generating enthusiasm and energy so that your protégé keeps moving forward toward their goals. We discuss these topics in a chapter called "Short-Term Mentoring Skills" because these are skills you'll need in the moment, at every mentoring contact.

Listening and reflecting skills: how to make the most of what your protégé tells you

Even before your protégé opens their mouth, they have begun to communicate with you. The posture they take, the gestures they make, their facial expressions, all hint at what goes on inside their head. By developing your observational skills you can learn to calibrate and find connections between outer behavior and inner thoughts and feelings.

We substantially enlarge on this matter in our book *7 Steps to Emotional Intelligence*, where we explore all the facets of verbal and nonverbal communication, both in terms of receiving information and in terms of reciprocating in kind.

Even when they speak, people use far more than words to express themselves. Your protégé's words are supported by an ongoing tapestry of tones, pitches, rhythms, intonations, emphases, on which the words appear "embroidered". This tonal substratum can reinforce the message of the words, or detract from it, conveying to you a different message than the language itself, or a message of a different order, the words often expressing intellectual, conceptual, or even metaphorical information and the tonality— what professionals call *paralanguage*— expressing emotional information. The mistake people sometimes make is to ascribe universal meanings to behavior that may actually be idiosyncratic and whose meaning may vary from person to person.

Congruence occurs when a person is of one mind with themselves, when their values, beliefs, attitudes, actions, and speech all tell the same story, leading in the same direction. Congruence is usually denoted by symmetry, balance, well-modulated, harmonious, resonant tonality, rhythm, flowing language etc.

Incongruence is when different parts of a person's message go in different directions either at the same moment in time or across time. Incongruence is usually marked by asymmetry, moving about, jerkiness, fidgeting, halting speech, disparity between the various modes of communication.

The words say "Yes", the voice says "I'm not sure." The word and voice say "Yes", the body says "No way".

Learn to calibrate congruence, behave congruently and encourage your protégé to be congruent also.

To give you an example, one of us was coaching a woman who had her arms tightly closed. This is commonly labeled as "defensive". Her tonality and the expressions she used nonetheless intimated that she was fairly easygoing and relaxed. So much so that, after a moment of working with her, she ended up by candidly revealing that she had sore breasts and needed a new bra! A behavior that might have been evaluated as "defensive" turned out just to manifest some physical discomfort. Too often, we jump to conclusions, putting 2 and 2 together and getting 22. What gave us the clue that she might not be on the defensive was the apparent mixed messages we received, the body saying one thing, the tone of voice and the words saying another. In other words, we detected some *incongruence*. Had her tonality been sharper and more level, her facial expression tense, her sentences short and her words mainly noncommittal or negative, all her means of communicating would have reinforced each other. She would have been *congruent* and we would have probably been right in thinking her defensive. As it happened, holding her arms that way was a manner of supporting herself.

Get into the habit of just observing, just seeing, just hearing, and let the information come in freely at the descriptive level, before interpreting what you observe. Although, indeed, many behaviors, postures, gestures, and tones of voice have a broad cultural meaning that we can easily interpret when we share a culture, these are by no means universal enough to generalize inappropriately. Practice observing your protégé and draw your conclusions based on what you receive and not what you had acquired before. You may make correlations later on, but in the meantime your protégé will appreciate your attentiveness and your sense of their uniqueness. It will enable you to make comments of far greater pertinence to their own needs, made-to-measure instead of some ready-to-wear or, even worse, hand-me-down remarks.

In the same way that you seek to observe them, reflect back cleanly, too, using the same language and words as your protégé, as this will give them the sense you have been attentive to them. All too often, people are encouraged to reflect back information using different words and expressions. People use the words they use for a reason, usually because they approximate most closely to what they have in mind at the time. If you reflect back what your protégé tells you using different words or type of language, you may distract them from their train of thoughts or make them feel that, although they were listened to, they were not heard. In addition, just reflecting back is easier to do than paraphrasing, so why make things harder for yourself than you need to?

Communication skills: dos and don'ts of feedback in the mentoring relationship

Brian van der Horst, an American living in Paris, France, says that, when the French really appreciate you, they will tell you exactly what you did wrong and what could be improved. The same is true for mentoring: sometimes the biggest gift we can give our protégé is truly telling them what went wrong or which capabilities they need to develop. The goal of feedback is to make the protégé learn from their mistakes. Everyone makes mistakes every now and then, so it doesn't help to blame persons for making mistakes, as long as they learn from them and don't repeat them.

Trust but verify.

Ronald Reagan

In some large organizations, the contrary is sometimes true. In *Jack: Straight from the Gut* (2001), Jack Welch tells us that, in the late 1970s, appraisal at General Electric (GE) meant being nice: the boss would usually write "fully qualified to assume the next position", even if they both knew this wasn't true. A negative feedback would be so exceptional that headquarters would ask to get rid of the person.

Those things that hurt, instruct.

Benjamin Franklin

In countries such as Japan or in the Arab culture some caution may be appropriate as well. Giving negative feedback may be seen as embarrassing for the person on the receiving end or may be taken as a personal attack. In those situations you might want to give the criticism indirectly and include praise for some good points and assure that you have high regard for the person.

Guilt manipulation

Guilt messages often signal a meta-emotion. The person feels angry, hurt, or sad and projects the responsibility for that on the "guilty" person. Because this often works, this is easier than looking into one's personal role in the issue at hand. And this "technique" may even help getting what you want. However, everyone is responsible for their own emotions.

To cope with guilt manipulation, check for the facts underlying the issue and whether you have trespassed any boundary or made a mistake. Don't take the blame if this is not needed.

The message is, "Before giving feedback, know your culture." If you want to give your feedback differently from the way it is ordinarily done, make it part of your own frame of operation within the mentoring process. Unless you manage to find ways of changing your company's culture, use its traditional way of giving feedback outside the mentoring.

Well-delivered negative feedback isn't about finding a person guilty and condemning them. As the American management consultant W. Edwards Deming advocated, quality thrives only in a situation where fear is driven out, so that people speak freely and can admit their mistakes. When we deliver feedback our focus should be on how we can make sure it is understood, and on what it takes to make a message stick. Four important factors make the difference:

1. Building rapport

Much of the mentoring relationship is about just "getting along". Your protégé must feel that you, as mentor, are committed, feel concerned, and care for them. The issue at hand is often less important than the relationship. Separate negative emotions linked to the issue from your emotions toward the person. For example, you can be angry because a salesperson missed a deal because he was selling too aggressively, and that put off the prospect, but overall you still can appreciate the motivation this salesperson has for getting your product sold. The worst you can do is show an unmanaged emotion of anger, as expressed through your words, your tone of voice, or your body language. As mentor you need to communicate that you want to help, and not hurt, your protégé. One of the questions feedback should answer is, "What are the needs of my protégé? What's necessary for them to improve in this area?"

2. Timing

Feedback usually works best when your protégé invites the feedback or, at least, allows you to give them feedback. Asking permission is important: for instance, when your protégé is stressed because of a heavy work schedule, it might make sense to find a more appropriate time to deliver your feedback, and to find a time when your protégé is more receptive. Also, check for the right location: giving negative feedback in front of others will often be taken badly. On the other hand, don't postpone feedback for too long: it should be sufficiently close to the event being discussed to be quite fresh in the protégé's mind.

After asking permission, what do you do if your protégé says no? You can either temporarily back off and put the issue on the agenda for the next session, or tip your toe in the water: you can decide that the issue is important and just give a hint in a nonconfrontational way.

3. Form

The facts have to be expressed specifically enough, precisely formulating the incidents in terms of your protégé's behavior and double-checking the facts, so that they cannot be denied. While the facts should remain separate from your feelings about the incident, expressing these feelings is important as well, so that your protégé fully grasps the impact of their behavior. Explain what the impact was on you, the team, or the organization. When delivering a value judgment on how other people have reacted on the incident, make sure you focus on their behavior, what they did, and how they did it, not on attacking them as a person. Finally, check whether your message has been received clearly.

Check the facts

Remember playing the "Chinese Whispers" game as a kid? A message starts being passed around a circle of people, being whispered in the neighbor's ear. The person at the end has to tell what they heard—and the result invariably had little in common with the original message! Try getting facts from the source instead of at second hand. The more persons between you and the source, the more the story tends to change.

4. Flexibility of behavior

If your protégé cannot address the issue at hand, or doesn't feel supported to change the behavior, the feedback won't have much effect. Find different ways of saying what you want to say that might ensure a better reception.

Except for negative feedback as mentioned above, *positive* feedback is also welcome. Whereas the goal of negative feedback is to stop someone from doing something (and to encourage them to *do* something else instead), the goal of positive feedback is to reinforce good behavior and to keep them motivated to keep moving in the right direction. In that case you tell a person exactly what was done right and explain what made this action right. Saying, "You did a good job" is weaker than saying, "Your presentation yesterday was great: you used exactly the right arguments to convince them and your speech was short enough, which made it more powerful." The underlying suggestion is that you like to hear the right arguments presented in a concise, punchy manner and that you want to hear more of it.

Finally, there is *improvement feedback*. As a format, this third type of feedback has many elements in common with negative feedback. The person did things right, and you see an opportunity to enable them to do even better.

DESC[18] feedback format

Taking into account the preceding elements, in our book *7 Steps to Emotional Intelligence*, we recommend chunking a feedback moment in four steps—the DESC (**d**escribe, **e**valuate, **s**olve, **c**ontinue) format:

Tip: Remember that your protégé's behavior has a positive intention for themselves (of course, the effect won't always be good for others).

You might want to "mindread" them to figure out what may be the positive expectation of that behavior for your protégé. Odds that a solution to the problem that will stick often increase if the solution takes into account this "advantage" for the protégé.

The DESC format

D: Describe: Explain (as precisely as possible) to your protégé the facts you want to communicate about. Use descriptive and/or sensory-based language, as few people can quibble over these.

E: Evaluate: What is your opinion about these facts? What effect do these facts have on you? How do you feel about them? This is the place for evaluative language. Wherever possible, endeavor to use constructive comments.

S: Solve: What is to happen? What course to take now? Either you suggest a solution, or you look for a solution together with the involved person. Our experience has taught us that the solution reached with the other is usually more powerful (the person "owns" the solution and the possibility for correctly understanding and executing the solution is larger).

[18] We developed our own variant, but the DESC acronym can be traced back to a popular assertiveness handbook: *Asserting Yourself: A Practical Guide for Positive Change* (Bauer, 1975).

In addition to this, if you get into the trap of suggesting a solution from the start, the protégé may become dependent on you, instead of developing self-reliance. Unless you wish to become a guru, we suggest you rely on enabling your protégé to find out a course to take based on their own thoughts/feelings. Nothing, however, prevents you from making useful suggestions, dropping hints, giving pointers, beginning with, "Perhaps ...", "What about ...", "You might want to consider ..." We find that this type of suggestion is very readily accepted and hardly ever perceived as intrusive.

Avoid "necessity" language, such as "must", "have to", "need to", "should", "ought to", and use "possibility" language instead, such as "can", "could", "may", "will", "would", "want", because the former narrows down the range of options and the latter widens them.

C: Continue: What is the conclusion of the communication? How do you deal with it further on? What follow-up is appropriate? If actions were planned in the "solution" phase, agree on when you expect each result. Agree interim evaluation delays if necessary.

The problem with advice

Suggesting a solution that your protégé hasn't thought of presupposes you have superior knowledge related to the issue at hand. Often, even if we have come across a similar problem in the past, the protégé is will be able to point out the differences and use the "yes, but" objection to explain why our solution won't work for them.

Win–win?

Is the solution coming out of the feedback a win–win? If not it may lead to an outcome your protégé won't commit to.

Just as you can look at a glass as being half full or half empty, instead of focusing on the things your protégé does wrong, you can focus on things your protégé does right. Many people appreciate getting some recognition; they like feeling valued. The feedback format above can also be used to encourage a person, reinforcing positive behavior that has been observed, because we would like to see more of it. The fact that the person was chosen as your protégé probably means that they have the potential and do more things right than wrong.

In order not to be seen as a criticizing person, you might want to give several positive messages for each negative message you have to give and, phrasing the negative one constructively, in terms of what to do better instead of what went wrong, insert this constructive comment among several more encouraging ones.

Feedback sandwich

You may want to package a negative feedback between two positive ones.

The power of "and"

"But" is a word that warns the listener that a disagreement will follow. Instead of using "but" use "and". For instance, "I liked the way you were assertive about that issue and I think that being a bit more friendly might even have had more impact."

A great advantage that the role of mentor gives you is that of experience, real or fictitious. A good way of giving feedback or comments is often to present them in the guise of something else, as if somebody else had said it, which you in turn would quote, as in, "If my friend/colleague/relative had seen me doing that, they would have said …" This way the potentially hurtful truth is not attributable to you, but is disguised within quotes—sometimes quotes *within* quotes. Indeed, the more nested quotes you add, the more acceptable the comment becomes. Milton Erickson, the great hypnotherapist, would frame his comments within multiple set of quotes, usually beginning with: "My friend John …" Listening to him, one would have the impression that "my friend John" had been everywhere, seen everything, done and experienced everything, and shared this wisdom with Erickson, who was just sharing it with somebody else.

As part of the mentoring role also comes the talent of storytelling. Many a truth cannot be told openly, but has to be presented by analogy, or metaphorically. The psychologist Bruno Bettelheim explains in his book *The Uses of Enchantment* (1976) how fairy tales teach children very important facts about life and allow them to explore ways of thinking and behaving that would normally be abhorrent to society, but in metaphorical terms, so that they will understand the morality of the story without feeling chided for unconsciously thinking or feeling this way themselves.

To give feedback metaphorically, you may want to use what are called *isomorphic metaphors*, i.e. a metaphorical story with a similar structure to the matter at hand in its components, situation etc. In such a story you can also make recommendations which would not be acceptable if you yourself had come up with it. A tale beginning "That reminds me of …", or "Funny you should say that: something similar happened to so-and-so. It went like this …", or "I couldn't help getting a *déjà vu* when you were speaking because …", or "What a coincidence! I was just reading about something like this other day that happened in [faraway country or long ago] and …" As we saw a little earlier, you can nest a story within another and insert quotes within further quotes. These approaches have a way of communicating directly with the unconscious at a deeper level than when one remains purely factual. They relate to our natural ability to suspend our disbelief when somebody says something approaching "Once upon a time …" in meaning. Your role as mentor gives you de facto the right to use such communication devices. In addition, you probably also know by now what makes your protégé tick, so you can set your story in a context that makes them even more interested in it (see also p. 102).

The review practice

Benjamin Franklin ascribed the greater part of his successes as a diplomat, inventor, writer, social reformer, and adviser to his habit of taking five to fifteen minutes at the end of the day to ask his unconscious mind to pick out two or three really important successes and also two or three things that could have been handled better.

Do this, and then review the successes, asking your unconscious mind to organize things so that you behave in such a way that this kind of thing happens more often.

As for the other events, ask your unconscious mind to run them differently, i.e. better, where the ball actually lands in the goal, the person of your dreams does say yes, the sale is indeed made, your father does smile and does make you feel welcome at home etc.

Self-evaluation

Where feedback comes from a third party, a protégé should also take the time to evaluate themselves: for instance, at the end of the week, by reviewing what they learned and what they could do better; or, at the end of the quarter, setting learning objectives for the next quarter and evaluating how well the current objectives were met.

As mentor, you could for instance ask for a summary of the self-evaluation at each encounter or each quarter, whatever seems more appropriate. This will give you something to start working with.

The "Johari Window"

Since Jim Collins's book *Good to Great* came out, it's official: having a big ego, a jealous attitude or focusing on individual success may help you to get the front cover of *Fortune* or *Newsweek*, but it will not help you to contribute to the success of an organization you're working for. For one thing, these issues may come in the way of being humble enough to figure out how you can improve. If they're not careful, "larger-than-life" people have a way of trampling on their colleagues or acting in their own interests, which may not coincide with those of people who are close to them or with whom they work. Or perhaps it may be that they behave like this because they compensate for inner feelings of inadequacies.

	Known to self	Unknown to self
Known to others	Public	Blind spot
Unknown to others	Hidden depths	Mystery

Figure 4.1: Johari Window

There are some things that we know about ourselves that others know about also; these form our public face (see Figure 4.1 above). However there are many things that we wouldn't dream of sharing with others, because they are too private, too precious, or too embarrassing. For a range of reasons, we wouldn't dare share some of our beliefs, values, or thinking. There are also many things we don't really know about ourselves, but that other people know about us. We tend to be our own blind spot and others can detect patterns in our behavior that we are unaware of, because we "can't see the wood for the trees". Finally, there are aspects of us that nobody—neither ourselves nor others—knows, a source of mystery, of wonderment. Introspection is a technique to learn to know ourselves better.

When the psychologists Joseph Luft and Henry Ingham developed this model, they were primarily thinking about communication: the larger the public window, the easier interpersonal communication becomes. The size of the public zone differs from culture to culture: it is far larger in US culture than in that of most European societies, which like to cultivate a private garden and have strong privacy laws to prevent and deter inappropriate snooping by paparazzi. In the US, virtually anything can in theory be found out about anybody, usually around election time. When Luft and Ingham developed this model, they were primarily thinking about communication: the larger the public window, the easier interpersonal communication becomes.[19]

---

[19] The diagram took its name from their abbreviated first name: Jo + Harry = Johari.

As a mentor, you can enlarge the public window through feedback. Your protégé will appreciate your showing them their blind spot, provided you use constructive terms to tell them. Helping your protégé to face their blind spots, or self-disclosure, will allow some private information to surface, usually as a consequence of feeling safe. Your ability as a mentor to create a safe context conducive to self-disclosure and one that ensures confidentiality is paramount. Many a mentor–protégé relationship has foundered in the past because the mentor has shared or divulged some privately disclosed matters without the protégé's permission. Your question-asking skills will help your protégé to gradually expand their public area and still feel that it's OK. The safest people in the world are those who have nothing to hide. It's as if they had become "transparent" and people generally appreciate this. Compare this with the obsessive need for secrecy some politicians manifest, which, like a red rag to a bull, is like an invitation for some investigative journalists to dig out some dirt. Compare the language: "transparent, like an open book", versus "opaque, a close book, cards close to his chest". Which do you spontaneously respond to?

Contrastive mentoring

You can even learn from people who by example inadvertently show how things *shouldn't* been done. A bad boss may teach you how *not* treat an employee. If you take a difficult decision, try to remember how it would have felt if your boss imposed such a thing on you.

In the Johari Window, the zones that are most important for personal development relate to what we don't know about ourselves and your protégé is no exception. They probably see you as the person who can enable them to identify what these zones contain, either because you can see what they can't or because you have the means of enabling them to identify it for themselves.

Process: unstructured 360-degree feedback

The Johari Window shows us that our proper image often escapes us. You may wonder what others know about you, and what they think. At the same time there may be a lot they can teach us. The format described below can help your protégé to discover the four quadrants of the Johari window.

A: Invite your protégé to describe themselves in at least five different ways: what they do, what their competencies and qualities are, what they value etc.

B: Invite your protégé to ask at least five people in their environment to describe who they (the protégé) are, preferentially in writing, since this may be less confrontational than giving the answers "in the face". Invite them to choose people who know them well (friends, relatives) as well as people who know them only superficially. Ask your protégé to explain to these people that this is only an exercise and that they won't "shoot the messenger".

C: Invite your protégé to read the answers as if they were describing a stranger, and to let the answers resonate within without wanting to react. Let them analyze the answers "objectively". Where do these assessments match the way they describe themselves? Where do they differ? What comes as a surprise? If they experience part of the descriptions as "criticism" or "fiction", ask them what they could do so that others would describe them "better" or "more correctly" in the future?

As mentor you can help your protégé by facilitating this exercise, in the same way this is generally done in 360-degree feedback exercises. You can serve as intermediary between the persons giving feedback and the protégé, help them to constructively face the criticism etc.

Perceptual positions

Another excellent way for you and your protégé to find out more about the bottom two panes of the window is a process known as the "meta-mirror", also known as "perceptual positions".[20] The process presupposes that we actually know a lot more than we know, but that ordinary ways of experiencing things prevent us from making conscious use of this information. Aldous Huxley, in *The Doors of Perception,* was the first person in the West to refer to this ability.

---

[20] We present this at greater length in our book *7 Steps to Emotional Intelligence.*

How often do you hear people say, "Put yourself in my shoes"? And how many do it? Very few, in fact, and those who do hardly ever do so cleanly, often letting their own thoughts and feelings intrude and impinge, clouding the issue. This process allows you to cleanly assume the position of another person and view the world from their perspective.

Here are three main perceptual positions:

1. First position: "I"
You are in your body, perceiving the world from your own "point of view" and experiencing your own thoughts and feelings.

2. Second position: "you"
You are in the shoes of another person who is interacting with you, perceiving the world and yourself from their viewpoint, thinking their thoughts, feeling their feelings, and taking on their "frame of mind", their own way of filtering the world, with their beliefs and values, their map of the world.

3. Third Position: "he/she/it/they"
You are perceiving the world from the viewpoint of an uninvolved, dispassionate, benevolent observer.

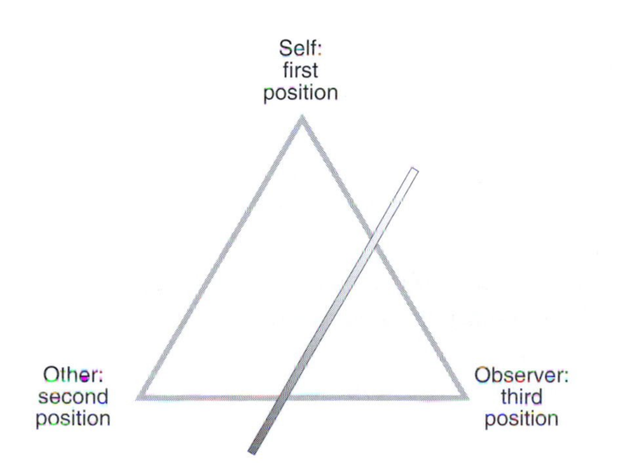

Figure 4.2

In addition to these, you can take a "meta-position" in relation to each of the above. In this meta-position, you stand beside the position you are currently in and evaluate in clear terms what you are currently doing in a manner that will not affect you emotionally.

You can also assume the "we" position whereby you experience "being" a group, collective, or system and perceive the respective inputs and outputs of each component of the system, the energies and frictions, the pullings and pushings inside the system.

Perceptual positions

1. Think of a person you have difficulties with.

    - What's their name (you could call this person X if you don't want anybody to know who they are)?
    - Remember or imagine a particular situation when such a difficulty arises.
    - What outcome are you seeking to achieve in this interaction.

2. Represent X somewhere in your visual field.

    - Where is X located in relation to where you are standing?
    - Observe X's posture, gestures, tonality, language in this interaction.

3. Now imagine that you are stepping out of your body, leaving it behind, and now step into the shoes of X. Get into X's posture, X's breathing pattern, make X's gestures.

    - What thought patterns come to you, as X, in this situation.
    - What metaphors and symbols come to your mind?
    - What has to be true for you, as X, to take this posture, to make these gestures, to speak like this, to say these words?

- What is your positive intention for yourself, as X, when you are behaving like this?
- What outcome would you like to achieve as a result of this interaction with X for yourself and others?
- How do you perceive Y (the original you) over there?
- What would you like Y to know that would make the situation easier for the two of you (and any others who may be involved)?
- What would Y need to do? What resource would they need to have that might resolve this matter? Tell Y, honestly and sincerely. Notice how Y responds to this.
- Is there anything about Y that you actually like, that you approve of, that you admire? (If not, if you *could* like, approve of, admire something about Y, what would it be?
- Tell Y, honestly and sincerely. Notice Y's response.

4. Now step back into your own body. Bring back with you and integrate the information you have acquired in your "out-of-body" experience.

   - How is this changing your perceptions of the issue?
   - Receive X's information, expressed honestly and sincerely.
   - Express your thanks to X. Notice what this expression of thanks does to X, to their body language, their location.
   - Receive X's honest and sincere compliment.
   - Express your thanks to X and reciprocate honestly and sincerely. Notice what this expression of compliment does to X, to their body language, their location.
   - How else would you like to respond now that you have this information available to you?

5. Now represent somewhere around you a detached, benevolent observer, one who is all-loving, all-knowing toward you.

   - Where is this observer located? Now step again out of your body and into the body of this benevolent observer.
   - Now observe the interaction between Y and X.
   - Tell Y what you think Y has been doing well and also give Y some suggestions about how to do it in a way that will work.

- What resources could Y do with that Y hasn't got?
- Give Y those resources in the manner you feel is most appropriate.
- Notice the difference having those resources makes to Y.
- Finally, if appropriate, give Y your blessing. Notice the difference this makes to Y.

6. Now step back into your own body.
   - Bring back with you and integrate the information you have acquired from your observer's perspective.
   - How is this further transforming your perceptions of the issue?
   - Receive X's information, compliments, and recommendations.
   - Receive the resources and allow them to integrate into your neurology. Notice where they are now located within you.
   - Finally, receive your observer's blessing and notice how this transforms your perceptions of the issue. How do you feel about it now?
   - How do you want to respond now that this information and those resources are available to you?

7. You can revisit the other perceptual positions if necessary, each time making the necessary adjustments until you are totally satisfied.

From feedback to action

In some cases, making things happen is the missing link. It requires robust, realistic strategies and "action" plans to succeed. A management book that discussed this topic is *Execution: The Discipline of Getting Things Done* by Larry Bossidy and Ram Charan (2002).

By itself, feedback, finding blind spots or solving mysteries isn't much use until some action follows. The eternal self-improvement question is, "What do I want to do about this?" But then what we risk ending up with may go the way of many of our New Year's resolutions: good intentions to do something, but a year later nothing has happened! Well-formed outcomes have a much better chance of being realized. Here are our SMARTEST guidelines to make your outcome well formed:

SMARTEST: Well-formulated outcomes checklist

Specific: The description is clear enough and contains enough details so that someone else would be able to understand it correctly (you might test this out!).

Methodological (action-oriented): Next to the outcome, you have specified the steps (in terms of actions) of how you will get there. Does the action-oriented plan have an underlying concept? Does it list the sequence of steps to take as well as the resources needed to reach the outcome?

Attractive and formulated positively: You are motivated to do it; the way it's written down appeals to you. The formulation states what you want to and will do (as opposed to what you don't want to or won't do).

Realistic: Is the plan, as it is written down, reasoned through? Have the possible pitfalls been taken into consideration?

Timed (target date): Setting a date may help against procrastination, but don't fall into the trap of minimizing your goal in order to remain within your schedule. Setting more dates (of intermediate steps) is recommended as well, and at each intermediate milestone you may want to revise the rest of the schedule.

Established (within one's area of control): Few of the goals you set will be 100 percent within your control. Either reformulate them or make sure that other persons involved really agree to help this outcome come true. Metaphorically speaking, is everyone "embarked", as on a ship or on a plane, toward the target? Is there now not much that can be done to stop them from getting there? Others acknowledge the right of the person to go there.

Systemic: Does it take into account the whole, in terms of the implications for both yourself and others? Are the goal and its implications acceptable (not at the expense of others)? Do the advantages of the outcome both for yourself and others clearly outweigh the disadvantages?

Testable: We know how to measure the intermediate and the final results.

The lack of up-front, clear agreements is at the heart of every relationship turned bad.

Ken Blanchard

Goals too clearly defined can become blinkers.

Mary Catherine Bateson

The rules in our checklist box, devised to define well-formulated outcomes, have a wide area of application: not only can they be used to set outcomes to remedy issues that came up through feedback or by analyzing blind spots, but they can also be used in any planning event, from personal goals to strategic goals at organizational level. One of the main advantages of well-formulated goals is that the formulation is specific enough, and that both deadlines and specific measurements are part of the goal's definition. As such, when the goals an employee has to reach by the time of their next job-performance review are well formed, this makes it easier to figure out to what extent these have been achieved.

Analytical skills for mentors

Being able to:

- identify
- order
- evaluate
- integrate

elements of a problem so that the issue becomes manageable for your protégé.

Exploratory skills: asking the right questions

On the one hand, your protégé may see you as a role model. On the other, they may benefit more by being confronted with the differences between the way they see the world and the way you experience things. Centuries ago, Socrates made his students learn and explore their thoughts and beliefs by employing what we now call the *Socratic method*. This is a specific structured format that, instead of using teaching material, continuously challenges the mind through a system of questioning that creates a context whereby students will discover for themselves what there is to learn. Applying three simple question-asking rules may be enough. In other circumstances, you can be of help by reorganizing how your protégé is structuring the experience.

Leaders do not need to know all the answers. They do need to ask the right questions.

Heifetz and Laurie, "The work of leadership", Harvard Business Review, *January–February 1997, Vol. 75, 1, pp. 124–34.*

Three rules for asking questions

In 1933, Alfred Korzybski was far ahead of his time when he coined the now well-known maxim "The map is not the territory". His message was that, wherever you are, if you take a look out of your window and compare it to a map of that area, you'll notice that you'll see many things you cannot trace on your map. For instance the map you are holding is flat, while the landscape you see through the window, whether it

Philosophical thought

Even scientists are not really sure that anything is "true". All science can do is tell us what, at a given time, cannot be proved wrong.

contains trees or buildings, will contain objects of different heights. And you may hear the sound of birds, or cars moving, which your map probably doesn't even mention. Similarly, when we talk about our experiences we can only present a shallow map of what we really live through. If somebody asked you how your last holiday was, you hopefully would answer, "Oh, it was excellent." If you knew each other very well, you might add a couple of sentences to that or even show them some photos, but that still wouldn't be enough for them to "relive" your holiday the way you lived it.

Book resource

Our book, *7 Steps to Emotional Intelligence*, contains a full chapter (44 pages) on the topic of asking questions.

To you as a mentor, at times the map your protégé is presenting isn't complete enough to really make sense of what they are feeling or thinking. The most hilarious example in recent history is probably the last public quotation from Mohammed Saeed al-Sahaf, the Iraqi information minister, to John Burns of the *New York Times* on April 9, 2003: "I now inform you that you are too far from reality." At other times, your protégé might actually be using the wrong map. When you want to head to the South of France over French highways, you probably won't be using a set of detailed army maps: one map showing the whole of France would be more suited. On the other hand, if you are going for a walk in the French Alps, your highway map won't be of much use …

Tip: Remember a time when you were really trying to figure out the ins and outs of an issue. Maybe it was finding the plot of a detective story; maybe it was solving a riddle.

The feeling that goes with this memory may be a good one to have while you figure out which question you could ask.

To get closer to the map, being really curious is key. Listening is one side of the coin. Are you able to grasp the meaning of what your protégé is saying? Are you figuring out what the issue is? Are you picking up their body language and their underlying emotions? If you aren't sure that you're getting what you need through listening, make sure you ask them about it!

The first rule to bear in mind when trying to fully grasp your protégé's experience is to get a complete picture. What has been deleted from the picture you are presented with? What's going on outside the frame of the picture? Which area of the picture is blurred? What's hidden behind the objects in the foreground? A general request to start with might be, "Tell me more about that."

Tip: It's more important to keep rapport with your protégé than to gather all the information—refrain from "interrogation". Rather, use nonverbal cues to motivate the protégé to tell you more. If rapport is working fine, you'll get a lot of information with very few questions.

The second rule is about making the picture come alive, so that it becomes a movie. What's going on beneath the still surface? The surface of a river you see in a holiday picture may look tranquil and peaceful, but at that very moment, a few feet down, one fish might be eating another. What are the pictures that precede the picture? Where does the water of that river come from? Where is the car heading that is crossing the river bridge?

Three-rule game

Get a picture from a photo album and apply the three rules to it. (1) What cannot be seen on the picture? (2) What was going on before and after the picture? (3) What else could have happened?

The third rule blurs the line between what a person makes of an experience and how else it could have been lived. It's about being in a discovery mode and finding out what else is possible, thus expanding options. For instance, the sound of a car in the distance may help you to appreciate the quietness of the landscape, because it means that it's silent enough to hear a car more than a mile away, or it may annoy you, because it makes you think about how difficult it is to escape from such noisy, polluting, killing objects. These two different ways of experiencing the same situation illustrate that it's often our beliefs and attitudes about events rather than the events themselves that create our emotional upsets and counterproductive behaviors. We can expand the rule by asking how it could have been different. What would the picture be like if it were raining? Or if it were night? Or, if I see the picture of an interior of a house, I might be wondering how things could be reshuffled and how that would change the space. Or I might wonder what it would be like if that room were painted in a different color. Maybe a provocative question such as, "Is this picture worth bothering with?" might be more appropriate. Queries such as, "Are we using the right map?" and "Is this the real issue?" might bring us to a different map altogether.

Our life is what our thoughts make it.

Marcus Aurelius

The third rule may also be appropriate when a person complains about the opposition or obstacles they are facing while trying to realize a goal. As a sailor would tell you, even if you have an opposing wind you can move toward your goal by setting your sail at a certain angle, even though it won't be in a straight line. Similarly, by exploring boundaries in one's thinking, one will probably find a way to circumvent problems.

If you want to learn more about a person's experience, the two first rules are enough. Using the third rule, looking for the boundaries of the map, figuring out what else would have been possible, what other interpretation may be given, is about enlarging the initial experience, maybe even changing how that experience is remembered. In that sense, one can "change" one's personal history.

Three rules in action

Re-experiencing

Rule 1: Get the picture
Keep asking questions such as "What does it mean? Could you be more specific?" until the description you get is enough to "reconstruct" the image, without extensive guessing.

Rule 2: Get the show rolling
A movie is a sequence of pictures succeeding one another at fast pace, so that we see "movement". Reconstruct the movement by asking, "What's going on? What are the steps?" Continue asking questions until you can re-enact what occurred.

Rule 3: Changing the world
Start changing the memory of the experience by looking for alternative meaning: "What else could it mean? What would happen if we move beyond the boundaries? What other possibilities are there?" Continue asking questions till the limits of the story become large enough to see new opportunities.

Dealing with emotions

The question-asking rules we described above will yield answers only if the person being "questioned" is willing to answer. This partly depends on their relationship with you, but it is also a function of their current emotional state. Until a couple of years ago business was thought to be purely rational, and many managers considered emotions to be completely out of place. Fortunately, recent research, partially triggered by Daniel Goleman's books on "emotional intelligence",[21] showed that emotions are important after all. Actually, when one takes a closer look, most business decisions seem to have an emotional element, and a choice might be taken following a mix of intuition and emotions, with the decision being backed up with rational arguments only afterwards.

Basic principle

When you have a "gut feeling" that something may not be right, heed it.

The first step you might have to take as a mentor or coach is to help to put your protégé into an emotional state of "serenity", so that they can explore their current situation without being overwhelmed by vicious circles of negative emotions. Negative emotions have a signal function, which works well as long as you get the message and then leave the emotion behind, while dealing with the message. In short, emotions function as our "internal response system". We will discuss some of these negative "responses", their messages and how to deal with them as a mentor.

Fight or flight?

Beware when a party seems to withdraw from the fight and starts to respond calmly. It may only be the calm before the storm.

Fear

Fear tells people they are in danger or that they risk losing something. For instance, one can fear the negative consequences of a business decision. There are two categories of response to this emotion: *fight* and *flight*. When the person chooses fight, the emotion may turn into anger, or be expressed by an aggressive reaction. When the person chooses flight, the question is whether this is a temporary or final withdrawal.

As a mentor, you should ask, "What are you afraid of? How big is the risk? What could you lose in the worst case?" Once the situation is clear, the next set of questions is about finding a way out—"What are your options?" "What can you do?"—and doing a cost–benefit analysis of the various options.

The meta-octant consequence system, which we present in the Appendix on page 203, can enable you to do that. You may want to consider the following quotation from William C.

---

[21] Daniel Goleman is the author of the bestseller, *Emotional Intelligence: Why It Can Matter More Than IQ* (1995).

Weldon, who became CEO of Johnson and Johnson in 2002: "Sometimes it is better to beg forgiveness than to ask permission."

Frustration

This feeling happens when something we expected doesn't materialize, or when someone doesn't keep their promises to us. The message of this emotion is that we need to take action, looking for other opportunities or different paths to reach our goal. The questions to ask as a mentor or coach thus become, "What did you want to achieve?" and "What other ways do you know in order to get there?"

Cross-cultural coaching

A diverse or complex workplace with many different goals, values, beliefs, cultural norms and attitudes leads to an increase in potential chances for misunderstanding and resulting emotional reactions.

Shame and guilt

Shame gives a feeling of worthlessness and unlovability and may leave the person feeling rejected and abandoned. Yet this feeling protects us from doing things that might be judged negatively by others and by ourselves. It indicates that we realize that something we did or said is not appropriate given the standards of the context we were in. For instance, while many of us find it perfectly normal to walk naked in our bathroom, most people would be very ashamed to be caught naked in the office. Or, while many parents think it perfectly normal to yell at their children when they don't obey, they might be ashamed when a colleague starts yelling at them in a restaurant and all eyes at the other tables turn to watch what's going on. In other words, the message of shame is that you may have violated a rule or cultural norm. The questions are: (a) which rule, norm, or value was violated?; (b) is shame appropriate given the circumstances?

Feeling guilty is similar to shame, but focuses on the responsibility one has or thinks to have for what went wrong. Responsibility is a very subjective thing: for instance, outplacement consultants have been known to feel guilty when a person they had placed didn't live up to the expectations the new employer had, while other outplacement consultants wouldn't have felt the slightest guilt in the same situation. One can feel guilty without feeling ashamed: if the person in the example feels they did the best they could at the time, there is

Other key basic emotions

Sadness and grief: These emotions have to do with something that is lost. Find out how to cope with the loss and what can be done to repair it.

Hatred and disgust: These emotions are linked to disliking some characteristics of a person, based on a set of culturally acquired values. Find out if the emotion is appropriate and how it can be expressed in a nondestructive manner.

little reason to feel ashamed, except if one thinks this is proof of incompetence. Questions related to responsibility are: "According to whom are you responsible?"; "Would a judge condemn you?"; and (if the person continues to feel responsible) "What can you do to repair the damage (if anything)?"

Anger

Anger may happen as a secondary emotion, following one of the negative emotions discussed earlier. In these cases, your task as mentor is to help your protégé get back to the real cause. It also may happen as a primary emotion, signaling that someone is trespassing on our boundaries. If this emotion is managed too late, the initial problem may escalate in an open conflict. Some appropriate questions are: "What's the boundary being trespassed on?"; "Is it worth fighting for?"; and "What other actions can we take to defend our territory (except fighting)?" A side effect of anger is often that the person's view of reality is reduced to a tunnel vision, where the person becomes unable to collect information about the other party (what are the other's views, motives, positive intentions etc.?).

Emotion: primary or secondary?

Often emotions come in chains, forming a vicious circle. For instance, you may be fearful of the consequences of the action of a competitor and then become angry because you think their action is "unfair". Then you might become disgusted with the way they act in the marketplace. As a mentor, you want to tackle the source of the problem. The question to ask is, "What causes the emotion?"

Contagious emotions

Some people blame others for emotions. For example, your protégé could tell you: "My boss makes me anxious." As a mentor, you can reply that a person chooses their own emotions. Gently remind your protégé that allowing others to choose your emotions means acting as a puppet on a string. Your protégé can *choose* how they react with regard to the actions of their boss.

Another case is when someone tries to put the blame for their emotions on you. They try to induce a feeling in you. In such a case, notice how you feel and know you don't have to accept the emotion.

Likewise, if you meet a bad-tempered person, they might spread this emotion even without wanting to do so consciously. Do you allow yourself to "catch" the emotion, and become bad-tempered yourself? Something similar happens during downturns in the economy. Suddenly, everyone starts to see things in negative ways: pessimism prevails and people don't dare to take risks, because of "the bad economic climate".

Dealing with negative emotions: a generic framework

For the emotions discussed in the text we applied the following structure:

First, ask the following questions:

- What's the meaning of the emotion; what's the message for you?
- What can you do to reply to the message; what will you do to tackle the issue (rather than remain overwhelmed by the emotion)?

Then take the appropriate, constructive action, taking away the cause of the emotion.

Systemic thinking

David Bohm, the famous physicist whom Einstein called "the only person I met who truly understood quantum physics", often used the metaphor of a broken watch to explain that the whole is more than the sum of the parts (Bohm, 1996). According to him, one of the big problems with rational thinking is that it often breaks up something in a lot of tiny pieces, as if they were independent of each other. The problem is that, in reality, these pieces aren't separate. As Bohm says (1996), "It's like breaking up a watch and smashing it into fragments, rather than taking it apart and finding its parts. Things which really fit, and belong together, are treated as if they do not." Breaking things apart may be useful at some moments, to get a better grasp of what is going on, but our thinking thus tends to generate fixed structures in the mind. Problems arise from the moment we forget that the way we have separated things is just one way of seeing the "reality" out there. How often is the "quick fix" the real solution, and how often does it cause

Today, systems thinking is needed more than ever because we are becoming overwhelmed by complexity.

Peter Senge,
The Fifth Discipline

The map is not the territory.

Alfred Korzybski

If the doors of perception were cleansed, everything would appear to man as it is, infinite.

William Blake

problems to be dealt with later? Maybe we need to look at the whole, or at the relationships between the parts, to really "solve" a problem.

One answer comes from Bohm's system of dialogue meetings, in which participants give serious consideration to views that may differ substantially from their own. Dialogue involves being willing to hold many conflicting possibilities in their minds simultaneously and to accept what is, however uncomfortable.

Likewise, our minds have ways of turning dynamic processes into static mind objects. This may allow us to manipulate these processes, but at the same time may cause us to become fossilized in old patterns of thinking and feeling. An example is the word "decision", as in "my decision is irrevocable". It sounds cast in stone, rigid, static. However, if we managed to recover the process that led us to reach this endpoint, we might choose to go in another direction. We live in a world of process. Even our bodies are continuously processing, reconnecting with this systemic *world* of process, to prevent our thought processes from becoming fossilized so that we can evolve and move on.

A person functions in relationship to the context. What may work in the context of one organization may be completely out of question in another context. For instance, a salesman we know had a hard time learning that hard selling techniques such as those practiced at Rank Xerox during the 1980s are completely unacceptable (and will backfire) when trying to persuade an HR manager to use certain recruiting tools. Rather than really changing his approach, the salesman changed his audience: it turned out that this salesman had more success explaining his approach and products to people within these companies.

Enabling your protégé to become aware that they operate in a system and to learn to take into account parameters usually left out will enable them to have a richer experience of the world. Many geniuses, such as Leonardo da Vinci, had a richer, more systemic way of perceiving the world. Thus they were able to make connections between apparently unconnected things to get a glimpse at deeper truths.

A four-step approach to systems thinking

The various approaches we encountered always seemed to contain the following steps:

1. When finding out about a problem situation, what's the current situation (take into account cultural and political factors, conflicting interests of various persons involved, etc) and where do you want to go?
2. Structure the information. Draw out the model: how does each element involved influence the others?
3. Discuss with others which changes would get you closer to the stated outcome and how the system might react to these changes (political effects, cultural acceptability, conflicting interests and so on). What are the alternative actions possible? Which criteria can be used to evaluate these actions?
4. Take action and follow up (if the action doesn't work, go back to step one, taking into account the new information).

Static and mechanical versus process and organic

Even a system's view leaves some challenges. As Peter Senge pointed out:[22] "If a company were like a big machine, one would be able to predict exactly how it functions." He admitted that this was the way systems were initially thought of and said, "unfortunately, each time we tried to implement those changes, we found there were some things not going completely as planned."

An organization is a living system, consisting of humans each with their own purpose and values. An oft-used metaphor to point out the difference is that a physicist can predict quite precisely what will happen when a football player kicks a ball. However, suppose you replaced the ball with a dog of exactly the same weight. How correct would the physicist's prediction be in that case? (Make sure you don't get bitten if you try this out!)

The least you should remember from this section on systems thinking is that it's almost impossible to take a decision with full information about an issue.[23] Newly born babies assuredly have insufficient data to operate in the world. That doesn't prevent them from doing their best. They gather data as they go along and so do we still, even as adults. Very early on, we learn to "make do", and many innovative approaches are the result of such "make-dos". Waiting for sufficient data to get started can be used as an excuse for remaining immobile.

Not only do you need the hard data, but some sensitivity to the feelings and needs of people is welcome, too. However, knowing that you cannot have "complete data" shouldn't be used as an excuse, either for postponing a decision for too long or for taking a decision too soon. Again, being able to weigh the

---

[22] Cited from Patrick Merlevede's notes made during Peter Senge's keynote speech at the First World Conference for Systemic Management (Vienna, 2001).

[23] Visual representations of the system, such as mind mapping, often help to clarify things. The 2002 book *Mapping Inner Space* by Nancy Margulies (2nd edn) is a great resource for learning about this topic.

positive and negative consequences of both an action and an inaction (which is itself an action), and choosing a response based on this weighing, is one of the keys of leadership. (See the section on meta-octants in the Appendix.)

As a leader, you need to learn to deal with two kinds of anxiety: holding a decision until enough information is available and making a decision when faced with incomplete information. After all, as Robert K. Greenleaf writes: "[A leader] needs to have the sense for the unknowable, to be prepared for the unexpected and to be able to foresee the unforeseeable." (Greenleaf, 1998). Looking at the whole system makes it easier to fulfill these requirements.

Structuring an issue

No experience is a waste of time, as long as one has learned from it.

Sometimes the point is not that a person doesn't collect enough information about the system, but rather gets lost in "information overload". Where our three rules for asking questions help to gather the necessary information about the experience and enable us to relive the experience as if we were involved ourselves, we risk getting as mixed up in the information as our protégé is. There are times when people get so caught up in the middle of their experience that they need someone else to act as a sounding board, helping them to reflect on what's going on in order to figure out how to unravel an issue so that it becomes manageable. Yet, if it's properly stated, a problem is half solved. Hence the need for structuring the experience.

SCORE!

As you may have heard in Quality Management 101, when one sees problem solving as a linear process, jumping as fast as possible from a problem to its solution, you risk ending up much further from home than you were before. Given that high performers are often proactive, they are more prone to fall into this trap than most. Solving a problem systemically, making sure that you reach your goal, requires taking some steps backwards.

Problem-analysis techniques of the kind included in quality management will teach you to represent all aspects of a problem. In general, a problem-solving technique will require you to answer at least four questions:

- What's the current *situation*?
- What's are the underlying *causes*?
- What *outcome* do you want?
- What *effects* may this outcome have?

Once the problem has been analyzed, finding a *real* solution becomes easier. The question becomes, "Which are the resources I need to put in place to bridge the gap between the problem and the outcome I desire?"

Find the "r" from the resources needed to get to your goal, as this helps you to SCORE! The following box describes this problem-solving procedure in a more structured way.

1. Analyze the problem by specifying the S, C, O and E.

    a. Start from the **s**ituation. Describe it.
    b. Then describe the **o**utcome you want, then the **e**ffects of having achieved this outcome.
    c. Having done this, return to the situation and take a mental step back to identifying the **c**auses of what led up to it. What underlies these causes? Which presuppositions does the protégé have?

2. Look for solutions

    a. Now ask yourself, "What **r**esource do I already have in me that, applied to the original cause would make think and feel differently about the situation?"
    b. Revisit the situation from a new perspective and add resources to achieve your outcome.
    c. Finally find a way to implement the solution: add resources to achieve the desired effects.

Resource

The SCORE model as described here was developed by Robert Dilts. A more extensive explanation and other problem-solving skills can be found in his excellent book, *Skills for the Future* (Dilts and Bonissone, 1993).

Tip: To help your protégé visualize the different problem aspects in the SCORE model, you could use four flipchart sheets and put them side by side. This will help your protégé to distinguish the four aspects of the problem.

Discovering patterns

The SCORE model as it is described above is mostly used to analyze a single problem. However, if you structure an issue and look at several examples of similar problems, you may find a recurring pattern. Learning what the recurring patterns are in your problems assures you that the experience has not been a waste of time.

Intuition is a feel for patterns, the ability to generalize based on what happened previously.

Robert K. Greenleaf

When looking for a pattern, we recommend that you study at least three examples. After all, one example on its own is just an anecdote. Two examples allow you to form a hypothesis. But it takes three or more examples in order to have a pattern.

Finding a pattern is not only useful when analyzing a problem, but is also a powerful learning technique when used for finding the pattern of one's success, a process that is also known as *modeling*.

Modeling

Whether you like it or not, a mentor often serves as role model to their protégé. Most of this modeling is unconscious: your protégé identifies with you and tries to soak in your values, beliefs, and competencies. Are you sure they will like what they get? When people model this way, they sometimes unconsciously incorporate the less resourceful aspects of their model's personality, as well as the good ones. Are you aware of any less resourceful ways of thinking, feeling, speaking, and behaving that you would rather were left out because they might not serve your protégé? Do you like the idea of passing on your foibles to posterity? If not, do your own cleanup or manage your state to make sure they get only the improved version.

I have never met a person so ignorant that I couldn't learn something from them.

Galileo Galilei (1564–1642)

In order to model cleanly, your protégé will need to be clear and specific about what they want to model. Otherwise, anything will do. This is why we want to introduce the COMET method for structuring an issue.

COMET

Ask a person to describe three examples of the competence you want to model. Use the following questions to analyze each example in five parts:

Context: When and where did *this example* happen? Who is involved? (Make your you get a specific example, otherwise the person may be rationally discussing the issue in general.)

Outcome: What was the goal? What did you want?

Method: What could you do? What alternatives are there to reach the outcome? How are you going to do it?

Effect: Did it work? Did you obtain what you wanted? What were the consequences for others? What are the advantages and disadvantages?

Tasks: What did you do exactly? Did things go as planned?

Once you have the three examples, look for the pattern: "Why did you choose these three examples? What are the common elements—what is recurring in each example that helps to explain why the protégé is dissatisfied with it?" Are there any underlying beliefs that are key to making the person's strategy work?

When using the COMET method for modeling, the next step consists of comparing your own approach (or the approach of your protégé) with what you've just learned from the model. What are the differences (steps of the method you're not considering, other ways of judging the outcome, the exact tasks or actions the person took, etc.)? What actions can you take in the future to ensure that you integrate these new learnings in your own way of doing?

Tip: If you want to make sure a competence model reflects the reality and the real competence linked to a job profile, you can apply the COMET method to interview the top performers for that job role.

The COMET method for deconstructing an experience has several applications. Not only does it allow you to identify the pattern in a demonstration of a competence (as it is used here), but you can also use it to find the pattern underlying an issue or during behavior-based interviewing (to check whether a person has the competence). You may want to use it yourself, to learn from excellence displayed by others, or to teach the five steps to your protégé, so that they can use it for modeling a competence they lack. We'll revisit the COMET approach later in this part as a step in the action-oriented coaching procedure we'll be presenting.

Virtual models

Instead of asking a "real" person, you can ask yourself the question, "What have would-famous people, or people I admire, done in similar circumstances?" How would Einstein have dealt with the issue? Is there a creative solution Walt Disney could have thought of? What would John F. Kennedy have done? And what about Winston Churchill?

One can even learn from counterexamples. Indeed, there is often more to learn from a counterexample than from an example, since they tend to stand out more in our minds, and evoke a polarity response in us. Like this, like this, like this, *not like that*! Suppose you know a boss who doesn't treat their subordinates in a way you find appropriate. What is there to learn from that? For instance, if you have to take a difficult decision, remembering how such a boss makes their staff feel may motivate you to act more carefully.

Some extra modeling rules

- Modeling means learning from the person who is proven to have the skill. The person has been there, and done that. This person is sometimes called "the exemplar". (In this case, this "exemplar" might be you as mentor, or someone else who is considered an expert for this skill.)

- Modeling means figuring out how what the exemplar did applies to the situation the protégé is in.

- The protégé may not have to do everything the same way the exemplar did it. What would be the top three elements to adopt, the elements that make the difference?

- The modeling effort will be most successful if it ends with an explicit action plan the protégé is willing to commit to. As a mentor you may want to help your protégé with follow-up, making sure the results are evaluated.

People skills: generating enthusiasm and energy

It takes commitment to achieve great results. People have to care and feel that others count on them. Remember an occasion on which you were full of energy and had all the enthusiasm it took to achieve a goal that was compelling for you? When was that? What was the weather like? What did you do? How did you feel? What can you remember seeing, hearing ...? Now go back to that moment, and replay the movie of what is happening, what you are feeling. What do you hear and do and say, either to yourself or to others?

If you have worked through these questions, really looking for such an occasion, you probably feel more energized now than a few minutes ago. Research has shown that we all have the ability to recall such past states, to relive the state and to use the energy that comes with it in order to face our current challenges. Whenever your protégé needs to face a tough moment, this kind of technique may help them through.

Education is not filling a bucket but lighting a fire.

William Butler Yeats

In this context, a mentor is someone who helps to bring out the unconscious competence from a person, to make the protégé aware that they have what it takes and to apply that subconscious competence to a new situation. Find ways of making your protégé reaccess good states and experiences. These will be used as resources to draw upon for motivation and also to counterbalance challenging times.

Find ways of encouraging their imagination too. The human mind is such that imagining is almost as good as reaccessing a memory to access a state, and sometimes even much better. A rich imagination also has the advantage that what you imagine tends to be better than what you recall.

You probably know about the two teams of basketball players who were of equal strength and tested out the above hypothesis. For a given period of time, one group would practice normally while the other did all the practicing in their heads. When set against each another, the group who practiced in their heads won! When asked why that might be so, one player answered, "When I practice, I sometimes get it wrong. When I fully imagine I practice, I get it right every time!"

So, give your protégé the means to imagine richly, in full Sensorama, what they are seeking to accomplish. They stand at least as good a chance of getting it right than those who practiced physically. Oh, and make them practice physically, too! Even though reality may not be quite as good as imagination, it's still an experience worth living through, isn't it?

Creating challenges

Experienced managers can often predict what might go wrong when a person starts a project. If you act as a boss, you will prevent errors from occurring by telling the person exactly what to do. This, however, has two shortcomings: (1) many people don't like to be commanded and (2) people don't learn as much from executing your orders as they can learn by making their own mistakes and correcting them. In other words, when tempted by someone to present your solution to a problem they face, help them instead to formulate their own solution. However, even if we have to allow people to make their own mistakes, we still need to protect them from making too serious mistakes. It's better to come into contact with a wall gently than to crash into it at full speed.

"Heaven helps those who help themselves" is a well-tried maxim … Help from without is often enfeebling in its effects, but help from within invariably invigorates.

Samuel Smiles, from the first chapter of Self Help, *1866*

People learn from mistakes, from taking risks, from trying things out. If you observe the game of an upcoming top-ten tennis player, such as Justine Henin in 2002, you will notice that, in each of the grand-slam tournaments, there is a slight change in her game, which further improves it. It's only because of this drive to continuously improve that a person can make it in the top ten. The same is true in a business context. During the last decade, everyone was saying that change is the only thing that is certain and that, consequently, learning now has to be continuous, to make learning as inevitable as washing dishes after a meal, although hopefully far more pleasurable. "High potentials" are people who tend to learn faster, who get more knowledge out of one example than others get out of three.

Positively challenging your protégé to do things better may help to accelerate learning. Queries such as, "Hmm, how else could we do that? Is there a more efficient way?" or "What's next?" are a way to take the initiative. Being curious about any new ideas your protégé has, testing them for possible flaws, and supporting them is another, more reactive, path.

One doesn't always need to move out of the current job to find new challenges. In many cases, your current job provides plenty of growth opportunities—even if after a couple of years it may seem just "more of the same". According to Robert Kelly, author of *How to be a Star at Work* (1998), initiative is one of the areas in which star performers excel. High potentials will literally "see" the work: they will see areas of responsibility that are left unclaimed in their colleagues' job descriptions and they will enrich their jobs by moving into these new territories. In an era where change is the only certainty, such new opportunities and gray areas arise all the time. Taking such initiatives is what will get someone promoted, because they will be noticed for doing more than the job they were hired for.

Contrary to what most people seem to think, one never gets promoted for doings one's job well. After all, that's what you were expected to do in the first place! Even if General Electric Credit Corp (now GE Capital) was making two-thirds of the profits of GE Plastics in 1977 with only one-seventh of the people and no money tied up in research and plants, Jack Welch wasn't impressed when the division came under his lead. He wondered how much more potential the business would have if it were filled with nothing but A players and challenged all of the GE credit managers. When he didn't get the results he saw as possible, he replaced more than half of the leadership team over the next couple of years. Welch writes (2001), "In 2000 the business had $5.2 billion of earnings with more than 89,000 employees—thanks to an incredible succession of leaders."

Another way of growing, as opposed to growing in breadth by exploring new areas or getting new areas of responsibility, comes from developing more depth. Mastery often comes from refining your expertise.

Adjusting the communication style

One of the Chinese Taoist philosopher Lao-tzu's famous remarks is, "Tell me, I will forget. Show me, I will remember. Involve me, I will understand." Several types of communication are embedded in this maxim. One of the presuppositions we hold about communication is that the meaning of our communication lies in the effect it generates. In other words, if your communication doesn't generate the effect you want, try something else.

Ask a number of people how they know that someone else does a good job. What convinces them that the job is done correctly? You may get some person answering, "If I've seen the results of someone's job three or four times, I'll be able to answer you." Another person may tell you, "When they've been doing that job for a couple of months, I'll ask their boss and their colleagues what they think about the work that's been done. And I'm sure I'll hear all I need to know!" Yet another person might tell you, "I keep checking regularly, by reading the reports, but one needs to continue to check every now and then." And we can imagine a fourth person, a coach, answering, "I'd like to do a coaching session with them, and I'm convinced I can provide you with an answer in no time!"

The four people above illustrate the four types of information gathering you'll typically come across. The first person needed to *see* the result, the second one wanted to *hear* what was said, the third was going to *read* the reports and the fourth wanted to *do* something with the person being evaluated.

Given that a person may choose to ignore information presented in a channel other than the one they prefer, you might want to adapt your communication to match their preference. For instance, suppose that someone doesn't like to read materials, but would prefer hearing what there is to know. In that case, sending an email will be far less effective than picking up the phone to explain it. Or, if someone prefers doing something in order to be convinced, it will be more effective to organize an exercise or a demonstration. In cognitive science these four styles of gathering information are also known as "input channels".[24] Apart from gathering information, the examples above also reveal four different ways of processing this information:

Tip: If you don't know the preferences of your audience, you may want to build in some flexibility and repeat the same information in several channels. Provide enough examples and discuss what it will be like after they've applied it for three months or more.

Some people will need a *number of examples* in order to be convinced. As long as they haven't been given enough examples, they'll remain in doubt. They will often tell you how many examples, but as a rule of thumb you may want to give at least three.

Other persons will be convinced almost *automatically*, e.g. because they give you the benefit of the doubt.

A third group of persons will take a *period of time* to complete the evaluation. This may be three to six months, which explains why some employment contracts have that as an evaluation period.

Finally, there are some people who are really never convinced. They want to obtain *consistent* evidence and will keep check-

---

[24] The input channels, which are related to our senses, get the necessary attention in our book *7 Steps to Emotional Intelligence*. Books such as Shelle Rose Charvet's *Words That Change Minds* (1995) will teach how to recognize these patterns during a conversation. Questionnaires such as jobEQ's iWAM questionnaire measure them (see www.jobEQ;com).

ing. While the fourth category is the hardest to convince, their pattern may be useful for some types of management. For instance, for a sales manager it may be important to remain motivated to check the performance of your sales staff week after week.

The previous observations about communication explain why it's important to adapt your communication style to the needs of your protégé in order to allow them to convince themselves. Figure out which input channel and which interpretation process they use and adjust your presentation of the information to match their preference.

Summary

Four input channels:	See	Hear	Read	Do
Four ways of processing:	Number of examples	Automatic	Period of time	Consistent

Metaphorical communication

As Lao-tzu said long ago, "He who knows does not speak; he who speaks does not know." There is also an Indian saying teaches us that words are like arrows: once they are fired they cannot be taken back. In the spirit of these wise words, one might wonder why we have filled a book with words.

In fact, as a mentor you face the same risk as we do: namely that your message doesn't "stick", in the sense that the person doesn't take it, because the advice given has been too direct, or because they thought they had a better approach for dealing with the issue at hand. A first indirect route is to ask leading questions so that your protégé comes to a reasonable conclusion that enables them to deal with the issue. If that doesn't work, you may want to use a technique that has been used by educators for centuries and that proved very effective: packaging your message in a story.

Storytelling has played a special role in all cultures throughout the ages. It has an educational function and allows people to look for a deeper meaning. Stories give answers to important questions such as, "What is life? Why is it worth living? How does the world function? What is happening around us?" This remains true even today. For instance, Milton Erickson, a famous hypnotherapist who lived in Phoenix, Arizona, used stories for his interventions.

Stories influence creativity: using a metaphor helps to substitute one experience with new understandings, normally linked to another type of experience.

One of the oldest stories known in Europe is Homer's *Odyssey*, which we touched on earlier, because this story also lies at the roots of mentoring. Other well-known collections of stories are the Bible, the Koran and *A Buddhist Bible*, edited by Dwight Goddard and originally published in 1932 (Goddard, 1994). Once known, these stories start leading their own lives, inspiring millions of people throughout the ages, often in unexpected ways. For instance, *A Buddhist Bible* inspired many US writers, and part of it became "translated" in books such as Jack Kerouac's *Dharma Bums* (1958), itself one of the books that influenced the generation of people growing up in the 1960s. This then led to the spread of Zen Buddhism in California.

Resources

Books about metaphors:

David Gordon (1978), *Therapeutic Metaphors*

George Lakoff and Mark Johnson (1980), *Metaphors We Live By*

Nick Owen (2001), *The Magic of Metaphor*

Technique 1: Comparisons

Giving color to the picture of a situation, by helping the person make a comparison with something else. This comparison helps to bring solutions or actions one would consider in that story to the "real" situation one is facing.

An example is comparing our brain to a collection of people, each with their own function. For instance, consider the "adult", a serious person, responsible for getting things done; the "child", interested in play and having fun; and the "parent", willing to help others etc.[25] At times, these people seem to have conflicting goals. The "adult" may want to get a task done, while the "child" wants to play. So they end up in a conflict. The parent starts yelling at the child, and says that the homework (task) needs to be done before the child can go out and play. We can apply conflict-mediation approaches to work

What we outline in the example has been worked in NLP techniques such as "parts integration":

If a person has some unwanted behavior, the question becomes, "Which part wants us to have that unwanted behavior and which part doesn't want us to have it?"

What is the part responsible for the unwanted behavior trying to tell us?

How can we work out a solution that respects the goals of both parts and that both can agree to?

[25] This approach was developed in transactional analysis (TA).

within an individual just as well as between several people by just putting these "people" together and letting them figure out a solution that takes into account the goals of each party, so that a win–win situation arises. In this example, the question may be, "How can we make the task more fun to do?"

Technique 2: Creating distance

When your protégé sees you as an example and thinks they can attain what you attained, telling a story that happened to you personally may be helpful. At other times, this may not work, with the protégé saying, "Yes, that's easy for you ..." In those cases, instead of telling the story directly, add something such as, "A while ago I read in a newspaper this story about ..." or "Once, Marc, a friend of mine was having this problem with his coworker ..."

Remember: The meaning of your communication lies in the effect it generates.

Corollary: If your communication doesn't generate the effect you want, try something else.

A variant on creating distance, which may even add more credibility, is referring to a well-known person who went through a similar situation, but then of course the "Yes, but I couldn't do that" might show up, unless you can show that the solution is in everybody's reach.

Integrating your short-term skills: a coaching procedure

Presupposition

All the resources are already in the person.

The presupposition of this coaching approach[26] is that the protégé has the knowledge to solve the problems they are facing, yet they do not seem to put this knowledge into practice.[27] One can, for instance, apply this technique when faced with a salesperson or a manager who has experience with the job and was given training but is not performing as we would like. As you'll notice, the coach or mentor mainly guides the protégé at the level of structure with this procedure, leaving the content

[26] Some of the material in this section has been taken from Merlevede (2002), "Action Oriented Coaching", *Rapport*, Issue 50.

[27] In some cases, the resources may be "outside the person". In those cases, the problem is probably not a coaching problem, but rather a management problem or a training problem.

to the protégé. It shares some features with the nondirective approach that the psychotherapist Carl Rogers recommended for use with people who should be able to come up with reasonable solutions to their own problems.[28] The procedure combines the DESC feedback approach, the COMET problem analysis and pattern-detection tool and the SMARTEST action formulation approach in four steps, which are indicated on the coaching form (see Figure 4.3 on page 109).

Step 1: Deciding upon a coaching topic

As mentor you want to let your protégé choose what issue they need coaching for, since this will create the necessary motivation to really address the issue at hand. Often, if the choice is made for them, the coach starts with the handicap of first having to overcome some reluctance or even some resistance to coaching on the part of the protégé. Still, there may be some reasons to gently guide the protégé in their choice of a coaching topic, since other sources of information may be available to you. Much information can be obtained prior to a coaching meeting, such as the results of an assessment procedure, personal observation of your protégé's work, notes from a performance-review meeting, feedback from the manager or from a third person. It may be useful to present your protégé with this information at the beginning of a coaching session. Likewise, it makes sense to review what they did with the actions that were planned in a previous coaching session. The principles discussed in the section on the DESC format above may help your protégé to get the most out of this feedback.

In addition to this, one can ask the protégé which other topics should be covered during this or a future coaching session. Topics may come from asking the protégé to review what kind of issues they had to face in the weeks prior to this coaching session. For instance, the protégé may wish to discuss how to handle a coworker they are having problems with, or how to face angry customers who complain about delays.

Choosing a topic implies having a choice.

One topic only is no choice.

Two topics present the protégé with a dilemma, or "false choice".

One needs three or more options to really have a choice.

[28] In the 1989 book *The Carl Rogers Reader* you will find a comparison between directive and nondirective approaches.

Finally, you leave it to your protégé to choose the topic they want to concentrate on for this session. While this doesn't guarantee that they will choose the subject that you had in mind for them, the essential issues will eventually be tackled in line with the priorities the protégé sees for themselves in that moment in time, and each new coaching session presents the mentor with another occasion to present feedback and to follow up on previous issues.

Step 2: Analyze a couple of examples

Remember: It takes three or more examples in order to find a pattern.

One example is just an anecdote.

Two examples allow you to form only a working hypothesis.

Once the topic is chosen, and if it's an issue that presents itself on several occasions, you can guide the protégé to analyze some examples of this topic. We will use the COMET method for this analysis.[29] For each example, we first verify whether it's a real, specific example. Then we break down the example according to the COMET steps. What exactly was the context? What was your protégé's outcome? Which approach did they have in mind to resolve this? What was the effect obtained? Which specific tasks did your protégé do?

Step 3: Pattern detection

Tip: Asking, "Why did you choose this example?" for each example after the protégé has answered the COMET questions may facilitate finding the pattern that connects.

In general, the pattern will be fairly obvious once the three examples have been analyzed using the COMET method. The pattern is indicated by answering the questions: "What is common to these three examples? What is reappearing each time?" You might explicitly ask your protégé these questions, since the procedure will work at its best when they find the answer themselves and grasp how this has been a pattern for them.

Sometimes the pattern will be fairly obvious—for instance, when one of the COMET questions has remained unanswered each time. It may be that your protégé reaches the conclusion that they failed to plan or weren't really motivated to take actions or kept postponing it till it was too late. The question is, "What underlies such a pattern?" In the example quoted it may be because they felt uncertain they were actually competent

[29] In case the coaching topic is an issue that presents itself only once, you can use the SCORE technique, as presented under "Structuring an issue" earlier.

to reach their goals. This seems to be a double bind: if a person doesn't know whether they actually do something, their uncertainly will last until they try it out! But, then, it's exactly this very uncertainty that prevents them from doing something!

Other pattern examples

The effect of a person's plan is resistance by other persons: this may point to lack of second position (not enough empathy).

Blaming the failure on others: maybe the execution of the action plan wasn't really within one's control (make the plan SMARTEST).

Sometimes, the pattern is less obvious. The good news is that your protégé may often intuitively "know" the pattern, and the problem becomes putting it into words, trusting the feeling generated by discussing the examples—in such a case the section "Dealing with emotions" on page 85 may provide a few clues. Or maybe using the question-answering technique to explore each example a bit further may provide the eureka! effect of "seeing" the pattern. In general one can say that each technique presented here and in the next part can be applied to finding patterns in the examples given by your protégé. For instance, in the next part we will be discussing values and beliefs. It's possible that a pattern is held in place by a limiting belief: e.g. the lack of confidence in the example quoted could be linked to negative beliefs about self-worth. As another example, suppose we find a pattern such as lack of assertiveness. Might this be because they didn't learn to be assertive (a competence issue) or is it because they hold a belief that prevents them from reacting in an assertive way, such as "assertiveness equals aggressiveness"?

Step 4: Making an action plan

Once the pattern has been revealed, the question becomes, "What actions can be taken to break the pattern?" The aim is to find several realistic solutions that the protégé endorses and that they can put into practice. By preference, seek to enable your protégé to find the alternative solutions. Beware of the "not invented here" syndrome: finding one's own solution is always more motivating than having to implement another person's. Moreover, if you presuppose that your protégé is competent, they should be able to find a solution.[30]

The more alternative solutions, the bigger the chance that the issue will be solved.

[30] If the protégé lacks competence, the first action to be considered may be to find a book or a training program so that competence can be learned. Finding a way to learn competence may be an action that can be formulated using the SMARTEST model.

Formulating each of the solutions in the SMARTEST way will increase the chance that they will actually do them. Even if your protégé seems really willing to try out the first solution, work out at least three choices of action, so that not only do they have choice, but that they are also *aware* of having choice.

Tip: Present your suggestions metaphorically if you really are tempted to present your own solution, or if your protégé really wants to know what you would do, because your suggestion will remain in their mind better.

Often, the first solution seems pretty obvious, which indicates that the question, "Why didn't you do this before?" might be useful to ask. If your protégé's source of creativity seems to run dry, before starting to suggest your solutions, use the "if" key: "And *if* you knew a solution, what would it be?" or "*If* a friend were to present you with a similar problem, what would you recommend them to do?" The "if" frame is the greatest creativity unlocker. It allows more resources to emerge than people think they have, because it has permission to do so.

Even if finding a second and third solution may take more time than coming up with than the first answer, enabling your protégé to work on them may help to get a breakthrough. Experience has shown that the second and third solutions are more likely to be implemented than the first answer the protégé came up with, usually with fewer side effects. At the next coaching session, you can close the loop by checking whether your protégé has really implemented one of the solutions. Perhaps you may want to offer them some encouragement to keep working on the solution, and we hope you'll be able to congratulate your protégé on the results they will have obtained!

The coaching form

You can use the coaching form on the next page as a guide for proceeding systematically through all four steps and ensuring you collect all the information needed. The form is also useful as a follow-up instrument. When preparing the next coaching session, you should retrieve the form and take a quick look at the actions the protégé had planned, in order to ask them how it went. A completed example of this form can be found on the website www.jobEQ.com/mentor.

Smartest action-oriented coaching

1. Topic

Follow-up	Feedback (DESC)	Self-evaluation
1.	1.	1.
2.	2.	2.
3.	3.	3.

2. Analysis

	Example 1	Example 2	Example 3
Context			
Outcome			
Method			
Effect			
Tasks			

3. Pattern

4. Actions

	Action 1	Action 2	Action 3
S			
M			
A			
R			
T			
E			
S			
T			

Figure 4.3: Action-oriented coaching form

PART 5 Long-Term Mentoring Skills

Earlier we pointed out that the difference between the short-term and the long-term in mentoring is that the long-term adds considerations such as values, mission, and vision. Long-term mentoring relationships, lasting from two years to a decade and beyond, generally evolve informally and are centered on career advice, helping the protégé to network, or even helping to create opportunities the protégé would benefit from, given the next career step in their personal development. Mentors will find they spend a lot of time discussing the meaning of behavior, making the link to motivation, personality, and values.

Other topics covered in this part focus on the fact that work is more than just a means to earn a living. Most people expect to find meaningful work in which they can invest a part of themselves. But there is more to life than just work. Finding your own balance as well as respecting your protégé and other people's need for balance is key.

Given that it would be too ambitious to cover all these issues linked to long-term mentoring in only fifty or so pages, we present a primer on these issues and suggest some further resources.

Control is not leadership; management is not leadership; leadership is leadership. If you seek to lead, invest at least 50% of your time in leading yourself your own purpose, ethics, principles, motivation, conduct. Invest at least 20% leading those with authority over you and 15% leading your peers.

Dee Hock, founder of VISA international

A primer on values, work attitude, and motivation

One of the executives we met in a consulting relationship wasn't able to take the necessary decisions to reorganize the insurance company he was leading. As a result, the conflicts between the underwriting department, responsible for selling insurance policies, and the technical department, responsible for calculating the "correct" price for the coverage sold in the

Tip: A question to ask about your current job: "Could I carry on like this till I retire?"

If you answer yes, this may well be the job of your life.

If you answer no, the question is, "What needs to be changed?"

insurance contract, increased. He had contacted us because he hoped that an expert system would once and for all solve the problem of calculating the "exact price". What he really needed was a mentor helping him to get hold of the organization and develop internal criteria to give a more directive kind of leadership needed by his managers at that point. However, one of his personal strengths was his ability to be a good follower, taking guidance from others. He had been a good lieutenant to the former CEO and was very motivated at that time, but had fallen into a black hole when he was promoted to the top job himself.

Behavior is always motivated ...

Identify the motive and you'll understand the behavior.

Satisfy the motive and you'll manage the behavior.

In the context of mentoring, we want to know what are your protégé's motivational "hot buttons", how they learn best, and so forth. You will get the best results if the job the protégé is doing, or the career they pursue, fits their strengths in terms of attitude and motivation.

What really motivates people? David McClelland (1987) would have us choose among *power* (hierarchical position, status), *affiliation* (belonging, being liked) and *achieving results* (or significant contributions to these results).

Contrary to common thought, few people are actually motivated to do what they want to do by material things for their own sake, such as money in the bank, by physical objects such as a powerful car, or closing a good deal on a contract, or even by situations and contexts such as getting the top job in an organization. Instead, they are motivated by what these represent in their minds. For instance, a powerful car may have to do with status.

These representations may in turn be intermediate criteria or prerequisites for something even more important or profound that they seek to have, to accomplish, to be, or to become, something that a person may be totally unconscious of, until you give them the means to allow themselves to think about it. When they emerge, these are usually expressed in very abstract terms.

Abraham Maslow judges that this highest motivation is self-actualization,[31] becoming who they really are, fulfilling their potential as soon as the more basic needs are fulfilled, and, if the person has enough self-esteem. This is what Carl Jung calls the drive toward individuation. Professor Frederick Herzberg[32] grouped all these factors together and conducted a study asking people when they felt good at work. For this, he derived that achievement is the most frequent factor leading to job satisfaction, followed by recognition for that work, the work itself, responsibility, and opportunities to grow.

However, these generalizations about the world's work population are not very helpful in dealing with a particular individual. In this case, a better question to ask is, "What motivates *you*?" and the conclusion one can draw from answers to this question is that each person is motivated in their own individual, specific way.

It is this uniqueness that enables each of us to focus on specific facets of an issue, offering multiple perspectives and so helping us to identify an integrated systemic solution to the problem. This solution is more likely to endure than one derived from a single-minded approach. Later, we present a process to enable you to elicit your protégé's hierarchy of values.

The Scottish philosopher David Hume (1711–76) posited that the highest aspiration of man was the search for happiness, closely followed by "making others happy", "making the world a better place", and "making the future a better time". These last three aspirations make sense when you realize that they are actually subsets of the first. If you ask people what would make them happier, being happy at someone else's expense or being happy and contributing to others' happiness also, the latter always wins. Likewise "happiness" is perceived

---

[31] Actually, in his 1971 book *The Farther Reaches of Human Nature*, Maslow proposes a list of meta-needs to which self-actualizers evolve, such as truth, beauty, and aliveness.

[32] Herzberg's theory is summarized in his 1968 article "One More Time: How do you motivate your employees?", which is *Harvard Business Review*'s most reprinted article.

as being further intensified when it can have the fewest deleterious consequences to the environment now and in the future (when one's own children could be affected, anyway). All the other motivational goals actually appear to be stepping stones to this ultimate one, which usually connects with people's sense of vision, mission and/or purpose (see below).

Meta-programs

A person's motivation can be represented by a range of parameters, called *meta-programs*.[33] The concept of meta-programs—or operating programs that influence other operating programs—derives from cognitive science. Meta-programs predict which "programs" (or behaviors) a person will naturally prefer to apply, both in a given context and also cross-contextually. They most often manifest themselves in terms of polarities.

As a mentor (or indeed any other human being), you, too, are continuously running your own set of meta-programs. By learning to identify them, you can detect which of these operational modes you apply at a given moment or in relation to a particular issue. It also allows you to do likewise with your protégé, which will enable you to ascertain whether this mode serves them or their goal.

If it does, you will probably want to validate their choice, responding in kind, and manifesting the similar meta-program, to create a positive reinforcement. However, should you perceive that their operational mode does not serve them, or does not serve others or their project, you may wish to take the opposite component of the polarity, even going so far as playing devil's advocate in order to redress any imbalance you may perceive. Gradually, your protégé will internalize this approach and do it by themselves.

---

[33] Our 2001 book *7 Steps to Emotional Intelligence* includes more than fifty pages discussing meta-programs in detail. Another good source is Shelle Rose Charvet's *Words that Change Minds* (1995). The principles of these books are applied on the jobEQ website: www.jobeq.com.

To go back to the executive we met in our example at the beginning of this part, we saw that he was externally referenced, meaning that he oriented himself to other people for direction. So his behavior was organized around asking other persons' opinions. This is great in certain contexts: e.g. in customer care it may help to start from the presupposition that the customer is right. However, executives often need to have their own criteria and their own internal sense of direction and must be willing to act on it. If you ask the question, "How do you know you have done a good job?" or, "How did you take that decision?" the answer you get will indicate to what degree you are internally referenced (the decision is based on personal criteria) or externally referenced (the decision is based on the opinion of others).

Evaluation reference

How did you take that decision?

Internal: decide for yourself, It is up to you

Versus

External: feedback, receiving advice and guidance

As a mentor you will typically act as an external sounding board. You can be an external reference point, but, as in the example, you may find it more useful to help your protégé to develop their own criteria. In other cases, when your protégé appears to be ignoring clear signals from the outside, you may need to help them to open up, and become more externally referenced. This will usually enable them to reconnect with the reality "out there" and, more often, to become conscious of the consequences, positive or negative of their actions or inaction on themselves, other people, the world, and the future. A balance of internal and external referencing, dependent on the given context or situation, is usually best to ensure most factors are taken into account.

Another set of meta-program patterns indicates the *action level* of a person. Will a person *initiate* projects or rather *follow* the lead of others? Our executive tended to wait for others to take the initiative. If he had to take the initiative himself, he would first be sure to take all the time required to gather all the information he deemed necessary. This motivation trait had been great when he was a lieutenant and had to compensate for the proactive drive of his former boss. While being too proactive may not always be the best strategy for a top manager, waiting too long didn't help our executive, either.

Action level

Who took the initiative?

Starts: initiate, start, just do it, begin

versus

Follows: patience, wait, all in good time

As a mentor, depending on the context, you may need to help your protégé slow down their decision process when they are acting too proactively; or, on the other hand, you may need to speed up the process, so that your protégé can take the initiative faster, ideally to achieve a balance between the two.

A third meta-program grouping indicates which direction one's actions take. Does someone prefer to operate as a problem solver, cleaning up the past (away from what went wrong) or rather to set ambitious goals for the future? Often executives have a clear preference and this can be deduced from the direction that their actions will take. For instance, Scott Adams, the creator of the cartoon strip *Dilbert*, seems an advocate of an away-from management style. One of his most oft-quoted statements is, "I'm slowly becoming a convert to the principle that you can't *motivate* people to do things, you can only demotivate them. The primary job of the manager is not to empower but to remove obstacles." Jacky Ickx—a racing driver who won the 24-hour Le Mans six times, eight Formula One Grand Prix victories, and one Paris–Dakar rally event—is an example of being more toward-oriented. "When you are young, you don't know fear. That's why the young can't be beaten. You don't take danger into account, you want to realize your dreams. As soon as you start to consider the risks your career is over."[34]

Action direction

Why did you decide that and why is that important?

Toward: Focus on goals, the outcome, have, get, obtain, approach

versus

Away from: Focus on problems, avoid errors, concerns, uneasy

If one looks at the history of many companies or divisions, one often sees phases of expansion, where the focus is *toward* achieving more growth, followed by phases where problem solvers have to take over, cutting costs and doing away with unprofitable business, to get *away from* losses.

Commonly, other managers guide these phases, e.g. the CEO in charge of the growth phase is fired because of huge losses, or because they weren't able to deliver upon their ambitious growth figures, as happens in times of recession. For instance, from October 2000 till the end of 2001, Lucent[35] was run by an

[34] Interview with Jacky Ickx, 2003, *Humo* (Belgian magazine), July 8.

[35] In September 1996 the systems and technology unit of AT&T, which includes the famous "Bell Labs", was spun-off and became Lucent Technologies.

interim CEO, Henry B. Schacht, whose main task was to shed unprofitable assets, revamp the product line, and cut staff by more than half, thus trying to bring Lucent back to a break-even. When Pat Russo started in January 2002, it was seen as her fist task to get Lucent out of these dark days and then get sales growing again.

As a mentor you can help your protégé to develop a better balance between a goal orientation and a problem-solving attitude. To a goal-oriented person, you may need to recommend doing a more extended risk analysis. To a problem solver, you may recommend thinking in terms of solutions and acceptable risk, again achieving a contextual balance of things to get away from and to move toward.

Both polarities are equally important, if for different reasons. Avoidance ("away from") gives you the energy to move. Goals ("toward") give you a direction to aim for. Without the initial impetus provided by a strong away-from, a person may be content to remain in their mediocrity. Without a strong toward to pull you in the right direction, you can spend as much energy as you want, but it will take you nowhere. The most motivated people in the world usually have an alignment of what they seek to avoid and what they want to achieve, i.e. instead of being at loggerheads these polarities take them in the same direction. We call such alignments a "propulsion system". Enabling your protégé to develop such a system will be invaluable in their progress, especially if it is itself aligned with their mission, purpose, and calling (see below).

The fourth meta-program category indicates one's task attitude. At lower levels of the hierarchy, companies often expect people to strictly follow the procedure handed down to them. After all, you wouldn't want a bank clerk to be creative when figuring out what they would do with your money if you just want to deposit it in your cash account, would you? Much of the quality-assurance movement of the eighties and of the ISO 9000 international quality management system standards and guidelines are based on procedures.

Task attitude

How did you do that?

Options: alternatives, possibilities

versus

Procedures: do it the right way, follow procedures

However, studies conclude that most people get bored with routine after a certain period of time, and that they prefer some options, finding other ways to do things, or, if they have to do the same thing, to find alternative ways of doing it. And yet not following the procedure would probably get our bank clerk fired. That's why some jobs seem to be of the kind where the company wants you to leave your intelligence at the door (together with your coat) and to operate on automatic subroutines.

The paradox is that, when asked, most managers wouldn't remain motivated for long if they had to follow these procedures all day long themselves! Luckily for them, in times such as ours, where the only constancy is change, most management functions require managers who are busy figuring out new options all the time. Managers constantly need to achieve a balance between ensuring predictability of work and using procedures, and flexibility of options to deal with unpredictable situations.

As a mentor, you can help your protégé to achieve, fine-tune, and sustain this fine balance between options and procedures.

There are many more meta-program series we could explore. However, the last one we will discuss in this part is *relationship sorting*. The name of this meta-program comes from the question that will help us discover one's sorting preferences: "What's the relationship between your job this year and your job last year?" (If you want to find out your preference, you might want to write down the answer before reading on.)

If you ask this question to a dozen people, this may include a person who recently switched jobs and answers, "Oh, basically, I'm still doing the same thing." Seen from the outside, another person of your test sample may be doing the same job as last year, but may nonetheless answer, "Oh, things have changed a lot around here."

The first conclusion one might draw on hearing this is that these answers don't sound "logical". However, this is a very important mode of operation. One of our customers, a logistics company, had truck drivers complaining, and even leaving the company. This was because, instead of transporting motor parts coming from the UK to the Opel plants in Rüsselsheim and Boschum (both in Germany) each day, they now had to take them to the German Ford plant in Cologne.

When you analyze the twelve responses you get (or your own answer) more closely, you'll find examples of the three following kinds of structures. Some will refer to the *similarities* between the current situation and last year's situation; these are things that remained the same, that are alike. Others will express themselves in terms of *comparisons* between today's situation and the previous one and finally evaluate whether, to their mind, it has improved, evolved or degraded, becoming better or worse, more or less etc. The remainder will express themselves in terms of *distinctions* or differences, focusing on what's different or new, or what has changed drastically.

Relationship sorting

What's the relationship?

Similarities: same, in common, similar, alike

Comparison: improved, changed for the better, different yet similar

Distinctions: new, change, different, unique, switch, flip

Why is this meta-program important? Simply put, the more you focus on distinctions, the more you like change in your environment. If you are working in an industry such as computer technology or in a startup, you'll probably have all the change you want. If you work in a mature industry, such as the steel industry, only a few things may change. Some industries, such as advertising, really focus on change: each advertising campaign has to create something new.

However, if you look at the workforce—apart from the fact that, to some degree, people self-select toward industries that have change patterns they like—you'll find you're surrounded by people with various sorting preferences. In other words, some people in a team may thrive on change and are constantly bringing in new ideas, while others would prefer more stability. This might be something to consider when someone seems "resistant" to change. They might just be defending the merits of stability! Not every change is for the better, especially not for the persons involved. Combining what's best about the current situation with some improvement might be better than radical change.

Do not set out to remake your personality. Learn to live with it.

Robert K. Greenleaf, The Power of Servant Leadership

As a mentor you can help your protégé to figure out what they prefer for themselves, what the people they interact with prefer, and how to develop enough flexibility in relation to their own preferences for stability or change. For example, suppose you want to reorganize a department. Guess who would be the people to call upon. Right, those who prefer change! On the other hand, how do you sell change to people who would prefer things to remain the same? You explain to them how much the new situation will resemble the old one (with some improvements, of course) and how the changes will benefit them.

We have outlined only a few meta-programs in this part of the book. Yet the number of combinations you can obtain solely with these patterns is huge. Suppose we just distinguish between a low, a medium and a high score for each parameter. The number of combinations then amounts to 3 to the 11th power or 117,147 possibilities. Given that we could even distinguish more parameters, this helps explain why every person seems to be indeed unique.[36]

Attitude and motivation assessment

What are your key motivators? What are your attitude preferences? How are these reflected in your current job?

Given that meta-programs act as filters through which we observe the world, the advice that you as mentor will give your protégé will be directed by your own natural meta-program preferences. For instance, if you are naturally a proactive person, you may urge your protégé to take initiative; or, if you are good at recognizing problems, you may suggest that your protégé first focus on resolving some problems. By recognizing your own meta-programs, you can learn to put them aside to focus on what your protégé will need. For instance, you can expect that, in a learning situation, your protégé may need a bit more support. They will be less proactive and be more on guard regarding potential problems than if they already know how to tackle the matter at hand.

---

[36] The chances of finding two identical persons are quite small: jobEQ's iWAM questionnaire explores 48 meta-program parameters. The 48 scales are continuous; yet just distinguishing low, medium and high scores gives 79,766,443,076,872,509,863,361 combinations, or billions of possibilities for each person who has ever lived.

If instead you were acting according to your own meta-program preferences, not only might you be setting your protégé to fail, but it might also put you in a position to create "clones" of yourself, which is definitely not a desirable trait in a mentor. In a guru, however, that would be different.

Meta-program activity

Keep a diary for one week, each day logging at least one issue you had to deal with. At the end of the week, figure out for each of the examples whether you:

- decided for yourself or did what others suggested
- were proactive or rather patient
- approached the situation or avoided it
- looked for options or took the "standard approach"
- figured out how this situation resembled what you already knew, eventually trying to improve upon it, or rather looked for what was new

Were the meta-programs you used the most appropriate given the situation at hand? If not, consider what you could have done better and what would be the effect.

Pacing Meta-programs

The table on the following page indicates what kind of behavior and what kind of thinking your protégé will appreciate from you as a mentor, given their own meta-program preferences.

Meta-program applications

Apart from avoiding the trap of putting your own meta-programs first and thus not pacing your protégé, knowing about meta-programs presents you with a range of opportunities.

First, you can help to balance your protégé's preferences where this is required. Widening their awareness may make their experience more meaningful. One way to go about this is by doing the opposite of pacing someone's meta-programs,

Resource

To know your own meta-program preferences, fill out the iWAM "Work Attitude and Motivation" questionnaire at the jobEQ website and take a look at the "Attitude Sorter Report".

www.jobeq.com

Starting	Allow for fast initiative: what is the next step to take after this session? How fast can that happen?
Following	Have patience, pace their speed. Have a "Zen attitude" toward time: things will come at their time.
Internal reference	Don't expect them to buy an idea from you: they will make up their own mind. Leave room for an opinion other than yours. Ask how they think about it. Figure out what criteria are important for them in that situation.
External reference	This person will want your opinion on things, and probably other persons' opinions as well. You may suggest some criteria that play a role according to you.
Toward	Figure out with the person what the goal should be.
Away from	The focus will be on problems met and how to deal with these problems, perhaps looking in the past to what caused these problems. When discussing an idea or a solution they will want to do some contingency planning.
Options	There is no such thing as the "one" solution. They want to choose from a variety of options.
Procedures	This person will want a procedure, a series of steps going toward a solution of the problem or issue they are currently facing. Bring enough structure in your meetings with them or else they might feel lost.
Similarities	Help them figure out how this is similar to other things they have faced, or how other people have faced similar issues.
Comparison	They will want to know how to make it better, how to improve upon what's currently there without radically departing from their current situation.
Distinctions	Things need to be framed as new, innovative, radical. The person may become bored if what's presented is not new enough to them.

namely taking the lead. Look back at the previous table and perform more of the behaviors that they wouldn't do naturally. This might be a stretch for them.

Second, you can help your protégé to make better use of their own motivational preferences. How can they do more of the things they are naturally motivated by and do fewer of the things that are in the area of their weaknesses?

Third, you can help your protégé to tackle development areas when their natural preferences do not match the requirements of the job. After all, if you always follow your natural leanings, your potential for development tends to be fairly circumscribed. However, when you seek to develop polarities you are not naturally familiar with, your potential for growth is phenomenal. In such cases, you may find that, in so doing, not only do you not undermine or reduce your natural effectiveness, but that you acquire a new set of operating tools in addition to the others, and an enhanced ability to evolve along the spectrum of extremes.

In a world that demands ever-increasing flexibility to cope with an ever-widening range of issues and development, developing this ability to shift between polarities according to the context allows you to identify an optimal way of responding to this situation. By their nature, the person you will choose to mentor will be a person for whom such skills will be invaluable. You might not have chosen them, or them you, had it been otherwise.

Human beings can alter their lives by altering their attitudes of mind.

William James

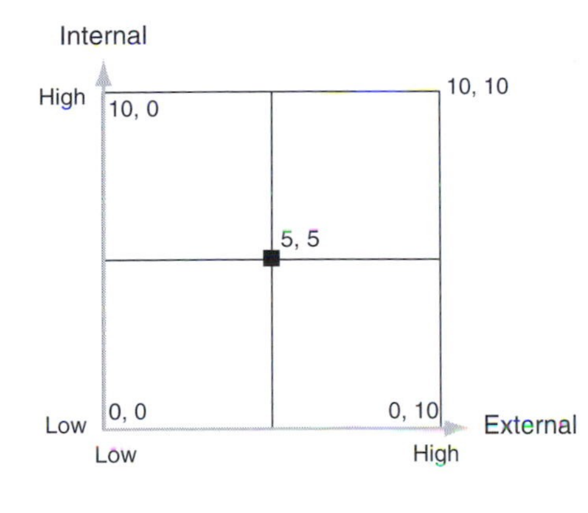

Figure 5.1

A way of making your protégé aware of their meta-programs and helping them to make better use of these patterns is the following exercise (see Figure 5.1). We will illustrate it with the action-direction meta-program grouping. Feel free to extend it to the other groupings, as the opportunity presents itself. We wrote the exercise in "you" form, so that you can present it to your protégé "as is", or try it out for yourself.

First, determine where you position yourself in the use of both patterns. Do you score low, medium, or high on internal reference (deciding for yourself)? Do you score low, medium, or high on external reference (involving others in decisions)? For a low score give yourself a low figure, between 0 for "not at all" and 3 for some. An average figure would be 4 for "slightly less than average" to 6 for slightly more than average. A high score would be a 7, for "most of the time", to 10, "Absolutely"! Once you have decided how to score yourself, draw a dot where your current position is on Figure 5.1.

Meta-program synergy

Instead of ignoring differences, pay attention to them.

Don't minimize them and avoid evaluating them (each pattern has its value; no pattern is inferior or superior)—but analyze the situation through all meta-program perspectives.

Integrate or leverage the differences.

A balanced use of both patterns would be, for instance, the position 5, 5: to some extent you use both internal and external elements in making your decision. If the position is 10, 0, only internal criteria play a role in your decisions. If it is 0, 10, you decide what others decide for you—a very single-sided approach. The most-developed position is 10, 10. If your natural meta-program use is single-sided, consider how it may be a strength in some situations and a weakness in others. Where it is a weakness, consider how you can make better use of the other meta-program pattern the next time when a context presents itself. If you consider that you use both patterns to some degree, the (5, 5) position, developing the use of both internal and external reference, would help to make even better decisions.

Team-coaching advice

Apart from balancing meta-programs on the individual level, you can also balance them inside a team, enabling each team member to play on their meta-program strengths. Some useful questions on a team level are:

- What are the tasks that individual team members will have to fulfill?
- Which are the most appropriate meta-programs for these tasks?
- Do we have a team of persons with the right mix of meta-programs (or can we add some team members to complete the mix)?
- How flexible are the individual team members to deal with meta-program differences?

Values and culture

Meta-programs act as filters through which you perceive the world that surrounds you. To some extent the filters we choose are culturally biased. For instance, the Internet culture, especially during the startup rage, was all about starting things up, being out there fast. This is almost the opposite to having to queue up in a line at a post office in the UK, where queuing is carried out with the necessary British stoicism. In other words, when we compare the scores on the meta-program category "action level" of the Internet entrepreneurs with the general population of the UK, the Internet entrepreneurs will be more biased toward "starting" than to "following".

If meta-programs tell us *how* we filter information, then the next question is, "What do we do with the remaining information?" The short answer is that we evaluate this filtered image of the world by comparing it with your values or criteria. In the example above, the underlying value might be "speed". We compare the situation at hand with this value and make a judgment, e.g. being "too fast" or "too slow". Whether some behavior is perceived as "too fast" or "too slow" will depend on our meta-program bias. Having the Internet entrepreneur waiting in the queue in the post office would probably be quite a stretch.

By helping your protégé become aware of their meta-programs and values, you'll help to:

- understand their way of thinking (filtering experience) ands its consequences
- identify their sources of motivation
- discover some secret aspirations

How does that affect what you do as mentor? If you want to help a person to gain better self-knowledge, to help them figure out their meta-program preferences, another useful way is to help them to clarify their values and criteria, which we all act upon. This may lead to challenging a protégé's values, which are not to be confused with their own intrinsic value, which is completely different. This inquiring includes questions such as, "How consistent are your values and actions?"

How about your personal integrity? Integrity means practicing what we preach, walking our talk, living our values consistently. Do people see a façade, or do they see who you really are? Integrity is what keeps us together. The more we set high standards for ourselves, as well as demonstrating the necessary self-discipline to follow these standards, the more others will trust us.

Assumptions or opinions are like computer programs in people's minds. Those programs take over against the best of intentions—they produce their own intentions.

David Bohm, On Dialogue

Some values

Aliveness, beauty, belonging, care, coherence, creativity, esteem, equality, fairness, freedom, friendship, fun, goodness, growth, happiness, harmony, health, independence, integrity, justice, learning, love, meaningfulness, order, peace, playfulness, power, quality, respect, safety, success, truth, unity, wealth, wholeness

Exercise: Hierarchy of values

Nietzsche[37] was probably the first to identify that we operate in ways that manifest our values and that these follow a hierarchy. While he was thinking of an absolute list of values that would hold for everyone, this particular exercise is about seeking to identify your own personal hierarchy of values. We have yet to meet two people who come up with the same list for this exercise.

Step 1: List five to ten values that are very important to you (you may look at the list we provided for inspiration).

Step 2: Check your list, by asking the question, "Is there anything I forgot that is maybe even more important to me?"

Step 3: Comparison in pairs: take two values from the list and ask yourself the question, "If I have to choose between those two values, and I can keep only one, which one would I keep?" Opposing them two at a time, work down the list. Write the value that wins at the end of the round on another column and remove it form this list and start again with the remaining ones. The new list you end up with will have your values in order.

Step 4: Validate your choice by asking the question, "Is there anything more important to me than X?" (Replace X with the value you found to be the most important.)

Step 5: Now rank the rest of the list according to the same principle as explained in Step 3.

Optional step:

Values assessment: give a score from 1 to 7 for each value, indicating to what degree you are honoring each value, "1" meaning "completely dissatisfied, this value doesn't get the attention it should" to "7" meaning "I fully live this value as I want".

---

[37] *The Genealogy of Morals* (1887).

The list you have ended up with reflects your current outlook, attitudes, and assumptions. A year on they may be quite different. Should your circumstances, health or family situation change, your values probably will also.

Your hierarchy of values also reflects the groups and communities that you belong to today with those you presumably identify with. Clare W. Graves and other researchers came up with the concept of value systems: groups of values that belong together.[38] One such value system stresses competition and continuous growth, focusing on winning and monetary gains. Personal achievement is important in this system, which is prevalent in many companies today.

Resource

To learn more about value systems, fill out the "Value Systems Questionnaire" (VSQ) on the jobEQ website: www.jobeq.com.

Such a system clashes with another system, which puts more emphasis on the community, where every person has to have equal chances and where "groupthink" or consensus building is more dominant. This system prevails in more socially oriented organizations and public services such as education and healthcare. Contrary to what one may think, such value systems do not need to be incompatible. Each has its advantages and so the various value systems deserve to be integrated. However, in most cases, one system runs the show over the other. Would you rather be competitively cooperative or cooperatively competitive? If these systems could be hybridized, so that the best of both are brought together, what might be achieved? Corporate cultures that seek to ensure a win–win situation endeavor to achieve such a hybridization.

Discussion topic

Ask your protégé to answer the question, "What do you believe is *really* important?" in five simple sentences (without long words). Then challenge each of these sentences (ask why, what if and so on).

In cultural studies, the list of values you identified would be called your "espoused" values, at least if you are willing to make this list publicly known. Integrity means being willing to do that and to live in accordance with one's values. The strongest careers are those in which a person is fully involved and has found how to be truly authentic.

---

[38] You'll find Graves's value-systems theory in Don Beck and Chris Cowan (1996), *Spiral Dynamics*.

Value integrity check

Where are the actions you take "incompatible" with your top values? What could you do to act with more integrity in these situations?

A study of organizations reveals that the real organizational culture is not defined only by visible artifacts and espoused values. Maybe more important are the tacit assumptions typically made by the organization. The espoused values are often published, e.g. maybe as part of the "vision statement" of how the organization should be operating. The second kind has to be derived from behavior by looking for what is driving this behavior, what it implies, and what is not explained by the espoused values, or is perhaps inconsistent even.[39] How does the organization set its goals and how are they followed up till they are realized? How is the company structured, and why is that so? What are the underlying principles? If a mismatch is found between espoused values and the "real value", the question becomes, "Is the value that seems desirable achievable, given the company's frame of mind, attitude or way of thinking?"

Sometimes we value things which are in conflict with our hierarchy of values, which makes it hard to get all values harmoniously aligned. When it comes to values, your task as a mentor is not only to be a guardian angel to the values of your protégé, but also to enable them to develop values that will serve them best. To begin with, some of these values may be limiting, others may be incompatible with the values of the organization. If your protégé is from the same company, one of your mentoring tasks may be to help your protégé to synchronize their values with those of the organization or, barring that, to help them find a better place for themselves somewhere else.

Stand up for what you believe in!

The integrity moment

We are writing this book in 2002–3, while questionable accounting practices recently discovered in companies such as Enron, Xerox, Worldcom, Tyco International Ltd, Imclone Systems, Bristol Myers-Squibb Co., Merck and Co., and many others worldwide are ravaging the stock markets. Stock prices

One thing I preached every day at GE was integrity. It was our No. 1 value. Nothing came before it.

Jack Welch,
Jack: Straight from the Gut

[39] A good source for learning more about assessing a corporate culture is Edgar H. Schein, (1999), *The Corporate Culture Survival Guide.*

have been collapsing because of a total lack of confidence in the way businesses are being run. Millions of US employees risk losing their retirement savings invested in stocks.

As this doomsday scenario, caused by a lack of business ethics, amply demonstrates, integrity is an issue that needs to be emphasized much more. Unfortunately, it may be very tempting to forget about ethics every now and then. In July 2002, halfway through his fourth four year term as Chairman of the Board of Governors of the Federal Reserve System in the USA, Alan Greenspan used the term "infectious greed"[40] to describe how the desire for money makes some executives forget values such as truth and honesty. Another observer spoke about "pay for pretence instead of pay for performance". Lester Thurow, professor at the MIT Sloan School of Management, acknowledges (2002) that current reward systems have a perverse effect: "Sales representatives, for instance, can get fired if they don't hit their numbers. They don't want to get fired. So they make adjustments [to their figures]. Sooner or later, small adjustments become large adjustments. And then no one wants to look too closely at the numbers ..." People hope that the real good numbers will make up for the faked ones, once the "good times" return.

The desire for ladder climbing and quick enrichment because of compensations plans (sometimes options-based) attracts misrepresenting figures or even fraud. Indeed, being a whistleblower may be hazardous to a career, and at times one can respect one's values by finding ways to beat the system, without openly defying it. At other times, one needs to question how much integrity one is ready to compromise in order to be on the fast track and what might be the consequences of that for yourself and others?

Of course, the problem of integrity is not limited to these big scandals. Donald Gibson and Sigal Barsade of the Yale School

Stock Exchange 2002

An explosive cocktail made up of corporate greed, fraudulent accounting, and a bubble created by optimist analysts, thus making huge profits for the broker firms they were working for, putting the customers at risk. No wonder the bubble now deflates and investors lost their confidence!

Willshare Associates calculated that between March 2000 and late July 2002 some 48 percent of the US stock market capitalization, or $8.2 trillion dollars, has disappeared.

Integrity theme

What was a moment in your life when you acted against your personal values? What was your intention? What was the choice you made? What would you have preferred to do instead?

When did similar moments occur in your life? What's the theme or pattern? How can you stop it from happening again?

[40] Speech for the US Senate Banking Committee on July 16, 2002, commenting on executives who fake profits in order to cash in on their stock options.

of Management, found that 24 percent of 1,000 interviewed men and women were "chronically" angry at work. The most common reason for this anger was that these employees sensed that their employers "violated basic promises" and didn't fulfill "the expected psychological contract with their workers" (Gibson and Barsade, 1999).

Borderline case

While the bureaucracy often frustrated me, I tried hard not to be a very visible critic of it—especially not to the higher ups."

Jack Welch, ex-CEO of General Electric, Jack: Straight from the Gut

Most people will be confronted with their values only when a choice needs to be made. The question is whether someone will walk their talk, be true with themselves, be authentic. In Linda Tobey's book (2001) the integrity moment is defined as "acting consistently with core values in the current context". But everyone encounters moments when the environment, the rules that govern a particular group we want to adhere to, or the situation we are in seems to require that we act inconsistently with our own values and beliefs, or all three conspire to make us do so. If we look back to a moment in our life where we chose the easier way and let our own values be called into question by others, a feeling of disempowerment or even guilt, fear or frustration may arise. You might want to be on guard for such moments in the future.

He always delivered on his commitments. I considered him Mr. Integrity—as high a compliment as you could pay anyone.

Jack Welch about Gene Murphy, who became a GE vice-chairman, in Jack: Straight from the Gut

As a mentor you can guide your protégé through such moments, helping them to discover possible patterns, where a certain value gets "run over" again and again. By discussing with them you can help them to identify how they might be able to combine the demands posed by the context, with their ethics and their personal values. You can enable them to become aware of ways of resolving such dilemmas and to identify where their integrity breaks down, in order to protect it.

Tolerance implies no lack of commitment to one's own beliefs. Rather it condemns the oppression or persecution of others.

John F. Kennedy

Fairness

Often people will reject an agreement because they don't consider it "fair". According to Robert H. Frank, a professor of economics at Cornell University and author of *Passions within Reason* (1998), fairness can be defined as a transaction "in which the surplus is divided (approximately) equally". It identifies the issue of balance, which we explore at greater lengths on page 159.

Beliefs

Another mentoring issue at the same level as values is about helping the protégé to deal with limiting beliefs. According to one dictionary,[41] beliefs are "the feeling of certainty that something exists or is true". You could say that a belief is a thought that one validates by consciously or unconsciously saying "yes" to it.[42] By doing so, we incorporate it into our worldview system.

Beliefs can be motivating, when we believe that we can do something, are worth something, etc. On the other hand, beliefs can also be limiting or demotivating, when we believe we are *not* worth it, *cannot* do it etc. When we ask a person what stops them from doing something, the answer we get will often take the form of a limiting belief.

Even when expressed positively, a belief can limit us when it is not supported by resources that it would need to be manifested. One calls such type of belief a self-delusion. A person who has delusions of competence or self-grandeur that are not backed by evidence or supported by inner skills and resources can be a very dangerous individual indeed, like a person driving a car who has not taken the necessary lessons and demonstrated their driving ability by passing their driving test.

As Mahatma Gandhi (1869–1948) put it, "Freedom and slavery alike—they are mental states. The moment the slave resolves that he shall no longer be a slave—his shackles fall. He frees himself and shows the way to others."

You can enable your protégé to identify beliefs that limit them, either because they prevent them from achieving something, or because they need to be backed by evidence and resources in order to truly become valid. You may point out where and how they can acquire these skills so that those beliefs actually become true.

Most of our thought originates in the whole culture and pervades us. We pick it up as children from parents, from friends, from school, from books, from newspapers, and so on. We make a small change to it; we select parts of it which we like, and we may reject other parts. But still, it all comes from that pool.

David Bohm, On Dialogue

Beliefs: Those things we hold to be true despite evidence to the contrary.

Joseph O'Connor

Our demons are our own limitations, which shut us off from the realization of the ubiquity of the spirit ... each of these demons is conquered in a vision quest.

Joseph Campbell

---

[41] *Cambridge International Dictionary of English*, 2001, (online dictionary), http://dictionary.cambridge.org/.

[42] A process called "meta-yes and meta-no" has been developed in neurosemantics to help you do just that. This is presented in the neurosemantic foundational training "Accessing Personal Genius".

Belief assessment

In his book *Visionary Leadership Skills*, Robert Dilts points out six statements one can check to assess whether a person really believes in an outcome:

- It's desirable and worth it
- It's possible to achieve it
- We can do it (we have the competence to do it)
- What we have to do is clear, appropriate, and ecological
- We deserve to achieve it
- The responsibility to do it lies with us

Pick a goal and indicate to what degree, from 1 as lowest to 5 as highest, you agree with each of these statements in relationship to your goal. The lowest one is probably the one that may prevent you from achieving your goal, or sabotaging your efforts and needs resolving.

Ask yourself, "What do I need to do, to have, or to be to believe this more?"

Some limiting beliefs that are overcome sound downright spectacular. Consider the story of the American football legend Rocky Bleier, who was severely injured in his right foot when he served in Vietnam. He was discharged with 40 percent disability. But then he received a postcard from Art Rooney, the owner of the Pittsburgh Steelers. Rooney had written only, "We'll see you when you get back." Bleier says, "The impact of these simple words was immediate. It was then that I determined that I would be back. I would fight this thing with everything I had."[43] The Steelers allowed him on their injured reserve and four years later, in 1974, he was playing in their core team, to win the Super Bowl with them. Bleier overcame a limiting belief instilled by a doctor but removed by Rooney, whose words and decision to put him back on the team illustrate what a mentor can do.

The following process helps a person to revisit a belief with the opportunity to achieve a breakthrough. It is based on the observation that human reasoning often isn't as "rational" as we'd like to believe it is. Often we believe something, because it is "to the best of our knowledge", i.e. "what I know and understand from the information that I have". Thus, it may be sufficient to realize that one was working with incomplete information when one made the decision, or that one's decision process has a logical flaw in it. Despite what most economists tell us, even "business" decisions are not as "rational" as they seem.[44] The same can be said about many other decisions we take during our lives, such as when we decide to believe that there are limitations we can't overcome.

---

[43] See http://www.pittsburghsteelers.co.uk/steelers/players/rocky%20bleier.htm. Rocky Bleier's life has been described in the book *Fighting Back* (1980) and a ABC-TV movie with the same title.

[44] To be fair, a limited number of economists have been dismissing the "rational customer" theory. In 1988, Robert H. Frank, a professor of economics at Cornell University, wrote *Passions within Reason*, in which he shows how we actually benefit from "emotional, irrational behavior". In 2000 Daniel Kahneman and Amos Tversky edited the book *Choices, Values and Frames* (Cambridge University Press, Cambridge, UK), which contains a multidisciplinary collection of articles presenting an alternative for the rational "*Homo economicus*".

Exercise: Overcoming limiting beliefs

Step 1: Write down the limiting belief

e.g. It's hard to find qualified staff nowadays

Step 2: Write down the evidence you have that supports the belief. Be as complete as you can.

e.g. When I place an ad, I only get a limited number of reactions.

I can't take into consideration most of the reactions I get, because either the people are not competent, or they are unionized.

Step 3: Write down the counterarguments that exist

e.g. My ad may not be appealing to my target audience.

Formal qualifications don't say everything, people may be self-educated

Not all unionized people are unqualified

Step 4: Write down the logic: How did you come to this conclusion, based on the evidence? Did you decide this for yourself, or did you pick up the belief from someone else? Did you take the counterarguments into account? Does this conclusion still hold today?

e.g. in the example given (a real "case" that came up during a "7 Steps to Emotional Intelligence" seminar), after listing the counterexamples, the person wasn't any longer convinced. In case your protégé remains convinced, you can use the "logical" reasoning of your protégé to help to come to other conclusions, e.g. after presenting a number of counterexamples over the period of time it takes the protégé to become convinced.

There is an infinite number of possibilities. There is a limited number of days. So, why have one of those days ruined by an "impossibility"?

Unknown participant in the INLPTA trainer's training, 1996

Step 5: Follow-up: looking at the future, suppose that it is three months later and you have left the limiting belief behind you. What new opportunities have arisen over these past few months that you have missed out on previously?

> e.g. the person imagines he has started a new advertising campaign, reworking the ad so that it comes closer to the work attitude and motivational elements that are present in other employees who have a proven track record in a similar function.

When a person gets stuck there is often a mismatch between how the person looks at themselves and the way their environment sees them. This exercise is an example of how your protégé may often be unable to see their own conflicts and inconsistencies. But, then, aren't we better at seeing the mote in our brother's eye, while we do not see the beam in our own?

In other words, as mentor you'll probably have enough occasions to help your protégé to sort out inconsistencies among their beliefs and actions, pointing out limiting beliefs and suggesting ways of resolving them.

Thought viruses

Much of our thinking is rooted in the culture in which we are immersed. People have recently compared thoughts and concepts to viruses that one shares unknowingly with people we come across. Some beliefs are as contagious as the flue, as if it were viruses that affect the mind. As children we start taking over the thought patterns of our parents, our friends, our school, books, newspapers, etc. We may make some changes to them, choose only those we like and do away with the rest. Still, the thought patterns and beliefs we adopt this way mostly come out of our own cultural pool.

In line with the theory set forth in Richard Dawkins's *The Selfish Gene*, scientists now describe values, ideas, thinking patterns, and beliefs as "memes", the mind equivalent of genes.

We take on such thought patterns by acknowledging them consciously or unconsciously. You can improve the immune system of your brain by making sure you accept only those beliefs you really want to have and rejecting the others.

Expanding your modeling skills

Instead of being "infected" by thought viruses, your protégé can also consciously choose to take over certain enabling presuppositions, beliefs, values, or meta-programs from you or another person serving as model or "exemplar". When modeling in order to master patterns of excellence, we recommend you consider at least where your model of the world differs from that held by the exemplar and how that might influence the excellence pattern.

Finding patterns

Most of the material discussed in this and the previous part of this book can be applied to discovering patterns.

For instance, which metaprograms, values, beliefs are underlying the examples? Was the outcome well-formulated? And so on.

Here are some suggestions protégés might want to incorporate into their modeling effort:

- Let them refresh the awareness of their values, both generally and in relation to what they're seeking to model. Why is that important to them?

- Let them compare their value hierarchies with yours. Are they compatible, complementary, or would absorbing your values jar with them. Let them feel them in themselves. Do they fit comfortably or do they cause them imbalance or discomfort? If so, let them identify the ones that jar. Are they indispensable or can they be left out? What values do they have within them that would do the job?

- Let them repeat the process with beliefs, about self, others, the world.

- Compare your respective meta-programs in relation to the modeling. If they differ from yours to achieve this, suggest ways they could develop theirs.

- Let them toy with your favorite metaphors. How do they respond to them?

Make sure your thought viruses are only benign or even benevolent ones.

You can also use these recommendations to your own advantage. This explicit modeling method serves as a mirror and it might help you to discover some of your blind spots. Or you might discover you've been infected by some negative thought viruses yourself and risk infecting others.

Along the career track

The brave carve out their own fortune.

Cervantes, Don Quixote

Knowing more about oneself in terms of motivation, attitude, and values will help your protégé to get more out of their career.[45] One way of creating more insight comes from analyzing your protégé's career track until now and studying their current career situation and then helping them to prepare the next steps. The career-coaching mentoring skills we discuss in this section are built around the CV/résumé-patterning exercise on page 140.

The learning journal

Learn more from your past, write down your learnings of the day every day.

Historical contexting

In many European countries you need to mention the historical-context question, "How is what you are doing today or might be doing tomorrow related to what you did in the past?"

This process starts from the observation that, as with other meta-program preferences discussed earlier in this part, some people will pay more attention to their past, others will be focusing on what's happening now, while others might be preparing for the future. Again, each of these three perspectives has its merit. Therefore the exercise helps you to get more out of the past and the present, in order to prepare for the future.

The past

Regardless of the time that has passed since the day you were born, how old do you feel? People who feel old, or behave as if they were old, often give more attention to their past than their future. People give the impression of being "old" when they are saying, "If only I'd made another choice when I was younger." Looking back, regretting what has happened in

We learn wisdom from failure, much more than success. We often discover what we *will* do—by finding out what we will *not* do.

Samuel Smiles (1812–1904)

[45] A book that focuses exclusively on succession management and managing the careers of future leaders within an organization is: William C. Byham, et al. (2002), *Grow Your Own Leaders: How to Identify, Develop and Retain Leadership Talent.*

your past, absorbs energy. A more useful question regarding your past is, "What can I learn from my past that can be useful today or that will help me prepare my future?"

What has been your life journey up till now? What were the ups and downs, the shaping events? Your past has shaped your ideas, your values, and it reflects your motivation and attitude. As we can't change our past, we should be grateful for what we learned and gained in experience.

Sometimes we discount what we have done well. It often leads us to underutilize a resource that we have, or to confine it into a narrower field of application than it needs to be. Revisiting the past to identify and refresh past resources is thus a very important stepping stone to creating a better and richer future. Even our past mistakes can help us to be stronger to face the future. They are often a richer source of information and resources than when we get things right the first time. Instead of being an invitation to despondence, revisiting one's past mistakes with an eye to doing something else opens before you the door to self-improvement. We now know better what we want and what we don't want.

In addition, labeling something a mistake is a very "digital" way of representing it. Hardly anything in life is ever 100 percent successful or 100 percent failure. Learning to represent achievements and mistakes in a more "analog" fashion reinstates a sense of proportion and a sense of achievability and validates our past experiences, whatever they were, for the teachings and learnings they have to offer us. This certainly cannot not be useful in a world ever more governed by "fuzzy" logic.

When mentoring you can enable your protégé to revisit their past to reawaken in them an awareness of resources they were not aware of having, by saying, "You must have done something in the past that might apply in such a case. It may not be identical to this, but it may be similar enough for you to apply it. Or it may be in another aspect of your life. Maybe you could map it across and see how it applies to this."

Nobody is perfect

One is completely qualified for one's job. Either some aspects of a job can be a stretch on one's motivation, or one may lack some skills. Either work on your weaknesses, or find someone in your team who can compensate for your weak points.

Complete the past

Some people carry along a heavy burden by spending a lot of energy on past events. Help your protégé to bring closure to events about which they still feel grief, guilt or resentment. It will lighten them up and free their mind for doing something else!

To review past mistakes and learn from them, you could ask, "Although you may not have thought that at the time, in retrospect you must have done something well even there. Recollect and list what you did well, before, during, and afterwards. Now, how could you have done it so that it would have made a difference? What factors did you not take into account then that, in retrospect, you wish you had? How can you ensure that you will in the future? What did that teach you? How can you make good the teachings of that experience so that it, too, can become a resource in your life?"

The present

If you have ever discussed the past with other people, you'll notice that nobody is perfect, that no one is fully qualified for their job. Sometimes aspects of the job are incompatible with a person's motivation; on other occasions, some competencies may need to be developed. It may be that you will have to deal with your protégé's shortcomings or you will perhaps need to help them to compensate for their own shortcomings by surrounding them with a team that complements them.

Job assessment

How far does your current job give you work experiences you enjoy?

What about your current job do you find tedious? What drains your energy?

What do you find attractive and unattractive about the organization you work in?

How far does your current organization offer you career-development opportunities that attract you?

Dealing with the present, as such, is more related to short-term mentoring, coaching, or counseling, which we have covered earlier. In the margin, this part of the book has included several present-related topics, linked to integrity. In such very short-term contexts, the question is, "What matters *now*?", or, more specifically, "What can we do *now* that will deal with the urgent, direct problems?" or "What makes you happy, excited, challenged—*now*?"

For the CV/résumé-patterning process we have an additional series of questions in mind, which are more process-oriented. The goal is to create more clarity around one topic, namely, "How does the current job fit within the thread that is woven throughout my career?" To quote the late philosopher and writer Alan Watts, "No valid plans for the future can be made by those who have no capacity for living now."[46] On the other hand, too much focus on the present (and the very near future) leads to a desire for instant gratification and short-term benefits.

The future

One of the questions to ask yourself as mentor, whether or not your protégé works within the same organization as you, is, "Given my protégé's aspirations, their values, their current skill set and the challenges they need to develop further, do they belong to the job they're in?" If the answer is no, it's time to start planning the next career step.

Tip: Don't limit your planning of the future to what is going to happen next quarter or in the coming year.

The future can be seen as *short-term*: "What would your next career move be, given what we learned from the patterning exercise?" Following up a person's career and ensuring that they get the next opportunity as soon as they are ready for it is an important step in retention management.

Effective leaders are looking for both short-term success and long-term opportunities.

Or we could take the *long-term* vision: "The day you retire and you look back at your career, what would you like to see? What would you like to be able to tell? How do you want to be remembered?" At the very least, a background notion of one's long-term vision should be included when a job change presents itself. We'll address this long-term view, which is about learning more about life's purpose, in the following section.

[46] Quoted from *Brainyquote* (http://www.brainyquote.com).

CV/résumé-patterning process

Take at least four significant career steps/periods you made as a person (jobs, study choice, and so on), You might want to indicate each period with (an approximation of) its starting date and end date. For each period listed, ask the following questions:

1. What were your main activities and priorities in this period/ what was your core competence in the job?
2. How did you find the job/why did you choose it?
3. What did you like about the job/why did you leave it?
4. What did you learn?/What's the importance of what you learnt?

Write the answers to these questions in a table as the following:

	Period 1	**Period 2**	**Period 3**	**Now**	**Near future**	**...**
1.						
2.						
3.						
4.						

Look for patterns. Is there a common thread? What is similar/ different about these periods?

a. Attitudes, criteria/values

b. Meta-programs:

internal/external reference
proactive/reactive
toward goals/away from problems
options/procedure
sameness/difference

c. Mission: what does this period tell me about who I am?

d. What else can explain these patterns?

Discuss the patterns:

a. What surprises you? What is confirmed?
b. What are the implications (for the current job, for the future career)?
c. What new questions does this bring?

Next to the patterns that have already come up from the CV/résumé-patterning exercise, here follow some suggestions of extra questions you could ask for defining a short-term future career step:

- What business are *you* in (as opposed to what is the business of the organization you happen to work for)? What do *you* want to go into next? What's your "logical" next move jobwise, profession-wise?
- What do *you* want to learn, what challenges do *you* want? How is this next job going to add to *your* value?
- What are your competencies (hint: you'll find them by summarizing your most important learnings from your previous career steps)?
- What do *you* like and want more of? What do *you* dislike and want less off?
- Suppose you take that job you are thinking off. What do you think it will feel like in six months' time? Will it have brought you what you expected? What will be the problems you will be facing? How do you expect to overcome those?

Maybe a short-term solution is no *real* solution; such rarely are. One may dislike one's current job because one is still struggling to learn what there was to be learned. In that case, remaining six more months in the job may be more beneficial that getting away immediately. For instance, if you have seen the movie, you'll remember that the Karate Kid had to polish cars for a day, a job in which he didn't see the relationship to learning karate. As it turned out, the turning arm movement was a very useful one. On the other hand, if an opportunity presents itself, it may be interesting to go with the flow of opportunity, as long as you have checked for the angles.

Book resource

One of the classics when it comes to career advice and job hunting is *What Color is Your Parachute?* by Richard Bolles, with more than 7 million copies in print. There is also a website:

www.jobhuntersbible.com

People who live in the past generally are afraid to compete in the present. I've got my faults, but living in the past is not one of them. There is no future in it.

Sparky Anderson, American baseball manager and coach[47]

[47] Quoted from the *Baseball Almanac* (http://baseball-almanac.com/quomenu.shtml).

Resource

"Competence Versus Challenge" in the Appendix of this book, written by Stephen Wilkinson-Carr, expands on the question of how to choose a job for your protégé, taking into account competence and personal challenges.

Talking about opportunities: not so long ago a headhunter said that the best opportunities for change are often found within a company the person is already working for. Recruiters and headhunters prefer to hire someone who has proven competence in the area they are applying for. This means that at best you will be hired for the next step on the ladder in your area of competence (e.g. from sales team leader to regional sales manager), or for a job on the same level in a related area of competence (e.g. from sales team leader to marketing team leader).

So, if you want to make a bigger shift in your career, say from sales to managing operations, it may be more useful to look for opportunities within your current company. The advantage is that people know you and your qualities. It may not be a good idea, though, if you've already burned some bridges, or if your company isn't really growing and its situation doesn't offer many new opportunities. In that case, it might be useful to make a step sideways to another company or industry, and wait a while before really making the desired shift. Of course, if that's your attitude, another option might be to become an entrepreneur or a free agent.

Building a personal sense of security[48]

Jan Ardui, one of our Belgian colleagues, recommended that, in contexts where people have to face a lot of uncertainty, they should consider their present internal and external stability points.

He recommended asking the question, "Even if you currently may be facing some uncertainty, e.g. because you can't be sure that your current job will still be there tomorrow, what are the things that should remain stable?" Identify three internal stability points (such as personal competencies, degrees, past accomplishments) and three external stability points (such as family, owning a house without mortgage, a network of friends).

---

[48] This exercise is based on a project Jan Ardui carried out to coach the staff of Compaq Belgium through the merger with HP Belgium. He developed a four-hour workshop in which groups of eight people each were coached in order to get through these questions.

Subsequently, ask the question, "What are four empowering values or beliefs that contribute to my current success or will contribute to my future success?"

Once you have written those ten elements on a sheet of paper, ask, "What do these ten elements say about me as a person? How do they contribute to my future?"

Finally, ask the question, "Apart from my current job, what are three possible alternative jobs I realistically would see myself doing in a short term?" At least two of these jobs should be situated outside your current company.

Aligning the protégé's mission

While discussing values and culture we have already pointed out the challenging task of helping the protégé to live their values better. In this section we take this one step further. Helping your protégé to better align with their mission will help them to become themselves.

Work can often be seen merely as a source of revenue, to provide means for doing other things in life. Work itself can also be seen as a contribution, paying your "dues" to the human race, or to the community or field of knowledge you participate in. Missionaries were people who were sent to a foreign country to teach their religion to the people who lived there. They carried out their mission, and changed other persons' lives through it.

Writing down a personal mission statement is about figuring out what kind of message you have to bring to the world. Producing a good mission statement involves asking hard questions that will deepen your personal understanding of your role in the world. This means answering questions such as, "What am I deeply passionate about?", "What can I do as one of the best in the world?", "What have I got to share with the world that no one else has?" "How can I make a living out of my passion and my competencies?"

In every era God calls to every man, "Where are you in your world? So many years and days of those allotted to you have passed and how far have you gotten in your world?"

Martin Bruber, The Way of Man

Your effectiveness as a leader is more about who you are than about what your do.

Ken Blanchard

Gathering clues

Who have been the key influential figures, groups, and communities in your life? What have been key learnings from books, films, and so forth? What clues did these influences give you about your calling?

Aligning mission and calling

This can equally well be done with you there to ask the questions or by the protégé on their own.

Ask your protégé to take a piece of paper and, having drawn two columns on it, to write down their mission at the bottom of one and their calling at the bottom of the other.

Then, working with one column at a time, ask yourself questions such as:

- "What's behind that?"
- "What is my purpose in doing this that is even more important?"
- "What have I got in mind that is even higher than that?"
- "What am I intending to accomplish that is even more profound?"

Write down each answer above the previous one.

If you don't know, ask yourself, "If I knew, what would I say?"

Keep asking these questions until you feel you have reached the end of this series of answers, then move on to the next column and repeat the process. Upon reading back the answers in each column, you may be surprised to identify unexpected similarities or complementarities.

Marry the similarities until you feel you can redraft your mission statement in a way that is aligned with your calling.

As Martin Bruber writes in *The Way of Man* (1995), "Everyone should carefully observe what way his heart draws him to, and then choose this way with all his strength." Whether you see work as a means or as an end in itself, sooner or later you are confronted with the questions, "Why bother? What's the meaning of my life? What's my mission, my calling?" What has been called the "midlife crisis" can often be attributed to the period in life when people discover that they don't have an answer to that question.

They also discover that an answer to this "problem" is not to be found overnight. Rather it's a learning process to find out how you can best put to use the talents you developed earlier in life. And isn't helping a protégé to put their potential to better use precisely the aim of mentoring? Ultimately, we are all responsible for ourselves; however, it takes some self-awareness and inner direction to put us in the right gear to figure out our personal path.

A person's sense of mission often relates to the higher values that they seek to manifest. Surprisingly, even for nonreligious people, these are usually expressed in quasi-spiritual or religious terms. The word "mission", like the word "missile" derives from the Latin root (*mitto*), which means "to send". The very concept of mission presupposes therefore that one is "sent", i.e. propelled from behind. A good question to ask is, "who" or "what" does the propelling?

Conversely, the concept of "calling", related to the word "vocation", presupposes that somebody out there does the calling and one is pulled toward that which "calls" us, usually to "higher" or "better" things. The question to ask is "who" or "what" calls us?

The term "purpose" itself derives from the Latin (*propono*), "to propose, to put forward". The question to ask is, "who" or "what" does the putting forward? Is somebody putting me forward, which is often the case when others, usually parents, put a path before you, sometimes in the family company, or does it come from within? A purpose that arises from without is usually a mission by another name, while an inner-driven purpose will tend to be sustained even when external factors are absent.

The issue arises when the direction of the "mission" or "purpose" does not coincide with that of the "calling". One may push toward B and the other may call toward C, D, or E. Much heartache can be generated by such discrepancy.

Your role as mentor will be instrumental in enabling your protégé to identify whether such discrepancies exist and to give them the support to go with the one that they resonate with. Most often, in such discrepancies the "calling" has been known to win out. You often hear, "Although I was doing this, my calling was elsewhere."

Another thing you could inquire about is: Are B, C, D etc. really incompatible. What do they have in common that I could choose to go for that would align the two?

If no similarities emerge and incompatibilities remain, ask your protégé to imagine weighing each in their hands. Depending on the person, the heavier one or the lighter one will win. You could also ask, "Which one feels warmer or cooler?" Creating metaphorical contrasts such as these will enable them to clarify which one to go for.

Sometimes incompatibilities are more apparent than real, usually a consequence of conceptualizing different timescales. In this case, invite your protégé to align them on a timeline. Usually the one on the nearer timescale will be of a lower order of logic than the one on the longer timescale.

Eventually, I learned I was really looking for people who were filled with passion and a desire to get things done.

Jack Welch,
Jack: Straight from the Gut

When the pushing appears to go, or the pulling dies away, usually in mid-career a "midlife crisis" often occurs. One is then left becalmed with little energy, as if the motion were sustained by energy sources that lie outside your control. "Who am I? and What am I for?" are questions often heard at this juncture. This is often the case when people are pushed into a profession by parents who die or pulled into it with a lofty goal that may appear unrealistic. Unlike a person with a mission or calling, a person with inner purpose usually finds the energy within that sustains them and gives them stability, even in times of difficulty.

> You only live once (according to western religion), so you can't have someone else run your life for you!
>
> *Steve Catlin,* Work Less and Play More, *1997*

As a mentor, you may want your protégé to structure their life purpose in a way that will serve them, not only in the short tem, but also the long term, so that it is not subject to faltering if either pushing or pulling fails.

Earlier sections in this part of the book should already have provided you and your protégé with a series of clues in order to define your mission and theirs. In fact, we can revisit the CV/résumé-patterning exercise and, for each significant period, ask ourselves, "What does this period tell me about who I am?" We can ask the same questions about our core values: "What does holding such values tell me about who I am?"

A mission statement's usefulness comes from choosing to focus on the mission. Peter Van Damme, one of our colleagues, once declared, "When you are young you have the time and energy to go after many things at once. Once you cross the psychological age of forty, you realize that there are many more things you would like to do than things you have time for. It then becomes time to learn from all the things you have done, and be committed to do the things you really want to do."

> Sometime, we have to learn to say "No!" to good things, so that we can say "Yes!" to even better things.
>
> *L. Michael Hall, PhD*

If you feel you aren't focused enough or could even focus more, here are some additional questions:

- To what length am I willing to go after it?
- Of the things I'm doing today, which is not "compatible" with my mission?
- What's the purpose of the things I'm doing?
- What should I stop doing?
- Do I have the courage, resolve, and other inner resources to stop it?
- What about the things I should stop but don't want to stop—what do these say about my mission?
- What do they do for me that I may fear I would lose?
- Are they indispensable?

- How can I make sure that I still have that and yet move on?

Answering this series of questions boils down to having the discipline to go for your mission, doing whatever it takes to become the best on the path you have chosen. If you find that you can't really develop a path for yourself that is compatible with your mission, you may want to go back one step, and continue the quest of finding and defining your mission. If you manage to develop a path that is compatible with your vision, you'll find that life becomes simpler as you focus on the things that are right for you. You will do your protégé a huge service by enabling them to clarify their personal mission.

Your sense of mission also extends way beyond your work life. You rarely hear a person on a mission say that it's a "nine-to-five" job. It's a whole-life issue, involving whole-life balance, and, as such, requires a whole-life development plan—many professional goals and challenges will have an impact on an individual's personal life.

To be effectively carried out, your mission must therefore also benefit other aspects of your life, otherwise these will suffer and the mission will suffer. If we are to believe what the Rev. Ralph Abernathy writes in his book *And The Walls Came Tumbling Down*, Martin Luther King may have had "an immoral liaison" with several women. Nobody's perfect, but ensuring that the high values you profess in one life area are mapped across to another will benefit all your life areas and not just one, and will reinforce your personal congruence.

A good question, therefore, to ask when dealing with issues unrelated to work is, "How can I extrapolate my learnings to all elements of my life?" The resources that you have available in one life area should be accessible to other areas to ensure this balance. The anthropologist Gregory Bateson called an awareness of this "ecology of mind". A well-balanced ecology of mind ensures that all aspects of your life benefit from the actions that involve a specific one.

Mission integrity check

To what degree is your current job a good "translation" of your mission in life?

How will your next career step be a better translation?

Book resource

Jim Collins's book *Good to Great* illustrates what companies do in order to achieve greatness. Much of what is written there can be mapped onto the content of this chapter. Here's just one quotation: "Get involved in something that you care so much about that you want to make it the greatest it can possibly be, not because of what you will get, but just because it can be done."

I think the person who takes a job in order to live—that is to say, [just] for the money—has turned himself into a slave.

Joseph Campbell

Although achieving this balance may not always be possible, as we are all human, at least aspiring to this balancing will keep it in your mind. Balancing can manifest in time, i.e. at a given moment in time, or across time, allowing some temporary imbalances may lead to greater overall balance later. The key point is to ensure that the "later" in question is as early as possible. Case studies abound of people who pushed this "later" further and further away and ended up never achieving it at all!

Linkages between behavior and company strategies

The previous sections of this part focused on helping to clarify your protégé's values and mission. People who are clear about their missions and who have jobs that are aligned with their them will be passionate about their work. If a job doesn't fit a person's mission, the organization won't get full commitment from the person. Clarifying an eventual mismatch will help the person to come clear and hopefully to draw the appropriate conclusions. A person without clear mission and values is as dangerous as a loose cannon was during a storm on a sixteenth-century sailing ship: it can cause serious damage! A cannon needs to be held fast and aimed to fire in the right direction. The table below indicates some other possibilities that are less appealing for company and individual.

	Low clarity	**High clarity**
High commitment	Loose cannon (blurred mission)	Passionate (focused on mission)
Low commitment	Lame dog (no energy, no direction)	Mission doesn't fit

When needed, you can help your protégé by clarifying either their personal mission and values or those of the organization.[49]

[49] Organizations increasingly become more aware of the need of a clear mission and explicit values. Corporate branding techniques are used to communicate these elements as part as the organization's image.

What do you do if your personal values or your mission seems to be incompatible with your job context? Often-heard advice is that everyone should put aside some "go-to-hell" money: a cash reserve on which you can survive in case something goes wrong and when you quit because your integrity risks being violated. However, Joseph Badaracco, author of *Leading Quietly* (2002), recommends facing the problem head on, having the moral courage to stay and figure out how you can do the right thing without bulldozing over everybody and risking your reputation in the process.

Try to change the organization by doing what is right and even hope to improve your reputation and relationships in the process. After all, if you go, the same thing will probably be happening to somebody else. Are you even aware of people who would have left before you for the same reason. Somebody, somewhere, somehow has to make a stand. Why not you? If it's worth it, your mentor will support you.

Walking your talk isn't good only when it comes to hiring people: it also helps increase commitment. Watson Wyatt's "WorkUSA 2000" study indicates that in the first place people need to feel they support the company's direction in order to feel committed to their employer. People younger than thirty also want to see senior management act consistently with core values.

From an organizational perspective, some companies, such as Walt Disney and South West Airlines, have always considered aligning employees as a must. In these companies, your actions will be followed up from a values perspective and persons who behave in a way considered incompatible with the companies' values will get extra attention and help to adapt them to become compatible. If they fail to adjust, the company will ask them to leave, regardless of how competent they are. General Electric did not discover the importance of values until 1992, but at that time they also decided to ask managers who didn't share the company's values to leave, even if they were performing very well financially.

Mission and value alignment

Connect with the vision and mission of your company or organization and conduct all your activities from this focus and perspective.

Look for the value you provide not only to external customers but also to coworkers and collaborators inside your company.

The spiritual level

Over the doorway of Carl Jung's house, one can read an inscription, "Invoked or not invoked, God is present". Whatever spiritual power you feel connected to, whatever you choose to call it, for both mentor or protégé it may be a source for deriving the energy to feed your values and your mission. Somehow, deep down, some of us feel that in some way we must be connected to one another and to the whole universe.

From personal recollections of our years in Jesuit schools, from ages five to seventeen, we learned that, whether Catholic or not, the Old and New Testaments and Jesus's life in general can serve us as inspirational forces. Later on, we noticed that the spiritual level is rarely mentioned publicly in the business world. When I (Patrick) studied for my master's degree in applied economics at the Catholic University of Leuven, most of us seemed to regard the mandatory class on religion as an anachronism. The only exception I even witnessed was a workshop by Ken Blanchard and Bob Pike at the annual conference of the American Society of Training and Development, where both well-known trainers discussed their spiritual insights, but most Europeans present dismissed this as "typically American".

When we are motivated by goals that have deep meaning, by dreams that need completion, by pure love that needs expressing, then we truly live.

Greg Anderson, US athlete

In many European countries, faith, religion, and spirituality are perceived as very private things that shouldn't be mentioned in a secular context, such as work, and thus, in some sense, writing this paragraph even feels like breaking through a "taboo". Yet during some of the deepest mentoring moments that we each have lived as a "protégé", at a certain point the spiritual element surfaced and it felt great to be able to share some personal experiences on that level.

Even humanists and downright materialistic people sometimes have spiritual moments, often before a wonder of nature or an achievement of mankind, or perhaps a small baby. Such ineffable moments that seem to break through all your barriers and leave you wide open to the world make you feel connected to something utterly lofty and profound and are among the most powerful resources for motivation or sustaining energy one can ever have. Recollect for yourself such moments in a quiet place now and take the time to relive them fully in your mind: how do you perceive them as connecting with your mission, vision, purpose, calling?

Giving permission to your protégé to access this spiritual level of being may serve them in times when all other resources may appear to have vanished. This need not be a "religious" experience per se, perhaps simply one of communing with nature or something that is bigger than we mere humans are. Just allowing ourselves to experience this way of living "beyond words" and to draw resources from it nourishes our highest values of love, care, affection, respect, courtesy, esteem, and ethics. It makes us better, more tolerant human beings.

The changing workplace

In the 1950s, the workplace was a very different environment. A job for life was common and, for many, this actually meant doing the same job in very similar settings and situations year on year. The intervening years have not only brought about significant changes in the technology used, but in the very concept of work in industrialized or post-industrialized societies. For example, few people today expect their current employer to offer them lifetime employment. The nature of work itself seems to have changed, as more and more people now work on projects instead of "having a job". Companies now demand high degrees of flexibility, and productivity. Performance is all that seems to count nowadays; loyalty and seniority have lost their value.

Claims that soon all employees will become free agents may be a strong exaggeration. Nonetheless, the more skills an employee has, the more independence they seem to demand and expect. Where companies now call their employees their most important asset (although they may not always act accordingly), many employees get the message that they indeed represent such an asset. Therefore, if they feel undervalued, they give themselves the right and the choice to go where they want. Following the "downsizing" of the early 1990s, many of these became independent.

Although much has been said about Generation X, far less research has been carried out.

According to jobEQ.com, overall, Generation X are not that different from other generations, except that they learned that the old concept of "loyalty" doesn't pay any more.

As a result, they won't always "grin and bear it". If they aren't treated well, they may vote with their feet and just walk out, if necessary.

Events such as the Oklahoma bombing and the September 11, 2001, attack make it very clear that, while we may put our lives at risk by working in office buildings, considering the number of road accidents, even commuting to work isn't without danger.

At least we should be able to give people a good reason to work with us as they reappraise their priorities.

By the year 2000, one in six Americans— some 25 million people—was working outside corporations. This is more than double the number for 1990. Many of these independent professionals are highly talented and have the inner confidence that they can make it on their own. Working independently allows them to align who they are as an individual and the way they want to live with the way they work. What many of these like most about their self-employment is the ability to do a variety of things instead of just one and to have the flexibility to adjust their schedules to their requirements.

Another significant change compared with the 1950s is that, while women then accounted for fewer than 30 percent of the workforce in the industrialized Western world, they now make up close to 50 percent.[50] In the book *The Time Bind* (2001), Arlie Russell Hochschild writes that, "... between 1989 and 1996, middle-class married couples [in the US] increased their work outside the home with more than three extra forty-hour weeks of work per year. Most of these hours are added by wives."

And this extra work is really necessary: 55 percent of working mothers provide half or more of their family's income. For Hochschild the biggest problem is that, while our work habits have fundamentally changed over the past three decades, we still think about work in the way we used to do thirty years ago. Even if the number of children per women has declined, this means that modern parents have to take their parenting issues with them to work.

No wonder that, according to a study done by Towers Perrin in 2001,[51] among 6,000 employees of all ranks in companies with more than 500 employees, balancing one's life is an issue for at least 42 percent of the US workforce today and even

[50] For instance, in Belgium in 1961, women accounted for 27 percent of the workforce versus 42 percent in 2000 (source: Belgian National Institute for Statistics, August 2002).

[51] "New Realities in Today's Workforce" (2001), Towers Perrin Talent Report, a presentation given at the IHRIM conference in Orlando, Florida, June 9–12, 2002. According to Chris Michalak, even if the study was done prior to September 11, 2001, a small follow-up study in 2002 shows that these unfortunate events have only reinforced the search for a work–life balance.

more of an issue for people aged forty and older. These people put priority on achieving balance between life and work and may not match the 2000s stereotype of ambition, professional restlessness, or dreams of wealth.

The cycles in the economy, with a busy season, followed by a quieter one, with its upturns and downturns, can be reflected in some people's work habits: some people are now willing to give their all for some periods, and then to slow down at other times.

On the other hand, a British study conducted by Professor David Birchall from the Henley Management College and published in *People Management* shows that fewer than a third of the 150 managers interviewed agreed with the importance of this work–life balance. What is worse is that they don't even see the importance of this balance for the motivation of their own employees, nor the effects this has on productivity, staff retention etc.

This is in strong contrast with surveys among the organizations considered the best places to work at, which tend to make achieving this work–life balance a high corporate priority. The provision of flexible working hours, the ability to telecommute, compressed workweeks, allowing people to leave work for personal reasons, etc. are now becoming standard practice and even on-site childcare and fitness centers are being considered, but all these programs require managers to understand the importance of such measures for their staff.

The cycles in the economy, with a busy season, followed by a quieter one, with its upturns and downturns, can be reflected in some people's work habits: some people are now willing to give their all for some periods, and then to slow down at other times.

In addition to this, trends such as the use of the Internet, employee portals, distance work, distance learning, and so on are blurring the boundaries between work and the rest of our lives. You can't stop people from developing their own blend of work and private life.

And yet, for the 12 percent of the people in the Towers Perrin study who consider themselves fast-trackers, such balance isn't that important. This may have consequences that need considering. We know about a person who wanted to double his earnings in a year and he indeed succeeded. However, during that year, he had three car accidents and one heart attack, and, having lost touch with his wife and children, his wife was filing for divorce and she wanted the house and custody of the offspring! It's a shame when one hears of the CEO of a big multinational saying that he stepped down, aged 55, because he realized he had lived too much on the fast track and felt that it was time to spend more time with his family before it was too late.

People are more effective when they feel a sense of completeness. People have to know that they can integrate other aspects of their lives into their jobs.

Ella Bell,[52] associate professor at Dartmouth's Tuck School of Business

As a mentor, you will certainly owe it to your protégé to make them consider the consequences, both short- and long-term, of their life priorities. You may even be called upon to enable them to identify ways of protecting themselves against themselves, as their search for high involvement, high rewards, and quick advancement may indeed help to advance their careers but, at the same time, might lead to significant deterioration in private life, health and perhaps even life altogether. One should question whether the fast track doesn't also mean "quick burn". After all, literature abounds with examples of "meteoric rise" followed by a spectacular fall, and the overwhelming majority of meteors burn up on re-entry through the atmosphere.

Also, a fast-tracker who, drawing on their own perspective on life, makes unrealistic demands on their colleagues and staff may sow dissension, animosity, or absenteeism, perhaps even causing burnout in other people. This may, in turn, be counterproductive with regard to achieving their own goals. As the example above showed, similar demands on a life partner may be even more detrimental.

As mentor, you will also need to enable your protégé to identify how their life priorities fit with those of other people—their colleagues, of course, but also their life partners. You will need to help your protégé to understand that, although they might not feel like this themselves, many of the people around them are looking to achieve this balance, something that fast-trackers may find hard to appreciate or even to understand.

---

[52] Quoted from article about the circus acts exercise with commentary from Bell (Hammonds, 2001).

You may want to invite them to find ways of synchronizing their respective rhythms, so that they can satisfactorily meet both their goals *and* those of their colleagues or life partners.

The balancing act

Balance in time

Balancing work and life has little to do with working from 9am to 5pm (and not even with working "only" from 8am till 9pm for that matter). That kind of definition may only add stress to your life. The first form of balancing is about figuring out how your job fits with you as a person. Do you have enough time for your personal life, according to your own standards? Does your protégé have enough time for theirs? Depending on the age you see them, they may not yet be in a relationship. Is there room for life outside work in their life?

Drawing the balance

The size of the ellipses in Figure 5.2 can show the degree to which you are satisfied with it, or how much time you spend. The overlap indicates how blurred the boundary is between your work and your personal life.

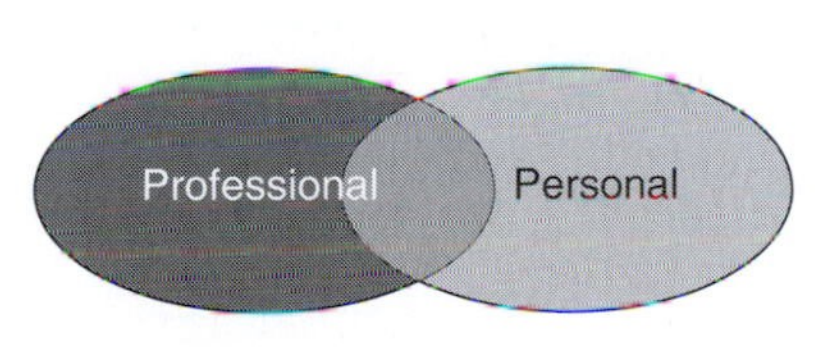

Figure 5.2: The best of both worlds

In addition, there is probably more to you than just you "as a person": Carl Jung considered the human psyche as having four aspects: physical, intellectual, emotional, and spiritual. For him, balancing meant attending to all these aspects. In the Western world we often point to the ideal of having a healthy mind in a healthy body, which is already a stretch for some people. Still, this downplays the importance of emotional and spiritual intelligence.

You can probably distinguish more components that form part of your personal life and that need to be taken into account. There are issues such as your finances, your health and what you do about it, time for your hobbies, friends, your family, your love and/or sex life,[53] your personal development, your spirituality,[54] and so on.

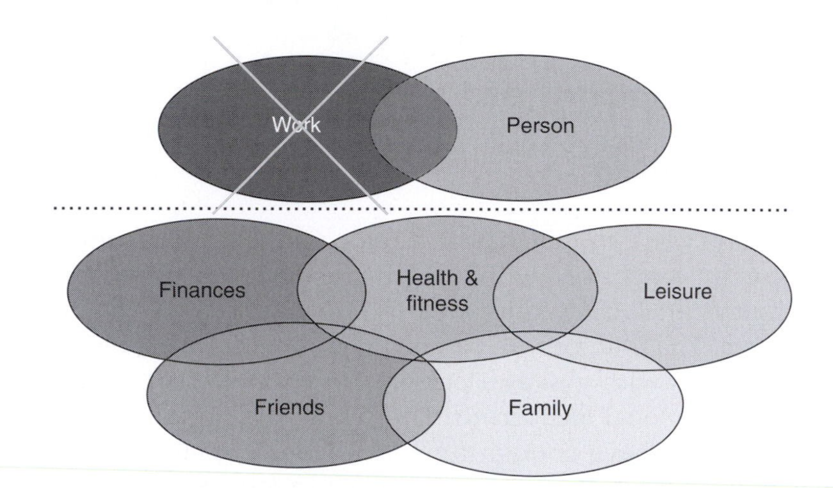

Figure 5.3: Work in a larger context

Other drawing formats

Each drawing or model you make from your balance may help to clarify some personal issues.

Other formats that are often used are a wheel or pie, in which each dimension becomes a piece of the pie, or a simple table, in which each dimension becomes a row and you have columns for answers to the questions.

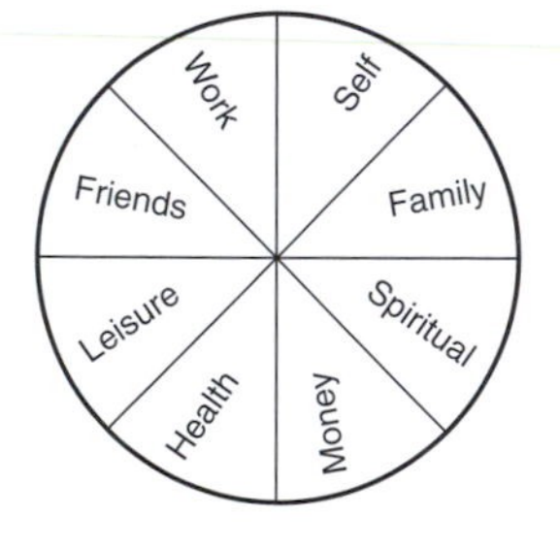

Variations on pie-model: You might draw the pieces in the right proportion to show your use of time. You can color each piece of the pie, filling it to the point that indicates your satisfaction with it (e.g. 50 percent satisfied = half-colored piece).

Draw your own balance model

Make your own diagram, taking into account the following guidelines:

1: Determine the content of your drawing to represent your current situation: What ellipses do you want to draw on your page? Elements to consider: next to your work life, include your social life (e.g. political, religious, and cultural activities, activities in nonprofit organizations, memberships of boards etc.), your family life (in the small sense: partner, children (if any) or in the

---

[53] For some people, this may be the same as your family life; for others it may be different. For some people, sex life and love life may mean the same; for others they may be quite different. We even know some people who put their sex life in the category of "spiritual activities" or even "sporting activities"! Each to their own.

[54] Although for many people this means belief in a deity and belonging to a particular religion, many humanists or nonbelievers also have a very rich spiritual life, often in relation to communing with the world we live in and feeling a connection with the universe.

large sense: grandparents, grandchildren, nieces and nephews), your leisure (hobbies, sports, vacations), your friendship life, your health life, your sex/love life (are they the same?), your creativity life, your spiritual life etc.

2: Determine the layout of your drawing: Where do you want to place your ellipses on your page? How large are they? Do the ellipses overlap? If so, which and how? How much overlap is there? Which don't? Are some ellipses nested inside others? Which?

3: Draw your balance model: Consider which kind of model you prefer. Do you want to use ellipses as we used in the example? Or do you prefer the wheel format? Would a mindmap suit you better? Use your creativity to come up with a format that will suit you!

4: Determine the future: If your drawing represents the current situation, how would it have to change to be the "ideal" model for now? For five years from now? What new ellipses might appear? (Maybe "mentoring" deserves its own ellipse.) Which will shrink? Which will expand? Which ellipses need to move and where to? Which ellipses should be bigger? Which ones should be smaller? What overlaps do you want to enlarge/reduce?

Mentoring at large: You can mentor others in various fields—consider for each ellipse how you could be a mentor to others.

Ella Bell, an associate professor at Dartmouth's Tuck School of Business, teaches a further variation on the ellipses model. She recommends listing your biggest stresses and your primary coping mechanisms for each of the ellipses: "How do people cope? Perhaps they eat more. Or they withdraw. Or they shop. How effective are these mechanisms?"[55]

[55] Quoted from article about the circus acts exercise with commentary from Bell (Hammonds, 2001).

Types of balancing

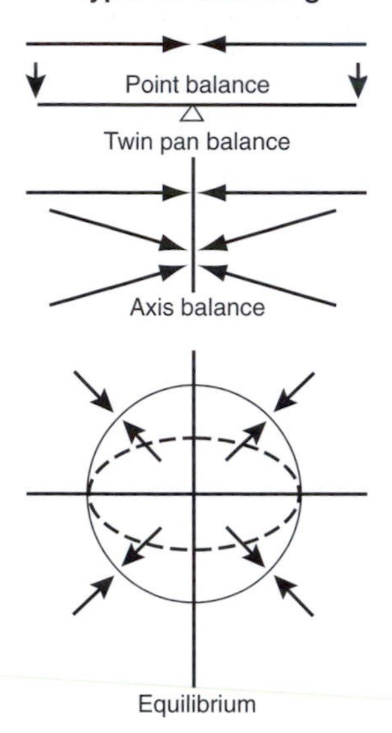

from Mark Johnson, *The Body in the Mind* (1987)

Further balancing exists where symmetry appears broken: these involve the concept of:

- **Proportion**, balancing the weight in relation (ratio) to the central fulcrum.
- **Pattern**, where the balancing or proportion occurs across space or time

As Fiona Harrold, author of *Be Your Own Life Coach* (2000), provocatively says, "Working excessively long hours on a continuous basis is actually a sign of failure. People who do this are usually avoiding other parts of their lives, rather than working creatively." Do you work because you really enjoy what you are doing and because you are fulfilling your mission? If you can truly answer yes, maybe you don't need to mind the hours that much. Indeed, those who work the longest hours are often the most motivated and highest paid employees. It's not because France currently has only 35 working hours in a week, compared with the UK's 48-hour working week, that the French would be more satisfied. On the contrary, only a quarter of the French were highly satisfied with their jobs, compared with 41 percent of the Britons and 44 percent of the even harder-working Americans.[56] If you're unsure about what your answer would be, feeling you "need" so much time off to compensate for workplace stress may be an indication. After all, vacations are a modern invention we now find we are entitled to have in order to compensate for an all-encompassing work life. If the answer is no, think about Harrold's remark. You might also want to ask yourself the question "What will I be left with the day my job ends?" Several companies now offer retirement training to help people cope with the transition from working life to retirement.

If your desired future differs from your current situation, the question becomes, "What actions can you take to close the gap?" For instance, if you notice that too much time and energy has gone in your work life, you might want to take actions such as sharing parental tasks, or engage in activities in your larger family, or organize a family reunion. Maybe you have been giving your friends less attention than a couple of years ago, or maybe you want to get more involved in your local community, increasing ties with neighbors, getting involved in local politics or in one of your local or even national associations.

---

[56] Recent study by Pew Global Attitudes, mentioned in *The Times* (London) August 7, 2003.

Whether your natural balance lies between all the elements that are important to you depends on your values, your mission, and your choices in life. In short, each person will have their own model of what "balance" means to them. Remember the value hierarchy process we met earlier? Repeat it within each of your various life areas (the ellipses above) and then draw it to put these life areas themselves in a hierarchy. Explore your personal satisfaction with the current place in the hierarchy for each of your categories by giving them numbers, as in the optional step of this process. If family comes before work, you won't have any problem spending more time with your family. If work comes first, it will naturally make sense for you to spend most of your week working. Consider Jack Welch (2001): "I had a tough time taking a complete vacation from the job. When we were on the Cape [for a two-week vacation in the summer], I'd often sneak off the beach to a pay phone to check into the office a couple of times a day."

If you feel "guilty" while not working, remember that, according to the Book of Genesis, even God allowed himself to have his seventh day as a "day off".

Balance across time

Even if you were fully congruent with your values at that time, many choices made earlier in life may seem incomprehensible when a value shift has occurred. We remember the tale of a workaholic father who suddenly saw a drawing that his little girl had made to portray her family. When the father saw that he wasn't on the drawing, he inquired about this, and his daughter replied, "Oh, Daddy, but you're at work." To be provocative a moment, you could say that if he had always valued his family more than his work, he had been acting incongruently with his values, or that if he valued working more when he got married, he should have thought twice before starting a family! But how many of us actually do so and repent afterwards?

If you constantly give more than 100% of yourself to your job, you'll find yourself with nothing left for friendships, family, or yourself.

Psychologist Ilene Philipson in Fast Company, *Issue 29 (November 1999)*

Balance and value conflicts

Values and life areas sometimes compete with each other. If you're clear which value is most important to you, making a choice will be easier, even if facing the consequences might not be.

If two values seem equally important, a question to ask in relation to each may be, "What do I want through this *value that's even more important* than this value? Do I want this because this is an end in itself, or a means to an end? If it is a means to an end, what end am I seeking to accomplish?"

Finding *what's more important* is commonly referred to as "chunking up". By repeatedly chunking up each value at a time, you'll eventually identify a value common to both, which will probably be an "end" value. This will, in turn, inspire you to find ways to manifest this at the lower level and resolve what appeared to be a dilemma.

For example, while working on this chapter, I (Patrick) was on vacation in Provence. Most of my writing took place early in the morning or late at night. In the morning I would be the first of my family to be awake, giving me time to write. Around 7 a.m. my son (aged four) would wake up and then ask me to play with him. At that time, this brought a conflict in me, between writing and family. If I don't write, this book will take longer to get finished. If I don't play with my son, he will be disappointed. So I managed to balance the two by playing for a while with him when he got up until he was absorbed in his play, usually within fifteen minutes. By then he would be so single-mindedly involved in what he wanted to do that he didn't really mind my going back to my computer, just a few yards away, thus retaining the comforting feeling that I was nearby, and knowing he could come back to ask me to play again whenever he wanted, while I can get on with my writing …

Invite your protégé to identify what their personal life consists of and to define in which proportion they would like to have it, at least for now. Then invite them to see how they see it evolving across time.

It is often difficult to achieve balance between all areas at any one time. What most people do is to prioritize one area on a temporary basis, so that balance is achieved in the long term. If this is the case, ask your protégé to identify how doing so could benefit those other life areas, so that they're not entirely left out.

All too often, however, this balance is never redressed and then it is too late to do anything about it. Usually, the goal was unrealistic or was a lifetime's work and, by the time you retire, the best balancing opportunities are gone.

Another question to ask your protégé, therefore, is, "If you commit yourself to this temporary imbalance in your life in order to secure a better balance later, by when do you realistically want to have achieved this? A week, a month, a year?" Invite them to be really precise.

Before they commit themselves to this choice, use the meta-octant system for questioning consequences (see "Competence Versus Challenge" in the Appendix on page 179), as it will significantly clarify all the implications of their choice.

Values naturally evolve and change over time, for individuals and cultures. If you compare the number of children a mother had in the Western world in the 1990s with the number in the 1950, you may be led to think that family values are on the decline, and this may be the case. There may, however, be more to it. Infant mortality was higher earlier in the century and, with nonexistent pension provisions, having many children was often the answer to long-term security and preserving the family name. Being a mother was a full-time occupation. This remains the case in countries in the developing world.

During the course of the twentieth century, the world of women changed beyond recognition with, among other things, the experience of working while men were on the World War II battlefront, the drastic decrease in infant mortality, the provision of better health and pension schemes, etc. All these have changed the social climate in such a way that many Western women nowadays work, maybe out of choice, but more often out of necessity, in order to pay the bills.

Working has, paradoxically, also enhanced women's desire to have fun unwinding from work. They can now control their fertility and choose to have fewer children, or choose to have them later. Thanks to better access to information, women may also be more aware than before of the long-term effect of over-population on the planet and seek a future of quality for their children: fewer children with more to share, rather than too many children with not enough and a ruined planet.

Maybe family values, rather than declining, which would be measured on an absolute scale, have evolved to cope with changing circumstances. It may also be that other life areas have evolved that did not exist before, and that family life, which for many, especially women, was the only life to have, has now become only one among many.

Likewise, your own values and the prioritizing of your own life areas will doubtlessly evolve over your lifetime and so will your protégé's. One of the biggest shifts in values, and certainly the best known, comes at a time that we commonly call the "midlife crisis".[57] When this typically occurred around the age of forty, people had already achieved a lot in their career and had, perhaps, accumulated enough material wealth to start worrying about other things, and a question suddenly arose: "Is this what I really want from my life, or is there something else?"

Today, this crisis moment may come at different ages. A successful stockbroker in the 1990s may have accumulated enough wealth by the time they are 28 to start worrying about what to do for the rest of their life. If people's values develop at a different pace, it may also help to explain many divorces: people who were "compatible" at a certain moment in their

---

[57] Another well-known life crisis is retirement.

lives may grow at a different pace or in a different direction. In other words, they may grow apart, discovering they now have different values and interests.

A midlife crisis usually occurs as a result of a previously uncorrected imbalance. Something has to give. Not everybody, however, goes through a midlife crisis, in the same way as not every woman perceives the menopause as a distressing situation. Others see it more as a transition point, or even as an emergence, like a butterfly emerging from the chrysalis. They will generally either have sustained a better balance, which prevented them from going off kilter, or planned ahead and had contingency plans in place that cushioned the impact, as a well-filled pension plan cushions a healthy retirement.

Acting old?

People who act old live more in their personal past than in the present or in the future. People seem old once they start saying, "If only, when I was younger, I'd made a different choice." Looking back, to regret the past is only draining your energy. We'd like to recommend a more useful question about the past, "What does it teach me that I can use today, or for preparing for tomorrow?"

Invite your protégé to frame their life priorities to ensure that this balance will cushion potential life crises or prevent them from happening. If they are in the middle of a crisis, enable them to make the most of what it has to offer. It was Marshall McLuhan who said, "Every breakdown is actually a sign of a breakthrough." Ask them what they are breaking through toward and enable them to achieve this breakthrough so that they can resourcefully get on their feet on the other side.

Dealing with our shadow side

In his 2001 book *Core Qualities*, Daniel Ofman describes the *core quadrant approach*. He notes that for each core quality in a person, there will be an opposite quality, which that person will probably have developed less. Instead of appreciating a person for having that complementary quality, we may criticize them for the possible excesses of applying too much of that opposite quality. To summarize the model, our personal core qualities will also predict what we are allergic to and what are our biggest challenges. For instance, take the following example based on meta-programs (and see Figure 5.4 overleaf).

Suppose that the core quality of your protégé is that he is perfectly able to follow procedures, and execute the task at hand in an ordered way. You can predict that he will hate it when

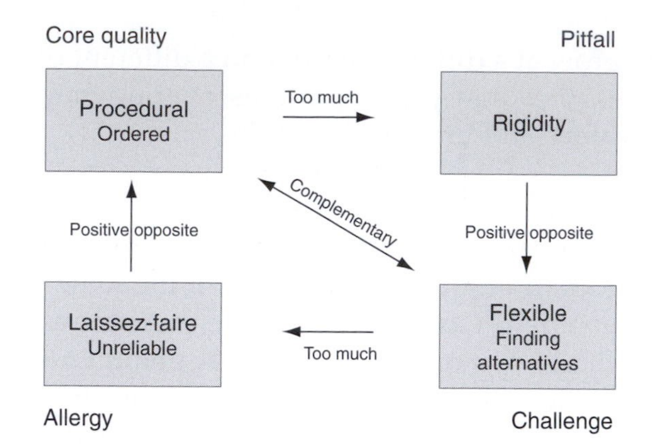

Figure 5.4: Core-Quadrant approach applied to options vs procedures

someone displays a laissez-faire attitude when it comes to following a procedure. He may dismiss that person as being unreliable. Also, in some cases your protégé may display too much of this procedural way of working, thus being experienced by others as being "rigid". Indeed, his challenge may be leading with situations where there isn't a well-charted path and alternatives need to be found, or where flexibility is needed to cope with the situation.

Flow states

When we are in balance, really congruently working in alignment with our mission, in accordance with our values, really doing something we like and feel passionate about, what we call a "flow state" often emerges. A flow state thus occurs when you create synergy, where the total effect of the parts working together is disproportionate in relation to the simple sum of the parts by themselves. Synergy is an interesting property of the world, which enables emergent properties to arise. In a flow state, your levels of productivity, creativity, and results are radically enhanced compared with laboring "out of flow", consciously trying to achieve the outcome you want.

One of the characteristics of the flow state is that, while you are immersed in it, time is not important. You are living "in time", just doing what it takes at that moment to work toward the goal, with little conscious awareness of what surrounds you. It's a kind of concentration or focused energy. And, as one can read in the Upanishads, one of the most important texts of Indian philosophy, "Those who reach greatness on earth reach it through concentration." Learning to be highly alert and focused, being at one with the moment while also being in balance, is key to such martial arts as aikido, judo, or kendo. It requires a sense of inner peace, so that you can fully attend what comes to you.

Paradoxically, when this occurs, your energy expenditure is drastically reduced and you may achieve much more in far less time. In a previous book we have compared such states to the property of superconductivity in physics, whereby in certain conditions energy flows freely with no loss or friction in some materials, and called these states of "superconductivity of the mind". The essence of any communication, whether within yourself or other people, is to achieve such states as to allow achievements to come easily and effortlessly.

As a mentor, you should seek to create and sustain such flow states with your protégé, as both of you will benefit far more from the encounter than if you don't have them. Most memorable mentor–protégé pairs you will know of experienced such flow states. If they had not, we doubt they would be remembered at all.

Live a balanced life—learn some and think some and draw and paint and sing and play and work every day some.

Robert Fulghum,
All I Really Need to Know I Learned in Kindergarten[58]

Rebalancing

When we are out of balance, we risk draining our energy reserves. Indeed, working in a situation where you cannot be truly yourself means that you need to expend much more energy on maintaining "compensation strategies": to keep up appearances, to resist saying or doing what comes naturally, and do something different instead.

[58] Fulgham, 1990, pp. 6–7.

As soon as you lose balance, you need to notice it to regain this balance as soon as possible. An interesting metaphor about balance is the way we walk.[59] Before actually moving our leg, each time we lean forward, we are off balance, literally falling over. As a toddler you learned to move one leg forward before you were too far off balance and ended up on the ground. To ride a bicycle, we learn something similar: we learn that we have to pedal and move forward, because we risk falling if we stand still. We also learn to adjust the position of our body so that we don't fall over on the bends.

Rebalancing in other areas of your life is just as easy. Once you realize you're off-balance, it only takes a few steps to correct this. The problem is that, without sufficient self-awareness about our mission, our values etc., it may take us months or even years to realize we aren't using our natural flow. Joseph Jaworski warns us of some traps that may make us lose our sense of balance.

Being overresponsible is the first trap, the thought that others rely on us and that the project will fail if we don't give all we have to make it work. This thought may lead us to fear, to be afraid that our best isn't good enough. In reality, the project probably will survive without us.

As a mentor you owe it to yourself and to your protégé to realize that you can't do the work for them, that it is ultimately their ball game. You are responsible for yourself and your own actions and that is already a full-time job. Furthermore, you're not perfect—no one is. You are human, which means being fallible. If it didn't work out, would anything or anybody else have managed it? Maybe not. Again, unrealistic expectations lead to disappointment.

Your protégé needs to realize this, also.

The second trap is about feeling dependent on others, thinking we wouldn't be able to function without their support. It's the flipside

---

[59] While writing this book we found the metaphor in Joseph Jawordski (1996), *Synchronicity: The Inner Path of Leadership.*

of the previous trap: it may not be easy without another person, but nobody is indispensable. Your protégé needs to achieve balance here also, between self-sufficiency to the point of loneliness and dependence to the point of powerlessness. The solution is to focus on the outcome you want to achieve, and, if reaching it one way is difficult, it's time to explore alternative roads to your goal. And there will always be alternative roads.

Your protégé may feel this more than you do, because the structure of the relationship, in a way, already lends itself to thinking or feeling this. Unless you're on an ego trip, you have nothing to gain from fostering dependence in your protégé, and doing this would actually betray their trust and your role. Your protégé needs to find balance in themselves also, between overresponsibility and dependence, steering the midline in their daily encounter with colleagues and partners.

The third trap is about being overactive: too focused on doing, and forgetting that running around like a headless chicken may seem "active", but may actually be a waste of energy—a lot of hot air, but not generating much lift. You may also be so engrossed in what you're doing that you're not noticing you're past your best and getting diminishing returns. Mistakes are often made in such circumstances, as when somebody falls asleep at the steering wheel From time to time, you need to take time to reflect, individually and collectively, in order to check you're still moving toward the goal, and adjust your course if need be. Communicate with others; make sure they know where the goal is and what is important about it.

The fourth trap is also the reverse of the previous one: being underactive, reflecting too much or too long, and not getting started. Although reflecting on something is useful, there must come a point where action must ensue. Balance, again, is required, so that one is neither hyperactive nor underactive; finding the cusp where acting meets reflecting is key.

How do you yourself notice you are off-balance? What do you do to relax? How do you regain balance? Do you lounge about with a good book, or refresh yourself at a health farm, or enjoy

There are basically three ways to use the energy we have available:

Think: What's the concept, the idea we are pursuing? What values, beliefs are important, etc.?

Organize: How will we do it? What's the plan? Who is involved?

Act: Take action, execute the plan

Every person has preferences on how to spend energy. Spending too much energy on one of these tasks may risk getting us off-balance.

a good relaxing meal in the company of friends in a setting that enables you to unwind? There are as many answers to these questions as there are people on the planet. While for some rebalancing means doing the opposite of what they did, for others it may be more a question of finding the still point of peace within, where all inner voices are quiet. Find out what works best for you.

Your protégé, too, needs to find their own balance for themselves between doing and being, so that they can apply their energies constructively and effectively and also set time aside for recharging their batteries. This balance will vary from person to person. Where one may need little energy to sustain extended activities, others may require a lot of pondering and reflection, followed by short but intense bursts of activity. Different activities may themselves require different energy use and management. Allow your protégé to identify a pattern that serves them well and to identify useful markers to shift to and fro—from one mode to the next.

Zenlike meditation

Find a peaceful place to sit down, find a posture that is upright and symmetrical.

For twenty minutes, focus on clearing your mind: let any thought that you notice pass by.

Rebalancing from the body

Which way does the off-balance go? How do you represent it in your body? Is it pulling you forwards, backwards, to the left, to the right? Is it top-heavy or bottom-heavy?

Shift your center of gravity so that you are balanced on your feet, with both hips evenly resting on your legs. Ensure your shoulders are evenly balanced, your neck is relaxed on your shoulders. Balance your head on your neck so that is upright, neither tilted nor turned either to left or right, with your eyes gazing directly ahead toward the horizon. When you have achieved this, smoothly turn your head and look around. Make fluid and smooth gestures and notice how, although you may take an asymmetrical posture, you may nonetheless be balanced. Look at yourself in a mirror and balance the features of your face, so that they are aligned along the mid-line.

Integration: Mentoring, a way of life?

In this part of the book we have explored motivational and attitudinal elements from the perspective of meta-programs and values. We discussed the impact of (limiting) beliefs and of the person's mission. Together, all these elements form the career drivers from which the patterns emerge that explain a person's career track.

Seen from the perspective of long-term mentoring, as a mentor you will add to most by addressing these elements and helping your protégé to make the personal choices that are in line with these career drivers.

Of course, knowing a person's career drivers is only the beginning. The main task of mentoring may be to help your protégé to achieve the career goals they formulate, goals that are hopefully in line with the career drivers as presented here. A person's calling and talents are a foundation to build on. As Eddy Merckx, six-times winner of the Tour de France, says, "Having talents is one thing, but one also needs the determination to succeed and then one needs willpower to stay at the top. This requires a lot of hard labor. If you're not willing to bring sacrifices, you won't make it. And, never, ever think that there is nothing left to achieve."[60]

Much of what we have so far presented in the second half of this book has focused on showing you some tools available for mentoring—there are many more—and on how we think you can help your protégé. Reading and understanding these materials isn't enough. Your task, once you have read this

[60] Interview in *Humo* (Belgian magazine), July 8, 2003.

book, is to internalize your newly gained knowledge, sift out what is useful to you and test it out in practice, adapting some so that it better fits with your way of handling things and making it your own, in order to respond even better to your specific requirements and those of your protégé. And what do you think Athene would say to that?

Success is guaranteed for whoever has a Big Goal in life and really goes for it.

Jacky Ickx

The protégé's summary

From insight to action:

What are my long-term career goals, in relationship with my mission and my motivational traits?

Given my career goals, what are the concrete top three actions I plan for the coming year (in terms of things to learn, experiences to gain)?

Integrity check: Do my goals and my actions match my values?

Well-Groomed Butterflies

During the 1990s, the personnel department, whose core business was paying salaries and performing personal administration, reinvented itself and became a human-resource management department. At the same time, the industrialized countries evolved to become knowledge economies, where closely monitoring the core competencies of the company is key. Suddenly, some general managers, investors, and financial managers started to feel very uncomfortable, as they realized that the most important assets of their organization were not showing up in the books and were leaving the organization each day, because the core knowledge is embedded in the core employees. Trying to keep the knowledge in the office, by building expert systems and other knowledge-management systems wasn't really satisfying.

The real solution consists in attracting the right human capital for the organization and making sure that their potential is fully realized. The current rise of coaching in companies certainly fits in with that line of thought. Mentoring fits in, too, given it's a great tool to retain your top performers when faced with the "war for talent". From a knowledge-management perspective, the biggest difference between mentoring and coaching is that mentoring has traditionally been reserved for high potentials, who were groomed for future positions in the top jobs by the current top management. In short, one can say that mentoring and coaching serve to create well-groomed butterflies.

Probably the most important message from this book is that most people have the resources they need to be successful. Therefore, as a mentor or coach, you have to help your protégé to catch the fish themselves, rather than merely give them fish. Parts 4 and 5 have been written with this message in mind. If you know that your protégé has the necessary competencies. It doesn't make sense to solve their problems for them. In such a case, use all your listening and problem-structuring skills to

Giving someone fish to eat is helpful only when the person is almost starving and doesn't have any energy left to learn to fish.

find out what stops your protégé from doing what it takes to solve the problem themselves. Even if Keynes[61] did postulate that in the long run we are all dead, the material presented in this book doesn't limit itself to the short-term problems. We have also covered figuring out which values do really matter, what is a protégé's calling and how to find a job compatible with all the elements that define your protégé's uniqueness.

As long as there will be persons doing some "work", there will be new challenges, possibilities for improvement, or unexpected problems, for instance because an old solution suddenly stops working. In all these circumstances as a mentor or coach you can be the sounding board that helps your protégé to set new goals and make sure their targets are met.

We expect that the competencies discussed in this book will remain useful, and that they may help to groom many caterpillars into wonderful butterflies. After all, who you are today is only the chrysalis of who you will be tomorrow.

---

[61] John Maynard Keynes (1883–1946), British economist. Cited from *A Tract on Monetary Reform* (1923).

Mentoring and Coaching Treasure Chest

APPENDIX

In Dutch there is a saying, "Why don't you behave normally? That's already crazy enough." We believe that you will be a great mentor or coach if you already apply everything that has been mentioned in the core of this book. But, then, if you have mastered all the above, and still want more, we as developers have more advanced material to offer you as well.

This treasure chest is just a glimpse of additional information we will be presenting on the website in the future. In fact, we have many more tools and processes we think would be useful to you, which didn't make it into the current edition of this book, mainly because of time constraints and our reluctance to make a book that would be too heavy to carry out of a bookstore!

Resource

We plan to expand this treasure chest on the jobEQ website: www.jobEQ.com/mentor

Modeling project

This section presents other elements that came from our original study, which tried to figure out what are considered to be important characteristics of mentoring. It is presented in an edited form, summarizing what we learned.

What are important characteristics for the ideal mentor?

Except for what we came to call the *mentoring attitude*, besides such values as knowledge, curiosity, willingness, trust, relating, unconditional regard, which are mentioned in Part 1, age was also identified as being significant, probably because eof the "older-and-wiser" stereotype, but there was disagreement about its being a prerequisite, maturity emerging as the key aspect behind it.

We then asked a set of questions to "up the antes" in order to identify and separate the *essential* criteria versus the *desirable* ones for the role.

Does a mentor have to like you for it to work?

- Not necessarily as long as you feel they're ready to teach you "all that's in the book".
- Not you personally. If they like their given domain of understanding they will like to enable others to enter this domain. They may come to like you as a consequence if they feel you do honor to the domain.

What would still make it work even if your mentor was not in the same field as you?

- It would work as long as I could make an analogy between our respective domains.

What would still make it work even if there was no immediate analogy between your respective domains?

This brought the answers to a personal level. In many ways, the mentor was perceived as a parent figure, to the mind, the personality, or even the spirit, if not to the body. Many answers we received to this question verged on the mystical/spiritual:

- They would need to exert a fascination, a sense of mystery.
- They would need to have attained something that I would like. How did they do it? I'd like to find out.
- An alignment or compatibility of our core values.
- They would offer codes to live by.
- A way of living worth being introduced to.
- An initiation carried out in an ecological fashion.

As age had been mentioned we asked the following:

What would enable you to make it work even if your mentor was younger than you?

- If I could feel they knew a lot more about the subject than I do. (This looped back to the domain of understanding (see above) that the protégé would be introduced to.)

- If I could feel that they were an old soul with mildness in a young body, someone who appears to have been through the various ups and downs of a life cycle. They can see where you are in your own cycle. (This loops into the mystical perspective).

This set of questions clearly identified two broad categories of mentoring:

- **Short-term mentoring**: a more formal type with a specific goal in mind, with a focus on practicalities, the latter usually an induction into a domain of understanding that the mentor would normally be expected to have *experience* in. This is the type people usually access in organizations.

- **Long-term mentoring**: commonly found outside work. This is more oriented toward the evolution of a career, of an identity, and the ongoing development of core potential. In this case the mentor is expected to display *maturity* of thinking and feeling.

As we pointed out in Figure (i-1) in the book's Introduction, these two categories, in fact, are not incompatible.

What skills does mentoring itself involve?

- being there
- looking at a situation "as is"
- looking without judging
- being aware of boundaries
- being involved but staying out of it at the same time
- being down to earth
- being provocative when necessary
- having an ability to "see" in your psyche
- having a knowledge of developmental approaches

- knowing what it takes to be firm
- being strong enough to take certain actions
- an ability to let go

Notice how these cover the three broad life-operating categories: to have, to be, to do:

- **To be** a good mentor—this relates to the identity, the persona you take on when mentoring.

- **To do**—this is about what you are actually involved in carrying out in the mentoring process.

- **To have**—this relates to the prerequisites that support your doing and your being: attributes, skills, knowledge, and resources. These can be external, but in the main will be found or will find a place within you by the time you finish reading this book if you read it in the way that serves you best.

A good mentor will have a balance of these.

Whom to mentor?

- someone who performs well
- someone who has the potential to grow
- an opinion former, a trendsetter, a person who is at a node of interactions, who can influence others just by being who they are

Mentoring: what's in it for me?

- it enables me to delegate

- it frees my time to do something more important

- it benefits my organization by cascading resources further down

- it motivates at one remove, via the opinion setter: i.e. people who see someone being motivated also get the benefits of this motivation and may also be motivated in turn

- it invites other people to transcend themselves by emulating the person who was mentored before

- it incites them to become worthy of my attentions and thus to improve their performance further

What we repeatedly noticed was that, whether as mentor or protégé, people kept using similar metaphors to refer to the relationship, usually mixing them within the same sentence:

Metaphors of feedback
- the bouncing board
- the mirror that reflects
- the crystal, which refracts back and casts a different light
- the shoulder to cry on

Gardening metaphors of growing, developing
- the gardener,
- nursing a rare plant,
- needs to prune occasionally to enable the plant to win "Best in Show"

Metaphors from the world of birds
- you take someone "under your wing"
- the fledgling
- fly the nest

Metaphors of guidance
- the guide, in the jungle or on a mountain, who shows you the ropes
- the ferryman, who moves you from one plane to the next
- the Steersman, who leads you through dire straits, or the narrows of life

Metaphors of change agents
- the catalyst, instrumental in the development of others just by its presence

- the chaperone (as in "chaperonins", molecules that guide and shape the structure of proteins); this led to the earlier meaning of "guardian", who protects you and grooms you to greatness

Metaphors of guardianship

- someone to watch over me; this in turn led to mystical/spiritual metaphors

Mystical/spiritual metaphors

- the Zen master
- the guardian angel, the tutelary deity
- the protector

These metaphors commonly overlapped with one another, from nursing to chaperoning, to taking under your wing etc. They reflect various facets of the mentoring role that have been explored in the book.

Conclusions

This study led us to conceptualize the change/development process as being multidimensional and multilevel, as Figure (i) showed. It also enabled us to usefully distinguish the respective roles and capacities of counselors, coaches, and mentors, with counselors and coaches more focused on the *what* and the *how* and the mentor on the *why* and the *who*. As these respective roles and skills are nested in one another, this also helps to explain why there would have been ambiguities in the definitions. Thus a mentor will on occasion need to apply counseling or coaching skills. In addition, mentoring appears to require a personal involvement on the part of the mentor, especially if long-term, which counseling and coaching does not. Indeed, personal involvement would probably be counterproductive in counseling or coaching, for it would muddy the relationship. As this sometimes occurs in real life, however, professionals need to know when it is happening, so that they can smoothly move from one role into the next.

Competence Versus Challenge

In this section by Stephen Wilkinson-Carr the assumption that you must be completely qualified and experienced before even considering applying for a promotion or a new job is revisited and challenged. As long as there is a match of about 60 percent between what you want and what the job requires then the protégé should apply for the post.

How many options do you have?

The intended outcome of this section is helping the protégé to consider far more opportunities than at present and widen their search to include elements previously excluded or simply not considered—a highly desirable outcome.

The jobs pie

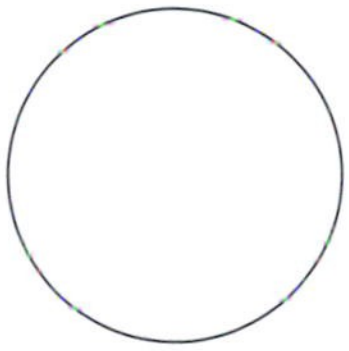

The circle on the right represents every possible job or role available to you. At the moment you could apply for any of them.

Let's imagine, though, that you have decided to work in marketing. This immediately excludes all jobs that are not marketing and reduces your slice of the pie to this:

Let's further imagine that you want to earn around €100,000. Your slice of the pie now looks like this:

You decide you want to work within thirty minutes commuting distance of your home. Your slice of the jobs pie will be much reduced and will look something like this:

What can you do to increase your slice of the jobs pie?

When considering what comes next in terms of change of job or role it is not always easy to decide on the most important factor. Most often there is a conflict between what you think the employer wants from you in terms of ability and how much or little you want to be stretched within that role. So where do you begin? Whether you are going for promotion or thinking about moving to a completely new job, the two primary factors that need to be taken into account are *competence* and *challenge*.

Competence
How much skill is required in this role?
Can I do it?

Challenge
How challenging will this role/job be?
How much personal risk am I prepared to take?

The relationship between these two factors is what drives our decision to apply for some roles and not others. In Figure (a) each factor is shown on a scale from 0 to 100 percent:

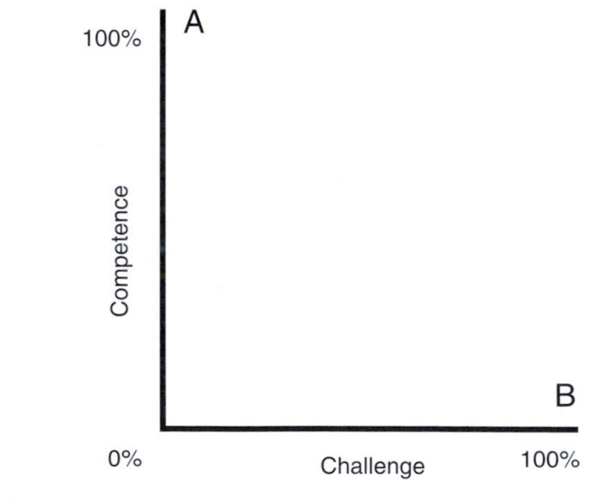

Figure (a)

Question 1:

Why would somebody choose a job or role at Point A, where the level of competence required dramatically exceeds the level of challenge in that role? Give three reasons.

1. ______________________________

2. ______________________________

3. ______________________________

Three of the main reasons, all equally valid, why you might choose a job or role where the level of competence required dramatically exceeds the level of challenge in that role are:

1. You are a technical expert and the role demands that you have a level of skill to meet the required standard. The amount of time you will stay in this role usually depends more on the duration of the project than any other factor. Examples include engineers, consultants, IT professionals, accountants, project directors, lawyers, and many other professions that cannot be undertaken without the necessary technical expertise and/or qualifications.

2. You are making a lifestyle decision where quality of life is the most important driver and will cause you to choose a job or role based on what you enjoy doing and value most in that context. You will usually stay in this sort of role for quite a long time, depending on whether you still enjoy it and value what you are doing. There are many examples in the business world of people who give up high-pressure, highly paid posts to spend more time on their hobbies or with their families. Occasionally, lifestyle decisions of this type result from health concerns.

3. You are highly averse to risk and need paid work, any work, to be able to continue paying your mortgage, hire-purchase plans, credit card bills, household expenses, schooling/education costs, and so on. The fear of not being able to pay for these items may cause you to apply

for any job you think you can do, even if it is an extremely unchallenging one. A case of "Get a job, any job. Get one now!" Mostly jobs are not offered to people who are obviously overqualified or overexperienced. This is because they are highly unlikely to stay in that job for very long and are much more likely to be seeking a job that they actually want, usually in another company. It is as though candidates say to themselves, "I'll get into the company by applying for a job I *know* I can do and work my way up from there." This is an overly optimistic strategy, which is usually unsuccessful.

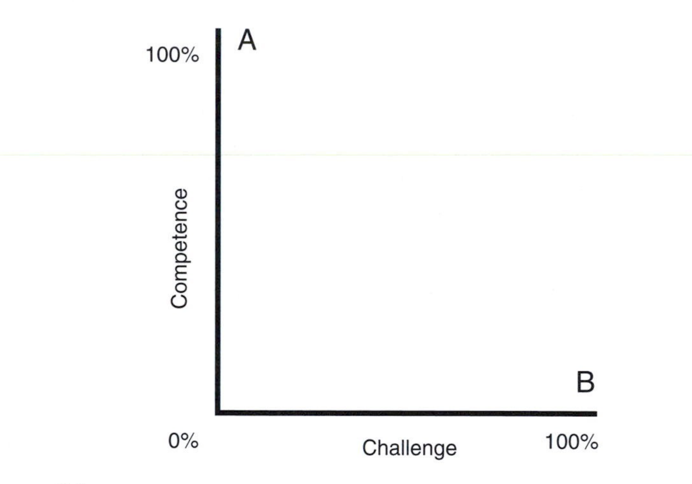

Figure (b)

Question 2:

Why would somebody choose a job or role at Point B, where the level of challenge in that role dramatically exceeds the level of competence required? Give three reasons.

1. ______________________________

2. ______________________________

3. ______________________________

Three of the main reasons, all equally valid, why you might choose a job or role where the level of challenge in that role dramatically exceeds the level of competence required are:

1. You relish the challenge of a job that will significantly stretch you, provide intellectual stimulation and test you to the limit. Often this is the sort of role where personal learning is a key driver or where there is a significant organizational problem to be solved. It could be that you are changing career completely, having learned all you can learn in the work you are doing currently. The time spent in this role is unlikely to be very long, as you will be motivated to move on as soon as the intellectual stimulation and motivation to learn decrease. This leads some people to adopt a portfolio lifestyle when working, whereby they undertake a number of different, often highly diverse, roles, all of which are hugely challenging in some way. These are usually relatively short-term roles, due to the fact that, as soon as the level of competence increases, the level of challenge decreases, causing motivation to dwindle.

When studying reasons why entrepreneurs fail or succeed, it was found that prior experience of running a business doesn't make much difference, while choosing an area of business in which one is already familiar (even if it was a "hobby") gives a higher chance of success.

2. You are highly motivated by money and financial reward, which for you is synonymous with the word "challenge". Many people this applies to undertake work where the opportunity to earn/commission rates are very high, as is the case in many sales roles. The length of time someone will stay in this sort of role is often linked to the perceived fairness of their pay/reward levels when compared with those of their colleagues both within the company and in the sector as a whole. It is much more often linked to the achievement of a personal financial objective, becoming a millionaire or buying an expensive sports car perhaps, which once achieved will cause motivation to decrease.

3. You have little or no idea of what you want to do (sometimes based on limited life experience) and have begun to experiment by applying for all sorts of jobs/roles. This usually results from being highly risk-prone and is sometimes referred to as being an adrenaline addict. It may also result from a combination of being risk-prone and wanting

to move away from something that is highly undesirable. Whatever your motivation, you are unlikely to end up doing work that suits you. You are likely to achieve inconsistent results and are therefore most unlikely to be selected/recruited. You will probably leave the job/role quite quickly.

At this stage it is useful to consider what is happening to your slice of the jobs pie. Whether it is becoming larger or smaller is equally valid as the movement will depend on your personal goals.

Question 3:

Why would somebody choose a job or role at any point on the dotted line in the diagram where the level of competence required in that role exactly matches the level of challenge?

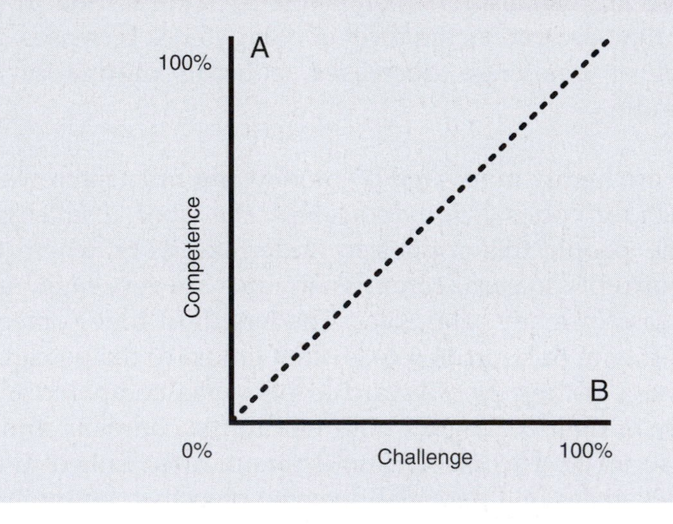

This question usually prompts people to talk about balance in the sense that there is a match between the employer's requirements and what the candidate values or enjoys. This sort of answer is the basis for many competency frameworks used in organizations to assess ability to do the work required. The trouble with that approach is that many people are now choosing jobs and roles based on whether their own personal values are being met and whether they would enjoy the work.

The sequence of events has now become "I want" in terms of personal values and challenge, followed by "They want" in terms of competence. This is equally important for employers when considering what sort of candidate they prefer.

Question 4:

Ignoring technical expertise and any work requiring repetitive activity such as production line jobs, mark a point or a zone on the diagram where you think most employers offer jobs.

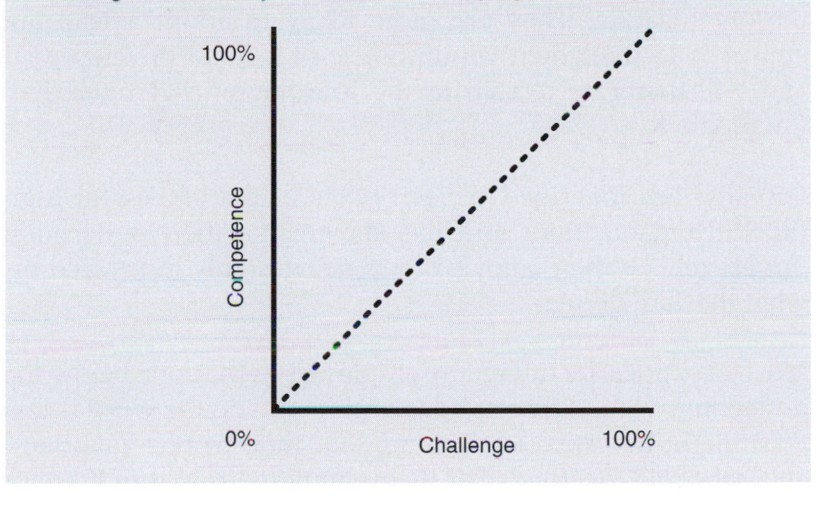

To help you answer this fourth question, imagine you are an employer considering the following two candidates.

Candidate X possesses the exact qualifications and experience you require and even has higher-level qualifications in the subject area. For sixteen years they have been doing the role you have advertised and in fact have been instructing others in exactly that role for the last four years. They possess all the knowledge required and could do the work with one arm behind their back while blindfolded.

Candidate Y does not have exactly the qualifications and experience you require. Has been working in a related area which requires many similar skills and attributes. Has a high number of very transferable skills, abilities and experiences with a track record of success at producing results. They are very willing to learn on the job and will do whatever is necessary to get themselves up to speed as quickly as possible.

Which candidate do you prefer?

Additional resource

Robert Kelly's book *How to Be a Star at Work* discusses the key skills found among top performers.

The majority of readers will have chosen Candidate Y. This is most likely to result from a belief that Candidate X would become bored in the role and would quickly leave the company. Candidate Y is much more likely to enjoy the work and be willing to learn about and identify with the culture within the organization. They are more likely to adopt a learning approach to their own continuing professional development and will therefore remain in the role for much longer than Candidate X.

The high fliers appear to be rather hard-nosed, calculating individuals but most managers would not be too surprised to learn that those who advance most rapidly to the top are: effective planners and organizers who take actions involving clear risk; show vision, inspiration, commitment, and enthusiasm …

Dulewicz and Herbert, 1999:20

Research has identified the attributes of the successful high fliers in organizations and has shown that their underlying drivers rely on their enjoying, and being highly motivated by, what they are doing.

Most jobs/roles are offered by employers in the zone below the dotted line, where the candidates' ability to do the work is less than might be expected. The amount they would value and enjoy the role together with their ability to grow into it are of much greater significance to many employers.

If you enjoy what you are doing, you tend to find a way to be successful at doing it.

Stephen Wilkinson-Carr

This is why many employers seek candidates who are in a zone very similar to the one in Figure (c) on the following page. This recognizes and takes advantage of the theme that, if you enjoy what you are doing, you tend to find a way to be successful at doing it.

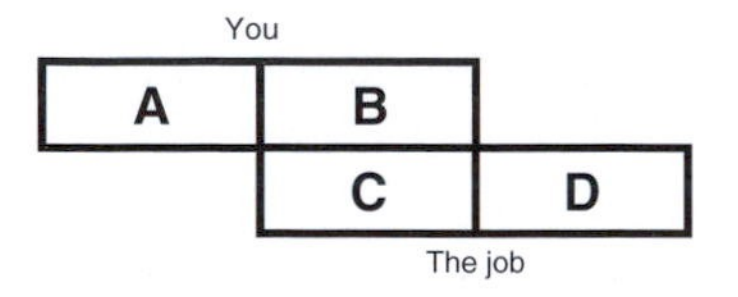

As a final thought let's consider your life and experience another way. Zone A in the diagram shown above represents

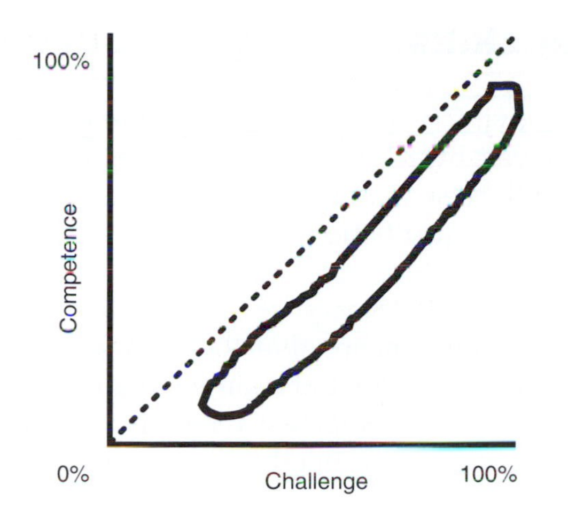

Figure (c)

all the talents, skills, qualifications, achievements, and interests that you possess but are not used in your work/job. This is why many people choose to put significant energy, enthusiasm, and commitment into their spare-time activities—because there they can do what they enjoy and value doing the most.

Zone D represents all the requirements of the job/role that you currently cannot meet or fulfill. When recruiting or selecting for most jobs or roles, employers are aware that you have untapped potential and this is why sometimes the most qualified person is not the preferred candidate.

As long as there is a match of about 60 percent between what you want and what the job requires (Zones B and C), you should apply for the post. If you have followed the exercises and answered the questions in this section your slice of the jobs pie should have changed size quite significantly. You will have added to the toolkit of techniques you can use as a coach and mentor to assist others at work to achieve their outcomes and make their slice of the pie as big as they want it to be.

Framing skills: setting the scene

In 1999 the movie *The Matrix* introduced the idea that Neo, the character played by Keanu Reeves, had to take a red pill to realize he had been living in a programmed world. If you thought that was "just fiction", think again.

Already in 1933 Alfred Korzybski argued that "the map is not the territory", which means that the map we have about the world is *not* the real world, but a kind of matrix. And one of the theories of artificial-intelligence research uses the notion of frames, a kind of skeleton filled with our default assumptions about reality.[62]

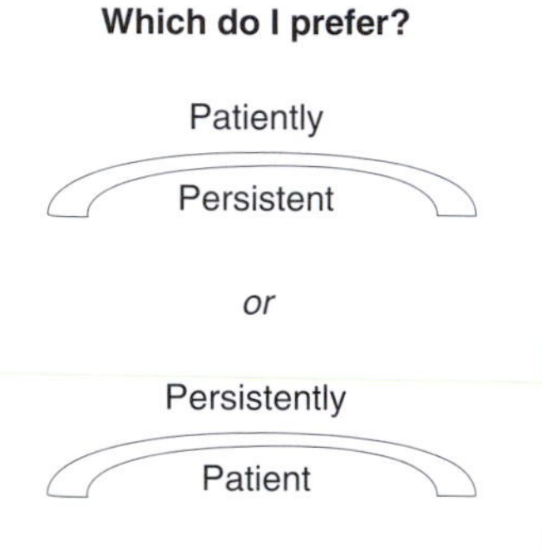

More recently, trainers such as Steve Gilligan and Michael Hall have drawn the analogy to our real life.

Frames[63] are a way of structuring the way we think, feel, and filter our information to extract meaning from it. Frames contain presuppositions we are most often unaware of, which limit our model of the world for the worse or the better. The quality of the meaning you extract from a given situation, as it occurs, as you recollect it or even as you imagine it, depends on the frame you will have set for it.

What frame of mind are you in now, reading this book? Is this the best possible frame to make the most of it?

If not, what could be the best possible frame for you that would allow to easily integrate its material with what you already know?

As a mentor, you will find an awareness of frames and their properties beneficial, as you will see from some of their properties we list below.

- Frames apply universally: everybody has them.
- They exist everywhere, all the time, simultaneously, although we are aware of only one at a time.
- They give a conceptual context to our experience.
- They govern and drive our experience. Change the frame and the meaning of your experience itself changes.
- A frame can always frame another frame. The higher frames guide, drive, modulate, and control the lower frames.

---

[62] Marvin Minsky, a cofounder of MIT's Artificial Intelligence Lab, discusses the notion of frame in his 1985 book *The Society of Mind*.

[63] For a detailed exploration of frames and other neurosemantic approaches, see L. Michael Hall (2001), *Frame Games*, Neuro-Semantics Publications.

- The order of the nesting is crucial to the effectiveness of the framing structure.
- The person who sets the frame therefore controls and governs the experience.
- If you "buy" into a frame, you are therefore constrained by its format into thinking, feeling, and responding in a particular way.
- Awareness of a frame gives you a choice to buy into it or not, or to set a higher frame that contains the lower one.

Even before you encounter your protégé for the first time, you will need to set up the scene, framing it in your mind to ensure that each encounter is the best it can be. Whether you want to or not, you will be setting frames both for yourself and for your protégé. The outcome of each encounter and of the overall mentoring process will depend on the quality of the frames you will have set.

We will explore a range of conceptual frames that will assist you to do just that.

Framing the encounter

Some useful frames—for mentoring

benign interest, observing, attentive, curiosity, focused, clarity, self-contained, lightheartedness, caring, flexibility, detached, supportive, uninsultability, fallibility, constructive, persistence, patient, humor, kind, trusting, thought-provoking, candid

For yourself

Ask yourself, "What frames of mind would I need to be in to mentor to the best of my ability? In what order would they need to be to have the optimal impact?"

For your protégé

Ask yourself, "What frames would I like my protégé to be in? What frames of mind would I like to instill in them? What frames would serve them?"

For the interaction between the two of you

Ask yourself, "What sort of frame would I like to set for the interaction to be the best possible one, both at each encounter and for the whole mentoring process?

Some useful frames—for a protégé

open, receptive, committed, motivated, observing, attentive, curious, focused, clarity, self-contained, self-possessed, trusting, light-hearted, ethical, spontaneous, sincere, honest, flexible, detached, uninsultable, fallible, resilient, persistent, patient, humorous, integrity, thought-provoking, candid

A good set of frames for any given interaction is some ground rules, to be set at your first encounter. Your protégé will expect confidentiality from you, with the proviso that, if legal or ethical issues arise, you may have to refer them to a higher authority and you may want the choice of keeping formal records. You will probably want confidentiality from your protégé also. Especially if you work together, you may want your protégé to avoid gossip, or what is known as "bitching about", or "mouthing" about a colleague, inviting them to describe any pertinent encounter in descriptive language only and focusing on behavior instead of identity.

Preframing

Where

If you work together, you may want to choose a venue that has no hierarchical associations, but appears neutral. Pick a room with space to sit, stand, and walk a few paces, preferably without a desk to hide behind. A drawing board or flipchart may come in handy.

To give the impression of a different "space", you may choose to wear something different, taking off the company uniform or professional garb and dressing differently. This will enable your protégé to distinguish between you the colleague/superior/etc. and you the mentor. Likewise, you may choose a different form of address. Different habits set up from the start ensure they will be preserved later and prevent eventual confusion of roles or "hats".

When

Choose a time when energies are available, avoiding late afternoons. A person's ability to think is contingent on physical factors also, such as food and hydration. Water and a few snacks might be handy, unless you choose to share a meal together. Unless you make a meal of it, agree an appropriate duration.

How

Sometimes, seeing each other face to face is not an option and you may want to work over the telephone. Phone sessions are usually more focused and task-oriented. Arrangements by prior agreement work best.

You may also work via email, in which case we invite you to maintain the appropriate "netiquette", be as courteous as if you were writing a letter and maintain your mentoring "frame of mind". Much of the "flame wars" one hears about on the Internet these days have more to do with the fact that this simplified form of conversation ignores most forms of politeness, an essential lubricant in any civilized society. Therefore, a comment one might accept framed by a "Hello, how are you?" and "Best wishes", is much more likely to receive a resourceful reception than one that merely begins "Joanne" (or whatever the recipient's name is, with no "dear") and that ends up only with the name of the sender, and no proper valediction.

When working on the Internet, we invite you also to weigh your words carefully, as the fewer channels of communication there are, the more those that are left acquire portent and meaning. Your reader cannot see, hear, smell, or touch you and has to compensate in their head. What representation your protégé will have of you will depend on what you gave them previously.

If using video links, remember that gestures are usually missed, unless the camera is set to catch them. Whatever our culture, we spontaneously handle "mind objects" in our "conceptual space", and this is therefore more important than it seems.

What

Depending on your protégé's outcome you may want to preplan what you are going to work on or allow yourself an "open frame". Experience has shown that open frames help to set up a scene. Once this has been accomplished, a mutually agreed plan of action is best, until the matter has been addressed and, hopefully, resolved in the desired way. Thus, open frames will commonly bracket set frames.

Some operational frames

Whatever the mode of communication, conversation or culture, some frames keep being applied and are immediately understood. We present how you could make a specific use of them in the mentoring process.

If you don't know where you're going, how will you know you got there?

Outcome frame

Set up at the beginning and at the end of each agenda item, this helps in identifying and obtaining agreement on what has been achieved. It also focuses the mind, instead of dissipating energies in all directions.

- "What specifically are we seeking to accomplish?"
- "Have we achieved what we set out to do?"

If you don't know what you want, anything should do.

Evidence frame

This enables you to gather information in order to decide what course of action to take, to make a judgment or reach a decision. When you calibrate your protégé, connecting a gesture, a tone of voice or mannerism with a state of mind or train of thought, you apply the evidence frame.

- What information have we got on this?
- How do you know this?
- How do we know this is the case?

Compare-and-contrast frame

You apply this frame to compare various options and weigh their respective pros and cons, to sort and sift evidence for what is pertinent. In order to do so, you search for difference.

You can also use it to contrast two states—the present state and the desired state—to distinguish where you're at from where you want to go.

- How do our options compare?
- What might be the difference between what you have now and what you want?

Agreement frame

Unlike the previous one, this frame is based on a model of similarity. Key to the effectiveness of rapport skills, it is used to find out points of agreement to match and lead to a mutually agreed outcome. You can also use it to identify components of the desired state you already have, such as key resources your protégé knows they have, or at least *you* know they have.

- What have you got in common to agree upon?
- What have you already got that fits the bill?

Relevancy challenge frame

Sometimes conversations, meetings, or mentoring sessions can go off track, one subject leading to another and so on. Using the relevance frame enables you to avoid unnecessary meanderings of a discussion.

- How does this relate to that?
- Where were we?

Recapitulation frame

This frame is useful at the end of a process to draw conclusions with, to summarize, or to review the journey taken. Jointly used with the relevancy frame, it can help to recapitulate after a digression.

- Let's recap.
- So, we have decided that ...
- First ... second ... third ... etc.

As-if/what-if frame

An essential frame to access resources, to gain information not otherwise available, the as-if/what-if frame enables you to conceptualize freely, to imagine, to anticipate in order to iron possible difficulties and iron them out, so that they need not materialize.

- Imagine you have already achieved this.
- How do you represent this in your mind?

- If you knew, what would you say?

Realization frame

We change all the time but rarely are we aware we are doing so. Using this frame enables you to become conscious of a change and therefore to start building upon it.

- How does it feel to realize this?
- Now that you know, what will you do as a result?
- How does knowing that make things different?

Ecology frame

This all-important frame enables you to relate an action or discussion to a greater system, to explore the consequences, consequences of consequences, and ultimate consequences and implications of an action or inaction on yourself, other people, and the greater scheme of things. It enables you to check whether or not an agreed outcome will unbalance the system. Applying it more systematically in a business or political setting would make a significant difference to the world.

- What might be the consequences of achieving this?
- How will it affect other people?
- Are the benefits we will draw from it justifying the costs?
- Will others suffer from our benefiting?

By becoming aware of the frames we set, we also become better at communicating. You will recognize them spontaneously as they manifest in Parts 4 and 5 of the book.

Action: Make your own frames

Take some time to consider what frames of mind about such things as business, your career, your work, money, and feedback would take you to the next level of your development and growth.

Given your answer, which frame of mind would you like to wake up in for the rest of your life?

The meta-SWOT analysis

Depending on circumstances, when you embark upon a mentoring project with a protégé, you may know a lot about them or very little. At the same time, they may know a lot about themselves, what they're already good at and what they need working on, or not, as the case may be. In either case, the meta-SWOT analysis[64] gives you the required structure to find out what you need to create a useful basis on which to work with your protégé.

The SWOT analysis—the letters stand for strengths, weaknesses, opportunities, and threats—originates in the world of management and organizational consultancy, where it is used as a diagnostic tool. In our previous book (*7 Steps to Emotional Intelligence*) we presented an extended version of this early model, which more precisely identifies the areas of life and personality where resources and limitations lie, and we have found it very useful to enhance the effectiveness of an assessment. Practicing with the model has enabled us to refine it further into the present model and to start using it, not only for diagnosis purposes but also to point toward ways of developing and integrating the resources of your clients and protégés.

The original SWOT analysis model, which mainly sought to establish a balance sheet that weighed the positives and negatives of a person's or organization's personality and structure, is fairly static. It is mainly a stock-taking exercise, which, depending on an individual's outlook, can make them feel less than at their best. After all, how often do *you* like your weaknesses pointed out and to see highlighted the threats the world may have in wait for you? The latter might put you in "fight-or-flight"[65] response mode, or even make us feel inappropriately

---

[64] The Meta-SWOT analysis is a tool for self-assessment and resolving limitations developed by Denis Bridoux.

[65] Anger and fear are interpretations of the 'fight-or-flight/face-or-flee' response, as you can face something without being angry and you can run away without being afraid. The Roman historian Livy relates the early Roman tale of the last Horatius left to fight against the three Sabine Curiatii brothers, who ran before his adversaries the better to ambush them and take them out one at a time. Some people also add 'freeze' to the list, and you can likewise be totally still and immobile without freezing.

angry, afraid, or out of control, while the former might make us feel inappropriately sad, guilty, ashamed, or hurt.

However, this need not happen. After all, there has to be something positive for us behind everything we do, otherwise we wouldn't do it in the first place. Our own perspective has long been that threats are actually opportunities in disguise, and weaknesses are strengths already existing in potential, or manifesting less well than we would like, and we are just waiting for them to emerge in the right way. Enabling your protégé to acknowledge the positives hidden behind a particular behavior will allow them to refresh this intention and to upgrade it so that it manifests itself in their life and actions without the side effects they had perhaps been accustomed to.

So, instead of inviting your protégé to self-flagellate or to castigate themselves for being less than perfect or to leave themselves vulnerable to external situations outside their direct control, you can instead enable your protégé to look for answers or solutions to these external or internal limitations. They will thereby cast a fresh eye on situations they may find themselves in for what these have to offer, i.e. create a resourceful frame of positive thinking for themselves. On the early earth, oxygen was a deadly poison until organisms found a way of utilizing it. So, if you can't avoid it, embrace it! Surfers, who develop skills to ride ocean waves that would crush less practiced people, know this well. The wave of change is upon us; we can erect a bulwark against it or learn to ride and "tame" it. Which would you rather do?

We usually perceive opportunities and threats as external to us, belonging to the outside environment, within external contexts and situations, and coming from other people. This forms the psycho-socio-cultural environment within which we all evolve. Concurrently, we perceive our strengths, resources, and weaknesses as being inside us, or, if not inside us, belonging to us at least, whether we like it or not. These may have to do with:

- Our **behavior**, *what* we say and do (external), *what* we think and feel, or not

- our **skills**, **capabilities** and **resources**, which qualify and potentiate *how* we do what we do, or not

- our **beliefs** and **values**, which explain and justify *why* we do what we do, or not, and *why* it is important to do what we do

- our **identity**, *who* we perceive ourselves as being or not being, professionally and personally

Our sense of belonging, or *connecting*, to something larger than we are—a family, company, community, culture, or deity—gives us a sense of vision, a mission to accomplish, a calling to follow, a purpose to fulfill, the greater whys and wherefores of living.

Meta-SWOT analysis

		Strengths	Weaknesses	From weakness to strength, via behavior, capabilities, beliefs, values, identity and mission					
Internal	***Level***	What am I good at?	What could I be better at?	How could I achieve this? What inner resource(s) can I put in operation that would enable me to achieve this?	What beliefs about myself, other people, the world would enable me to do it?	Why is that Important? What values of mine would this manifest?	Who would I need to become who could do this effortlessly? Which hat could I choose to wear that would enable me to do this?	How does this align with my vision, my mission, my purpose, my calling?	**Internal**
	Spirituality/ connectedness								
	Identity								
	Beliefs and values								
	Capabilities and skills								
	Behaviors and activities								
		Opportunities	**Threats**	***From threats to opportunities, via behavior, capabilities, beliefs, values, identity, and mission***					
External	***Level***	What supports me to achieve my goal? What is there out there that I can make use of to achieve my goal?	What external threats or constraints could prevent me from achieving my goal if I allowed them to?	How could I remedy this so that it doesn't prevent me any more from achieving my goal? What inner resource(s) can I put into application to face this external threat/constraint?	What do I want to believe so that, not only is it not a threat any more, but it becomes an opportunity?	Why is that important? What values of mine would this manifest? What new value do I need to identify that would turn this into an opportunity?	Who is the I that could make the most of this new opportunity?	How does this align with my vision, my mission, my purpose, my calling?	**External**
	Environment and context								

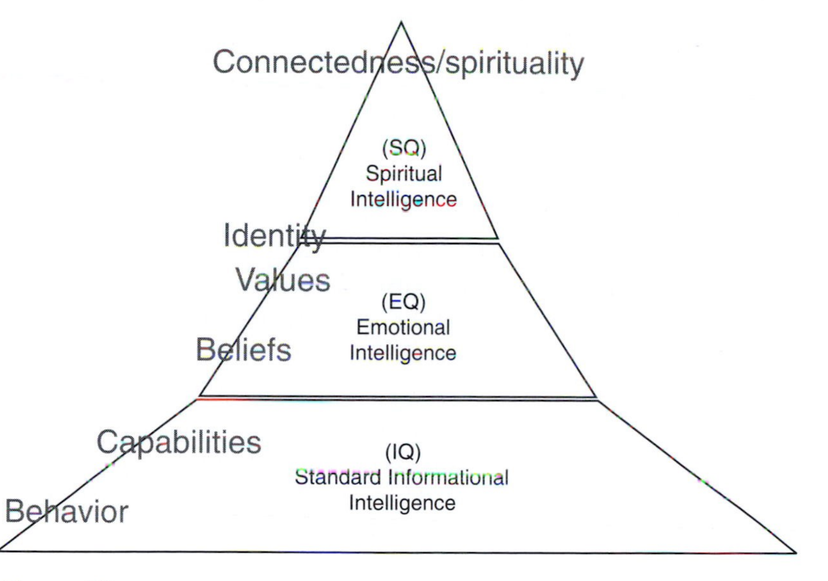

Figure (d)

Note here how these levels correlate with our levels of intelligence (see Figure (d) above):

- Our *"informational intelligence"* relates to our resources of knowledge, skills, and abilities and how we apply these in daily settings.

- Our *"emotional intelligence"* relates to the beliefs and values we hold dear, which allow for the use of our skills and resources to construct who we perceive ourselves to be.

- Our *"spiritual intelligence"*[66] relates to our ability to connect and interact and manifest our higher intentions in life with a view to self-realization.

Once we have identified our strengths (what we are already good at) and weaknesses (what we could be better at) what are we to do? The approach people traditionally take is that they focus on their strengths and ignore their weaknesses.

If you always do what you've always done, you'll always get what you've always got. If whatever you're doing isn't working, do anything else!

[66] This type of intelligence has only been recently identified. See: D. Zohar, and I. Marshall, 2000, *SQ: Connecting With Our Spiritual Intelligence*.

Thus George Leonard postulates (1991) that we can achieve mastery in only a few key areas of our lives, not all of them. So we may dabble in one area, hack in others, be compulsive in some, and master only a few. Similarly, Gregory Engels and Jay Arthur[67] suggest that we should focus on our mastery traits because these are the areas in which we excel already and where our true happiness lies, both in careers and relationships. However, if we strive only to continuously tweak our strengths to hone them further, the improvement in our life will only be incremental.

On the other hand, if you start working on what you're least good at to improve these, you stand a far better chance of making *big* changes in your life. This, in turn, will give you more all-round flexibility and make you a more balanced, more rounded human being.

While Leonard may be right in relation to your capabilities and skills, when you operate from a higher level of congruence and integration, you may indeed achieve levels of mastery that are much more pervasive and positively affect all areas of your life and not just those you initially identified. What do you think?

We are now expanding further our exploration of the SWOT analysis to do precisely this and enable you and/or your protégé to become better at what you were not necessarily good at to begin with.

So, give your protégé time to draw a list of their strengths and weaknesses, opportunities and threats. This may be a task you'll be giving them at the end of one session. You will be studying and analyzing the results together next time round. Enable them to identify at which level these are located. Thus:

- "I always leave things to the last minute" is a behavior issue.

---

[67] Engels, G. and Arthur, J., (1996) *The NLP Personal Profile Guidebook*. See also the discussion of metaprograms in Part 5 of this book. The jobEQ iWAM questionnaire comes with an Attitude Sorter report which helps you put Engels' and Arthur's advice into practice (see http://www.jobEQ.com/mentor for your free test).

- "I can't swim" is a capability issue.
- "I'm no good at talking in public" is a belief issue.
- "It's not like me to push myself" is an identity issue.

The meta-SWOT analysis continues from where the other left off. In the table, we suggest a range of questions adapted to the level at which the issue lies at any moment. This will enable you not only to identify points to resolve and means to strengthen embryonic resources but also to apply these recursively depending on the reply you get.

Example:

"I always leave things to the last minute."

What would enable you (a capability question) to plan ahead better?

What would you need to believe about yourself and your work to plan ahead in the best way?

"That I can start earlier. By starting earlier, I leave myself more time to polish what I am doing."

So an ability to polish and tweak is important to you (a value question)?

"I suppose I'm a bit of perfectionist."

So how do you reconcile this with leaving it to the last minute?

"Dohh!"

How does it feel to realize this?

What do you want to do instead now that you know? What's the first thing you're going to do to manifest this new way of thinking? What can you do to make sure you get about doing this the right way for you (behavior questions)?

We have also designed it for people to work on their own without recourse to somebody to ask them the questions. It may not achieve as much as if somebody asked them and followed them, but it will certainly allow for a change of perspective on the presenting issue.

If you wish, you could ask your protégé to fill the spaces below each question and bring the information back with them for discussion next time round.

The meta-octant consequence-evaluation system

"Knowing that whatever we do has consequences is the beginning of wisdom," goes a Chinese saying. Identifying such consequences can allow us to prepare for them. The meta-octant consequence-evaluation system[68] shows how to map out the positive and negative consequences of an action or inaction with much greater precision to better inform our choices.

We are most mindful of the positive consequences of an action, less often of its negative consequences, and even less often of an inaction and its consequences. It takes a genius such as Sherlock Holmes to track the last of these, as in the case he solved because "the dog did *not* bark in the night"!

Inspector Gregory: "Is there any other point to which you would wish to draw my attention?"

Holmes: "To the curious incident of the dog in the night-time."

"The dog did nothing in the night-time."

"That was the curious incident," remarked Sherlock Holmes.[69]

NLP charts this using the Cartesian grid illustrated below, which allows us to ask ourselves:

- What will happen if I do this?
- What will not happen if I do this?
- What will happen if I do not this?
- What will not happen if I do not this?

This will suit any ordinary exploration of consequences.

Consequence quadrants

What will/if I → ↓	Do this	Do not do this
Happen	+ +	+ –
Not happen	– +	– –

[68] Developed by Denis Bridoux as a tool for self-assessment and resolving limitations.

[69] Quoted from *The Adventure of Silver Blaze* by Arthur Conan Doyle.

However, for larger issues, involving changing jobs, location, partner, sex etc., this is insufficiently precise and we need to add more dimensions to uncover missing factors that may be crucial to making an informed decision. Recently, I (DB) expanded this model further.[70] See the table below to elicit the positive and negative consequences of an action or a lack thereof. Going through this grid enables us to best assess the pros and cons of our actions and inaction and is invaluable in all contexts.

What do I stand/by ➡ ⬇	**Doing this**	**Not doing this**
To gain		
Not to gain		
To lose		
Not to lose		

This can be represented by a cubic grid, instead of a square one. For a clear understanding of its structure, I (DB) have separated its sub-cubes or octants as shown opposite.

Furthermore, in the way that we extended the SWOT analysis by adding logical levels to it, we can do the same to the system of octants, replacing the question "What?" with "How?", "Why?" and "Who?"

We can thus ask not only:

What do I stand to gain/not to gain, or to lose/not to lose, by doing this/not doing this?

---

[70] Bridoux, Denis and Mann, D., 2002, "Evolving TRIZ using NLP and TRIZ", in the fourth annual conference of the Altshuller Institute for TRIZ Studies, TRIZcon.

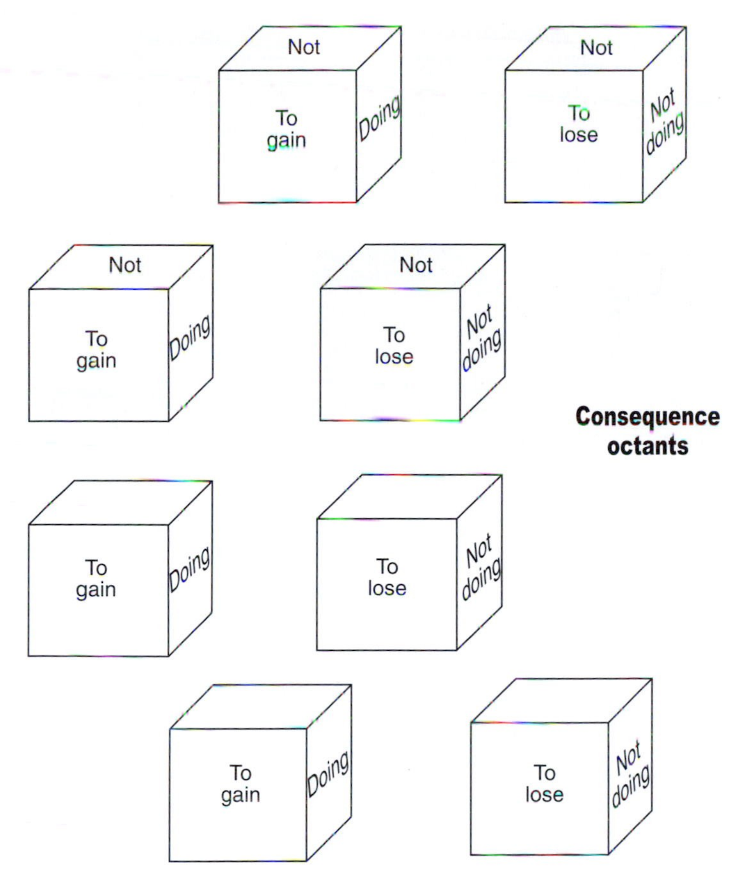

Figure (e)

But also:

How do I stand to gain/not to gain, or to lose/not to lose, by doing this/not doing this?

Why do I stand to gain/not to gain, or to lose/not to lose, by doing this/not doing this?

Who stands to gain/not to gain, or to lose/not to lose, by my doing this/not doing this?

See the whole structure of the meta-octant model in Figure (f) on the following page.

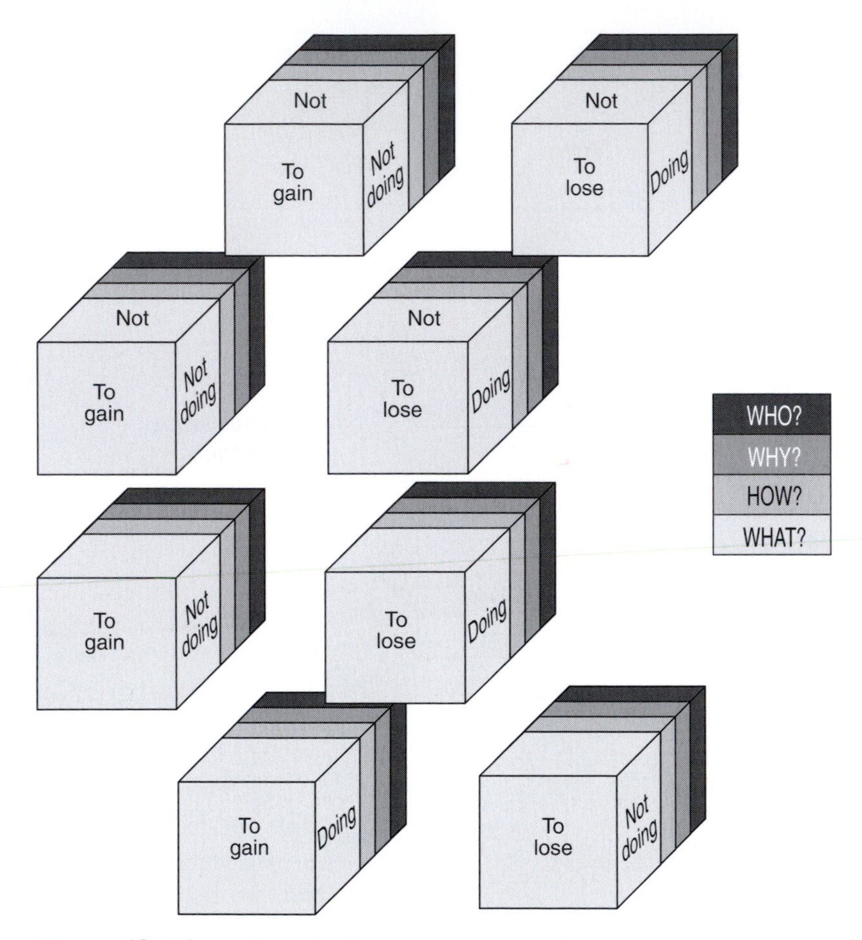

Figure (f): The meta-octant consequence system

We are often aware of the immediate consequences of our actions, but less often so of the consequences of the consequences of these. So, in the way that we looked for second-, third-, *n*th-order cause earlier, we can look at the second-, third-, *n*th-order consequence of an action. Chess players are very familiar with this concept and they can track in their mind the implications of an amazing range of combinations and permutations, which informs every move they are going to make.

Looking at the consequences of an action (or of an inaction, for that matter) makes us aware of the choices we have and enables us to put a value to a change. We can thus carry out a cost–benefit analysis, which is a universally applied tool in the field of management, but it is a very coarse instrument without the advantages of the meta-octants to quantify and qualify such consequences.

Most significantly for our welfare and wellbeing, that of others around us, and, ultimately, that of the planet at large, the cost–benefit equation as it stands omits one crucial component, namely the harm to oneself, to others, and to the world that a change might bring. It should now read:

$$\frac{\text{benefits}}{\text{costs} + \text{harm}} \geq 0$$

Thus a change is worth it when the benefits of the solution outweigh the costs involved in implementing it and the harms that such implementation will cause. Optimality is approached when benefits are maximal and costs + harm are minimal, as the ratio tends toward infinity.

This concept of optimality is key. This is not about achieving *quantity* of result but *quality* of result. After all, more is not necessarily better, and sometimes less is better. However, better *is* better.

To be optimal, results need to be contingent on time, place, relationships, and other issues, such as health/money/available knowledge and energy. *Optimality is not, therefore, an absolute amount, but a ratio that has meaning only in a given space/time/relationship (S/T/R) context.*

Today's optimality is not necessarily tomorrow's; in fact, it rarely is. Many of yesterday's optimal solutions may turn out to be tomorrow's problems. Extrapolating consequences can enable us to ensure that this need not occur for the foreseeable future or is kept to a strict minimum.

All too often we are so concerned by the here and now that we neglect to identify potential contradictions lying ahead of us, which, if we considered them and altered our course accordingly, need not arise in the first place. Being mindful of the consequences before we start can enable us to factor them into the equation so that they need not arise in the first place. The worthwhileness equation now reads:

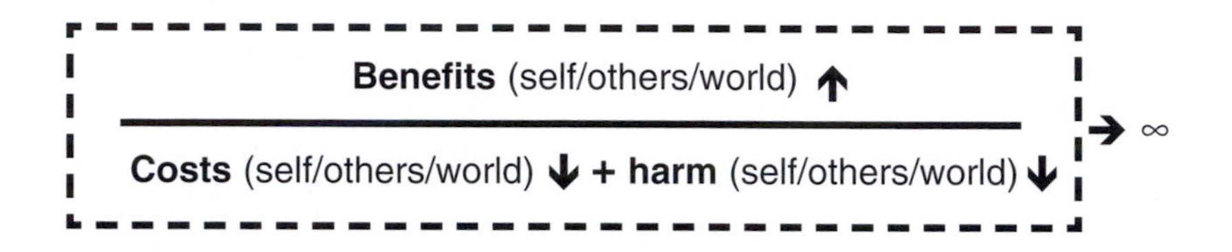

Timeframe:

- present, at this moment in time
- as long as possible
- within a given period of time/given date
- from now on
- for the foreseeable future
- indefinitely
- forever

Thus, we can qualify our choices and, for example, accept a temporary lack of benefit here and now provided it is tempered by long-term benefits within a given period of time.

By enabling us to look at the consequences of an action (or of an inaction) and the implications of that for ourselves and other people, the meta-octants system allows us to plan ahead, get the benefit of hindsight beforehand, and plan for contingencies.

The Coach and the Fly[71]

Jean de la Fontaine (1621–95)

Upon a sandy, uphill road,
Which naked in the sunshine glow'd,
Six lusty horses drew a coach.
Dames, monks, and invalids, its load,
On foot, outside, at leisure trode.
The team, all weary, stopp'd and blow'd:
Whereon there did a fly approach,
And, with a vastly business air.
Cheer'd up the horses with his buzz,—
Now pricked them here, now prick'd them there,
As neatly as a jockey does,—
And thought the while—he knew 'twas so—
He made the team and carriage go,—
On carriage-pole sometimes alighting—
Or driver's nose—and biting.
And when the whole did get in motion,
Confirm'd and settled in the notion,
He took, himself, the total glory,—
Flew back and forth in wondrous hurry,
And, as he buzz'd about the cattle,
Seem'd like a sergeant in a battle,
The files and squadrons leading on
To where the victory is won.
Thus charged with all the commonweal,
This single fly began to feel
Responsibility too great,
And cares, a grievous crushing weight;
And made complaint that none would aid
The horses up the tedious hill—
The monk his prayers at leisure said—
Fine time to pray!—the dames, at will,
Were singing songs—not greatly needed!
Thus in their ears he sharply sang,
And notes of indignation ran,—
Notes, after all, not greatly heeded.
Erelong the coach was on the top:
"Now," said the fly, "my hearties, stop
And breathe;—I've got you up the hill;
And Messrs. Horses, let me say,
I need not ask you if you will
A proper compensation pay."
Thus certain ever-bustling noddies
Are seen in every great affair;
Important, swelling, busy-bodies,
And bores 'tis easier to bear
Than chase them from their needless care.

This tale (see left) of Jean de la Fontaine was translated by Elizur Wright in 1841. The full translation of La Fontaine's *Fables* is a public-domain work distributed by Professor Michael S. Hart through the Project Gutenberg Association.

The official Project Gutenberg web pages may be found at www.gutenberg.net

[71] *Fables*: Book VII, Fable 9.

The counsels of Athene

This section of the book presents you with a process to help you to answer the questions we have raised when discussing the lessons of Athene in Part 1 of this book (the illustration above is an artist's impression). Going through this process will give you insights about mentoring in a metaphorical/symbolic fashion.

This process aims to create for you the optimal possible representation of Mentor, with the best qualities and attributes required for the role. It will also enable you to access the necessary resources to carry out this role to the best of your abilities—abilities you know yourself to have and those that you may not yet be aware of. It involves a bit of play-acting, a bit of "Let's Pretend", itself one of the oldest teaching tools in the world, where you will assume a different perceptual position or perspective on what you are working on.

From the self position, represent in front of you the following characters/people: Mentor in front of you and facing you, Telemachus to his left facing him, your own protégé to his right facing him too, and a step or more behind Mentor, Athene facing him also (see Figure (g) above).

1. Physically moving in the room, metaphorically step out of your shoes and into the sandals of Athene, taking her stance, her posture, her position, fully becoming her.

    a. Become aware of your external attributes as Athene: your helmet; your spear, which you sometimes use as a stick to walk with, which, when you smote the ground with it, caused the olive tree, symbol of peace, to rise and persuade the Athenians to give their city your name; your shield called the Aegis, which you loaned to Perseus and which now bears the head of the Gorgon Medusa to terrify your enemies with and turn them to stone; the Wise Owl that perches on your shoulder, which you use as an emissary.

Athene

Telemachus

Mentor

Protégé

Self

Figure (g): The counsels of Athene

b. Become aware of your inner attributes as Athene, your skills: you are a great weaver and embroiderer, able to weave together many strands and to make wonderfully intricate tapestries; your powers as you sprang fully armed from Zeus's head; your knowledge, for it is you whom Zeus seeks out for counsel; your wisdom, which you inherited from your mother Metis. You are also called Pronoia, the Foreknower, the Anticipatrix, for such is your power, too.

c. Become aware also of your good intentions for yourself, for Odysseus, for Telemachus, for this person seeking to become a good mentor and his protégé, for humankind and your intentions behind these.

d. Become aware also that, as part of your knowledge, wisdom and skills, you have those that enable you to veil your splendor—so as not to blind the mortals you counsel—and to adopt the best manner in order to channel all your skills and abilities so that only what is pertinent and appropriate emerges.

2. As you do all this, take a step forward and, as Athene, take on the persona—the Greek word means *mask*—of Mentor, the wise counselor of Telemachus and his benevolent adviser on his journeys. Turn toward him and:

   a. Become aware how you best observe him overtly and covertly, listen to him, respond to him in words, gestures and deeds.

   b. Become aware of your frame of mind as you do so and the reasons and motivations that put you in such a frame of mind.

3. When you have become fully familiar with this, step out of the shoes of Mentor and back into your own, becoming yourself again.

   a. Become again aware of who you are, your own attributes, external and internal, your skills and resources, your own powers of thinking, feeling, speaking, responding.

   b. Become aware of your own values, of what is important to you about the concept of mentoring, of mentoring this particular person.

   c. Become aware of what doing that well would do for you, for your own intentions toward yourself, toward your protégé, toward your organization or the context where this is appropriate. How would mentoring benefit you and the other people involved?

   d. Become aware of your own powers of presenting yourself that would make your mentoring not only acceptable to your protégé, but also rewarding and fulfilling.

4. When you have become aware of this, step again out of your own shoes and into those of Mentor, turning to look toward your protégé, bringing with you those realizations.

   a. Notice how this position has now become enriched with personal perspectives and become pertinent to your requirements and the situation.

   b. Consider your protégé and the best way you will want to interact with them. How are you going to initiate this approach to ensure the success of the whole process?

5. Now practice stepping in and out of the role of mentor (this step is crucial when you interact with people in several relationships: for example, manager–mentor, friend–mentor, colleague–mentor, parent–mentor, teacher–mentor).

   a. Become clear about what is pertinent to the role and what is not …

   b. where to do it, where not …

   c. when to do it, when not …

   d. how to do it, how not (and so on)

   By doing this, not only you but also your protégé and other people will see immediately when you are stepping into and out of the role. Find the quickest and most explicit way of changing hats to achieve this.

6. Finally, become aware that, wherever and whenever you need to, you can "take the counsel of Athene". Just ask "Wise Owl". How does it feel to realize this?

Annotated Bibliography

For several reasons we've chosen to add a bibliography listing books that particularly caught our attention while we were writing this one. Throughout the book we have tried as much as possible to pay tribute to the people who originated the ideas we have mentioned. Most quotations have the names of the persons who we think originally uttered them. A lot of footnotes quote the original sources of material we have mentioned. Also, given that more than two years have passed between the day we decided to write this book and the day we were rounding up this edition, we may have forgotten where we got some of the ideas from. This may be easier to understand if you realize that both of us probably read some four hundred books over this period, not to mention the number of articles we read and the number of seminars we attended. Therefore, we decided to write down a kind of wish list of books we would like mentors and coaches to read.

Resource

We have also reviewed some of these books on the Amazon.com website. Looking up these books is easy from the bibliography in the mentor section of the jobEQ website.

www.jobEQ.com/mentor

Additional skills

7 Steps to Emotional Intelligence, Patrick Merlevede, Denis Bridoux and Rudy Vandamme (2001)

This book aims at teaching you more emotional intelligence, starting from a practical framework known as NLP. Apart from really teaching you emotional intelligence, this book is recommended since NLP has been described as "the ideal toolset for a coach". Dutch and French versions of this book are available as well.

Flawless Consulting, Peter Block (2nd edn, 2000)

Peter Block wrote the original edition of this bible for consultants in 1978. It's a book for anyone who is giving advice to someone who is faced with a choice; who helps to change, but has no control over the implementation. In a sense, mentors and coaches are thus part of the intended audience of this book.

Business books

Alpha Leadership: Tools for Business Leaders Who Want More from Life, Anne Deering, Julian Russell, and Robert Dilts (2002)

This book presents a practical model focusing on nine skills good leaders should have.

Games Business Experts Play, L. Michael Hall (2002)

This book helps you to detect in which frames of mind or "frame games" you are involved and which frames lead to success in business. Knowing about frames is useful to a coach or mentor, but this book also helps to increase your business acumen.

Good to Great, Jim Collins (2001)

In order to come up with answers to the question, "How does a good company get into the league of the great companies?" Jim Collins looked through much of the management hype to define his "level 5 leadership".

For HR specialists, Ulrich's *Delivering Results* (1998) is also recommended.

Results-Based Leadership, David Ulrich, *et al.* (1999)

A must-read for anyone interested in leadership development, one of HR's strategic roles.

The Corporate Culture Survival Guide, Edgar H. Schein (1999)

This is a very practical book on organizational culture and values, even including process descriptions of sessions one can use to understand the organizational culture.

Self-help books

The Joy of Not Working, Ernie J. Zelinski, (3rd edn, 1997)

In a thought-provoking and fun way, Zelinski discusses some of the issues on balancing that were discussed in Part 5. Recommended as an antidote to feeling overwhelmed by work or suffering from workaholism.

Zen and the Art of Making a Living, Laurence G. Bold (first published in 1991; revised, 1999)

An inspiring career-design guide helping you figure out what you really want to do and taking steps in order to get the job you'll love to do.

Authentic Happiness, Martin E. P. Seligman (2002)

Seligman helps you to use the findings of positive psychology for getting more out of life.

jobEQ.com

The planned "Increase Your jobEQ" series of books is aimed at helping you to put best practice in place in various areas related to human-resources management.

Future "Increase your jobEQ" books will cover:

- recruiting and assessment
- management and leadership

JobEQ is a virtual organization providing tools to help organizations to get the right person on the right place, with the right attitude, values, and skill set. At the time of writing (August 2003), jobEQ's tools have been used in projects in Australia, Belgium, Canada, Denmark, France, the UK, Italy, Luxembourg, and the USA. Deployment of our tools to the Spanish- and German-speaking world is in progress.

Visit the jobEQ website at www.jobEQ.com

Bibliography

Alfred Korzybski, 1933, *Science and Sanity*, Institute of General Semantics, Englewood, New Jersey, USA.

Angelou, Maya, 1970, *I Know Why The Caged Bird Sings*, Reissue Edition, Random House, New York, NY.

Badaracco, J., 2002, *Leading Quietly*, Harvard Business School Press, Boston, Massachusetts.

Bateson, Gregory 1972, *Steps to an Ecology of Mind*, The University of Chicago Press, Chicago.

Bauer, Sharon A., 1975, *Asserting Yourself: A Practical Guide for Positive Change*, Addison-Wesley, Boston.

Beck, Don Edward and Cowan, Christopher, 1996, *Spiral Dynamics: Mastering Values, Leadership and Change*, Blackwell Publishers, Malden, Massachusetts, USA.

Bettelheim, B., 1976, *The Uses of Enchantment: The Meaning and Importance of Fairy Tales*, Vintage Book edition, Random House, New York, NY. Originally published by Alfred A. Knopf, Inc.

Block, Peter, 2000, *Flawless Consulting*, 2nd edition, Jossey-Bass, San Francisco, CA.

Bohm, D., 1996, *On Dialogue*, Routledge, London.

Boldt, Laurence G., 1999, *Zen and the Art of Making a Living*, Arkana, New York, NY.

Bossidy, L. and Charan, R., 2002, *Execution: The Discipline of Getting Things Done*, Crown Business, New York, NY.

Bruber, Martin, 1995, *The Way of Man: According to the Teaching of Hasidirm*, Re-issue Edition, Citadel Press, New York, NY.

Byham, William C.; Smith, Audrey, B. and Paese, Matthew J., 2001, *Grow Your Own Leaders: How to Identify, Develop and Retain Leadership Talent*, Financial Times, Prentice Hall.

Collins, Jim, 2001, *Good to Great*, Random House, New York, NY.

Deering, Anne; Russell, Julian, and Dilts, Robert, 2002, *Alpha Leadership: Tools for Business Leaders Who Want More From Life*, John Wiley and Sons Ltd, San Francisco, CA.

Dilts, Robert B. and Bonissone, Gino, 1993, *Skills for the Future: Managing Creativity and Innovation*, Meta Publications, Cupertino, CA.

Dulewicz, V. and Herbert, P., 1999, Predicting advancement to senior management from competencies and personality data: a seven year follow up study, *British Journal of Management*, 10, pp. 13–22.

Engels, G. and Arthur, J., 1996, *The NLP Personal Profile Guidebook*, Lifestar, Denver, CO.

Frank, Robert H., 1998, *Passions Within Reason*, W. W. Norton & Company, New York, NY.

Fulgham, Robert, 1990, *All I Really Need to Know I Learned in Kindergarten*, Villard Books, New York, NY.

Gibson, Donald E. and Barsade, Sigal G., The experience of anger of work: lessons from the chronically angry, working paper presented at the Annual Meeting of the Academy of Management, Chicago, 11 August 1999.

Goddard, Dwight (ed.), 1994, *A Buddhist Bible*, with a new Foreword by Robert Aiken, Beacon Press, Boston.

Goleman, Daniel, 1995, *Emotional Intelligence: Why It Can Matter More Than IQ*, Bantam Books, New York, NY.

Greenleaf, Robert K., 1998, The servant as religious leader, in *The Power of Servant Leadership*, Berrett-Koehler Publishers, San Francisco.

Hall, Michael L., 2001, *Frame Games*, Neuro-Semantics Publications, Grand Junction, CO.

Hall, Michael L., 2002, *Games Business Experts Play: Winning at the Games of Business*, Crown House Publishing, Carmarthen.

Hammonds, Keith H., with commentary from Ella Bell, "Circus Acts" in *Fast Company*, Issue 53, December 2001.

Harrold, Fiona, 2000, *Be Your Own Life Coach: How to Take Control of Your Life and Achieve Your Wildest Dreams*, Hodder & Stoughton, London.

Jawordski, Joseph, 1996, *Synchronicity: The Inner Path of Leadership*, Berrett-Koehler Publishers, San Francisco.

Kelly, Robert E., 1998, *How to be a Star at Work: 9 Breakthrough Strategies You Need to Succeed*, Times Books, New York, NY.

Kirschenbaum, Howard and Land Henderson, Valerie, (eds.), 1989, *The Carl Rogers Reader*, Constable, London.

Kram, Kathy, 1983, Phases of a Mentor Relationship, *Academy of Management Journal*, Vol. 26 (4), pp. 608–25.

Leonard, G., 1991, *Mastery*, Penguin, London.

McClelland, David C., 1987, *Human Motivation*, Cambridge University Press, Cambridge, UK.

Maynard Keynes, John, 1923, *A Tract on Monetary Reform*, Macmillan, London.

Merlevede, Patrick E. with Denis Bridoux and Rudy Vandamme, 2001, *7 Steps to Emotional Intelligence*, Crown House Publishing, Carmarthen.

Merlevede, Patrick E., 2002, Action Oriented Coaching, *Rapport*, Issue 50.

Minsky, Marvin, 1985, *The Society of Mind*, Simon & Schuster, New York, NY.

Murray, Margo, 2001, *Beyond the Myths and Magic of Mentoring*, 2nd edition, Jossey-Bass, San Francisco, CA.

Schein, Edgar H., 1999, *The Corporate Culture Survival Guide*, Jossey-Bas, San Francisco.

Seligman, Martin E. P., 2003, *Authentic Happiness: Using the New Positive Psychology to Realize Your Potential for Lasting Fulfillment*, Nicholas Brealey Publishing Ltd, London, UK.

Senge, Peter, 1990, *Fifth Discipline*, Currency, New York, NY.

Thurow, Lester C., Government Can't Make the Market Fair, article contributed to the *New York Times*, reprinted in the *International Herald Tribune*, July 23, 2002 (you can find the full article at: http://www.lthurow.com/articles/print/market.html).

Tobey, Linda, 2001, *The Integrity Moment: Making Powerful Choices in Life*, Kendall/Hunt Publishing Company.

Ulrich, David, 1998, *Delivering Results: A New Mandate for Human Resource Professionals*, Harvard Business School Press, Boston, MA.

Ulrich, David, Zenger, Jack, Smallwood, Norman, and Bennis, Warren (Foreword), 1999, *Results-Based Leadership*, Harvard Business School Press, Boston, MA.

Welch, J., 2001, *Jack: Straight from the Gut*, Warner Business Books, New York, NY.

Zelinski, Ernie J., 1997, *The Joy of Not Working*, 3rd edition, Ten Speed Press, Berkeley, CA.

Zohar, D. and Marshall, I., 2000, *SQ: Connecting With Our Spiritual Intelligence*, Bloomsbury, New York, NY.